About the editor

Tristan Anne Borer (BA, University of Texas at San Antonio; PhD, University of Notre Dame) is professor of government and international relations at Connecticut College in New London, CT. She is the author of *Challenging the State: Churches as Political Actors in South Africa, 1980–1994* (1998), the editor of *Telling the Truths: Truth-Telling and Peacebuilding in Post-Conflict Societies* (2006), and the co-author (with John Darby and Siobhán McEvoy-Levy) of *Peacebuilding After Peace Accords: The Challenges of Violence, Truth and Youth* (2006). She has also published several articles in the field of human rights in journals including *Human Rights Quarterly, Journal of Human Rights, Violence Against Women, African Studies Quarterly*, and the *Journal of Church and State*. Her research has been funded by the Joan Kroc Institute for International Peace Studies and the United States Institute of Peace.

D1508791

Media, mobilization, and human rights: mediating suffering

EDITED BY TRISTAN ANNE BORER

Zed Books

LONDON | NEW YORK

Media, mobilization, and human rights: mediating suffering was first published in 2012 by Zed Books Ltd, 7 Cynthia Street, London N1 9JF, UK and Room 400, 175 Fifth Avenue, New York, NY 10010, USA

www.zedbooks.co.uk

Set in OurType Arnhem and Monotype Futura by Ewan Smith, London
Index: ed.emery@thefreeuniversity.net
Cover design: www.rawshock.co.uk
Cover photo © Corbis
Printed and bound by CPI Group (UK) Ltd, Croydon, CRO 4YY

Distributed in the USA exclusively by Palgrave Macmillan, a division of St Martin's Press, LLC, 175 Fifth Avenue, New York, NY 10010, USA

A catalogue record for this book is available from the British Library
Library of Congress Cataloging in Publication Data available

ISBN 978 1 78032 068 7 hb
ISBN 978 1 78032 067 0 pb

Contents

Acknowledgments

In 2005, Nicholas Kristof published an op-ed about American apathy toward ongoing human rights violations in Darfur, Sudan. Trying to shock his readers into caring, he published pictures of dead and mutilated bodies. On a whim, I cut that op-ed out of the *New York Times* and brought it to class to discuss with my students. I did not know at the time that the ensuing, rather heated, conversation would light the first spark of an idea that would eventually become this edited book on human rights and the media. In the years since, I have had countless stimulating conversations with hundreds of students in my human rights courses at Connecticut College about a myriad of issues surrounding this topic. First and foremost, therefore, I wish to thank my students. Their intellectual engagement with the issues in this book has continually pushed me to hone and refine my ideas. Being their teacher has made me a better scholar.

As my interest in this topic grew, I issued a call for papers for a panel on human rights and the media for the 2010 annual International Studies Association (ISA) conference. The response was overwhelming, and I ended up organizing two linked panels. Some of the chapters in this book began as papers given at those panels; others were commissioned specifically for this book. I am profoundly grateful to the panelists and to the contributors to this book, all of whom responded promptly and graciously to my requests for revision after revision. I appreciate their willingness to be open to my many comments and suggestions. I hope I have done their work justice. On a more personal level, it has been deeply rewarding to come to know such a distinguished group of scholars, all of whom I respect immensely.

It was at that ISA conference where I met Ken Barlow, the editor with whom I have been lucky enough to work closely at Zed Books. Ken has been enormously helpful in shepherding this book from concept to final product. I am especially grateful for his respectful responses to my ideas and his willingness to negotiate on them. I also thank several anonymous reviewers, all of whom offered insightful and helpful comments; this is without question a better book because of them.

I thank the Dean of the Faculty's office at Connecticut College for granting me a sabbatical leave in the fall of 2011, during which much of this book was written or edited. I also thank the office for additional financial support through the R. F. Johnson Faculty Development Fund.

For permission to reproduce images, I thank: Fantagraphics Books for permission to reproduce images from Joe Sacco, *Safe Area: Goražde*; First Second for permission to reproduce images from Jean-Philippe Stassen, *Deogratias*; and Random House for permission to reproduce images from Marjane Satrapi, *Persepolis*, Art Spiegelman, *Maus*, and Guy Delisle, *Burma Chronicles*.

This book would never have come to fruition without the assistance and support of my husband, Dr. John Nugent, copyeditor extraordinaire. John gave of his time generously, reading, commenting on, and copyediting each chapter in this book. More than that, however, has been his unflagging moral and emotional support to me and to our family in the past year and a half. I cannot thank him enough. Finally, none of this work would matter if it were not for my beautiful Skye Mourne. Having a small child tends to bring world events into sharp focus very quickly, and the question with which all of the authors in this book wrestle – how to bring an awareness of, and an end to, the devastating human rights abuses suffered by so many around the world – are all the more real because of her existence in it.

For John, for his unwavering support

Introduction: willful ignorance – news production, audience reception, and responses to suffering

TRISTAN ANNE BORER

> An ample reservoir of stoicism is needed to get through the great newspaper of record each morning, given the likelihood of seeing photographs that could make you cry. (Susan Sontag, *Regarding the Pain of Others*)

> Most media consumers eventually get to the point where they turn the page. (Susan Moeller, *Compassion Fatigue*)

Twenty years in Somalia

On 20 July 2011 the United Nations (UN) declared a famine in southern Somalia, which was experiencing the worst drought in more than half a century. It was the first time that the organization had invoked the word famine in relation to Somalia since 1992, when its use, and the death of an estimated 200,000 people, resulted in armed humanitarian intervention to deliver food aid. Today, that intervention is best known for the 1993 Battle of Mogadishu and in particular the 'Black Hawk Down' incident that ended with the deaths of eighteen US Rangers and public outcry to end the intervention. Nineteen years later, famine again loomed large, causing massive displacement, starvation, and death. On the day of the declaration, Bloomberg news reported that almost 800,000 refugees had been forced to flee to neighboring countries (Richardson 2011), and Reuters (2011) reported that the UN estimated that 3.7 million people faced starvation inside Somalia, with 8 million more facing starvation in Kenya, Ethiopia, and Djibouti (Levitz and Abbany 2011). More than 30 percent of children in the famine-struck areas suffered acute malnourishment, with four of every 10,000 dying daily, Bloomberg further reported (Richardson 2011). Quite simply, the World Food Programme said, the crisis in the region 'ranks as the highest global humanitarian priority' (ibid.).

Two days after the UN sounded the alarm, the *Los Angeles Times* published an op-ed by UN Secretary-General Ban Ki-moon, who pleaded with the international community to intervene – if only by donating money and aid – to prevent the famine's spread and to help those already suffering. In his appeal, Ban described the shocking reality faced by Somalis: 'Every day I hear the harrowing reports from our UN teams on the ground. Somali refugees, their cattle and goats dead from thirst, walking for weeks to find help in Kenya and Ethiopia. Children who arrive alone, terrified and malnourished, their parents dead in a foreign land' (Ban 2011). Ban directed his entreaty to both states ('This means everyone. I appeal to all nations – both those that fund our work year in and year out, and those that do not traditionally give through the multinational system – to step up to the challenge') and individuals ('We must all ask ourselves, as individual citizens, how we can help. This might mean private donations ... or it could mean pushing elected representatives toward a more robust response'). In total, Ban said, 'we need about $1.6 billion in aid' (ibid.). The op-ed was accompanied by a photograph of hundreds of internally displaced Somalis, with the image's focal point being a severely emaciated man lying prone with a cloth over his head to ward off the sun. Other newspapers also resorted to the use of shock media – in their choice of both words and images – to describe the crisis. A BBC News reporter, for example, described a woman he met at a camp for internally displaced Somalis: 'Her five children were with her, but the youngest ones – aged two and five years – died on the way. She said she abandoned their bodies along the roadside because she was too weak to dig graves ... She said some of the mothers had walked up to six days without food to try to find help' (BBC News 2011). One of the most shocking images in the mainstream media was a photograph run by the *New York Times* on its 2 August front cover, depicting a severely malnourished child, with the caption 'More than 500,000 Somali children are verging on starvation.'

Celebrity activists soon entered the picture, often using social media to appeal for help. For example, several celebrities, including George Clooney, Bono, Clive Owen, Jessica Alba, Colin Farrell, and Ewan McGregor, joined the anti-poverty advocacy group ONE to launch a public service announcement (PSA) campaign to end the famine. In an online video entitled 'The F-Word: Famine is the real Obscenity,' the celebrities urged viewers to sign a petition, among other things (ONE 2011). On 15 August, Stephen Colbert, during an interview with US ambassador to the UN Susan Rice on his show *The Colbert Report*, urged his viewers to text the word 'AID' to a particular number, which would allow them to donate $10 directly to the World Food Programme.

Despite these frantic appeals by both the UN and celebrity activists, and despite increasing coverage in the news, the response by both states and individuals was tepid, prompting the United Kingdom's Secretary of State for International Development Andrew Mitchell to label the response by many European and developed countries 'derisory and dangerously inadequate' (BBC News 2011). The British charity Oxfam was equally condemnatory, accusing several European governments of 'willful neglect' in their response to the crisis (Reuters 2011). The mainstream media's coverage of the famine did not escape criticism either, when, in an op-ed in the *Guardian*, former British politician and UN diplomat Paddy Ashdown accused the media of ignoring the political and economic early warning signs of famine for years, 'reduced in a footnote in the media's eyes by more sensational events' (Ashdown 2011). On 28 July, the UN announced an $800 million shortfall in donations needed to respond to the crisis (Rhoads and Abdi 2011), and, on 5 September, the UN reported that the famine, which had originally affected only two regions in Somalia, had spread to six, and warned that 750,000 people could die within months if aid efforts were not scaled up (Gettleman 2011). Almost twenty years after the last famine, Ban Ki-moon summed up the frustrations of many in the humanitarian relief field when he asked, 'How is this happening again?' (Ban 2011). No substantial relief donations despite media efforts

Mediating suffering

How indeed? Today there is hardly a conflict – especially a large-scale one or a particularly violent one – that is not captured by photojournalists or television news journalists. In addition, anyone can witness atrocities by viewing amateur videos posted on online sites such as YouTube (see Jardin 2011, for example). We know and we see more than ever before. One of the central tenets of the human rights advocacy movement is the belief that information about human rights abuses leads to action to halt them. This conviction – that awareness of human rights atrocities has a mobilizing effect on an audience – seems so common-sensical ('of course people can't help but be moved to action by pictures of starving children') that it has taken on the quality of a truism whose factual basis is deemed almost too obvious to examine. And yet, as the 2011 Somalia famine, along with any number of other mass atrocities – the 1994 Rwandan genocide, the 1999 civil war in Sierra Leone, whose hallmark atrocity was the hacking off of limbs, and the epidemic levels of rape in the Democratic Republic of Congo, to name a few – make clear, this cause and effect relationship does not always exist. Indeed, one can easily imagine other responses to viewing and reading about human rights-related violence. For instance, it is possible that rather than spurring readers to action, media coverage instead desensitizes them to suffering, as Susan Moeller says in the epigraph at the beginning of the chapter. Another effect might be to overwhelm the audience with the magnitude of violence – so many atrocities in so many places – and make them feel helpless about what they deem to be hopeless. In this case, they may simply do nothing. Images and descriptions of atrocities may also elicit a different response: rather than evoking sympathy, they may result in the opposite – cries for revenge. Perhaps, most disturbingly, showing images of atrocities may hurt rather than help the victims of violence, turning the viewers into voyeurs of exoticized and objectified victims in an almost pornographic way. In other words, despite the repeated presentation of it as a simple causal relationship (exposure to images and stories of violence leads to action to prevent it), in reality the relationship between media portrayals of atrocities and individual responses to the portraits is anything but simple.

It is this complexity with which the authors of the chapters in this book grapple. Each chapter furthers our understanding of the multiple and varied ways in which viewing and reading about human rights atrocities can impact an audience. In other words, all of the authors are concerned with understanding how knowledge about human rights violations is mediated – what variables are at play between violence and its viewers? Thomas Keenan poses the question best when he asks: 'What links what we so loosely call "the media" and its images with action or inaction?' Furthermore, he asks: 'When something happens "in full view," why do we expect that action will be taken commensurate with what (we have seen) is happening?' (Keenan 2002, 548). Each chapter adds a piece to the puzzle of why news texts and images sometimes mobilize people but at other times are met with indifference. The book, then, sheds new theoretical insight into the complexity of the relationship between news and its reception – i.e. the process of news mediation. Indeed, the assumption of many human rights advocates that raising awareness of human rights violations is a precursor to political action is revealed to be anything but simple, clear, or direct. This is especially the case, some argue, when the suffering one sees or reads about is happening to people living far away and with whom the audience is likely never to come into contact. When this is the case, all of our knowledge of their suffering is mediated in some form. As Birgitta Höijer notes, 'it seems quite obvious that it

[handwritten: Media expected to make public 4 jump to defense but actually can have opposite response.]

is primarily through the media that we, citizens and politicians alike, meet depictions of the suffering of distant strangers' (Höijer 2004, 515). Luc Boltanski (1999) is also interested in the varying responses to distant suffering, asking: 'What form can this commitment take when those called up to act are thousands of miles away from the person suffering, comfortably installed in front of the television set in the shelter of the family living room?' (xv). Is there something in particular about both the distance of human rights violations and the reality that any awareness of those atrocities has by definition been mediated in some form that impacts whether people are more or less likely to act to stop them? When individuals personally suffer or witness abuses, violence or suffering, the reflexive response to resist, strike back, bear witness, or respond in any other way seems to make intuitive sense. But when knowledge is secondhand, it is much less clear what can and should be expected in terms of a response, despite the apparent certainty by many – or perhaps it is fervent hope – that 'if only people knew about what was happening, surely they would act.' This book deals primarily with responses (or lack thereof) to reports of violence and suffering that people do not personally witness or experience firsthand, but rather learn about through mediated accounts in newspapers, on television, through the Internet, through advertisements, or even through popular culture such as movies, books, or art.

The 2011–12 Somali famine and the world's underwhelming response is an obvious – albeit tragic – contemporary example of the reality that widespread coverage of suffering does not automatically translate into action to alleviate it. The Somalia case also features many elements covered in this book, including newspapers resorting to the use of shock (shocking images, shocking numbers, and shocking descriptions) to try to force a reaction from their readers; celebrities exhorting their fans to respond, often through new social media; the fact that these pleas often fall on deaf ears; and the responsibility of the media themselves, in part, for the tepid response because of their framing of crises. In sum, the chapters of this book help us understand why knowledge of human rights disasters sometimes moves an audience to action while at other times awareness of suffering barely registers. What follows is an overview of each chapter, embedded in a review of the theoretical literature, that illustrates how each advances our understanding of why and under what conditions exposure to the suffering of others sometimes leads to action to end it, while at other times ordinary people remain unmoved, complacent, and politically disengaged.

Second hand knowledge   5   doesn't elicit a strong approach.

States, the media, and humanitarian intervention

Both states and individuals have responded unevenly to human rights atrocities. The question of why states respond to some crises but not others has received much attention, especially in the aftermath of the Cold War. Between the end of the Cold War and the 11 September 2001 attacks, political space opened up for a debate about state intervention specifically to protect human rights. Regarding what has come to be known generally as humanitarian intervention, the initial question was whether the international community has the legal right and/or moral obligation to intervene militarily in the domestic sphere of another state to protect citizens whose rights are being violated by their government. Adam Roberts defines humanitarian intervention as 'coercive action by one or more states involving the use of armed force in another state without the consent of its authorities, and with the purpose of preventing widespread suffering or death among inhabitants' (cited in Weiss 2007, 5; see also Hoffmann et al. 1996 and Lang, Jr. 2003 for further theoretical review). The debate has now moved beyond this question, largely as a result of the emergence in the early 2000s of the principle of the Responsibility to Protect (R2P), which attempts to 'square the circle of state sovereignty and human rights' (Weiss 2007, 88). The core principle of R2P provides for military intervention for human protection purposes only when states do not, or cannot, act to protect their own citizens (for an overview of R2P see Weiss 2007 and International Commission on Intervention and State Sovereignty 2001). While R2P remains highly contested, most scholars no longer question *whether* a state has the right to intervene; rather, the question has increasingly become *why* they choose to intervene to stop abuses in some places but not others (see, for example, Power 2007). Various explanations for discrepant responses have been offered, including the strategic importance of the state in question, which includes the impact of a potential mass refugee influx; the amount of acceptable risk (how many deaths a state is willing to tolerate, for example); whether the conflict is perceived as intractable versus whether states perceive that intervention will help; and whether there is strong support from regional organizations, the UN Security Council, or both (Winter 2000). For the purposes of this book, the most interesting factor is the role of the media (see, for example, Soderlund et al. 2008; Allen and Seaton 1999).

As the concept of humanitarian intervention took root, scholars began looking at the role of the media in state-level policymaking. Scholars have analyzed how photographs and television news footage have impacted public opinion and how this opinion has in turn influenced foreign policy, a concept referred to as the CNN Effect. The 1992 Somali famine described earlier made this concept almost a household term. Operation Restore Hope, a US-led humanitarian initiative between December 1992 and October 1993, was the first large-scale post-Cold War humanitarian intervention. It was also the first intervention mediated live. In an analysis of just how hypermediated the event was, Thomas Keenan describes CNN's Christiane Amanpour reporting on the supposedly stealth landing of a joint Navy SEALS/Marine Reconnaissance unit. He quotes the *New York Times* as reporting that 'reporters were told when the landing would take place, and some network correspondents were quietly advised where the Marines would arrive so that they could set up their cameras' (Keenan 2004, 441). On 3 October, the 'Black Hawk Down' incident – in which two US Black Hawk helicopters were shot down, eighteen US soldiers were killed, and the bodies of several US casualties were dragged through the streets – was likewise reported live by CNN and beamed into television sets around the world. The images resulted in thousands of phone calls to US congressional representatives, many of whom themselves 'exhorted President Clinton to bring the troops home immediately' (Sharkey 1993). It was this sequence of events – media images captured as a result of twenty-four-hour news coverage leading to public cries for state action (first to intervene and later to withdraw), the resulting impact of public opinion on state policies, and a change in policy course – that has come to be known as the CNN Effect. Stephen Hess of the Brookings Institution defines it as 'the effect that continuous and instantaneous television may have on foreign policy, in the making of foreign policy, and the conduct of war' (Brookings Institution 2002), while Virgil Hawkins refers to it somewhat more facetiously as 'the do something syndrome' (Hawkins 2001). In terms of Somalia, Thomas Keenan asserts that the CNN Effect looked something like this: television pictures – in this case of starving children – brought US troops into Somalia, and television pictures – of dead US soldiers – pulled them out (Keenan 2004, 442).

Belief in a CNN Effect appears to have been at an apex in the aftermath of the Somalia intervention. Although the concept has subsequently been applied to other conflicts (see Bahador 2007) it remains most closely associated with 1992–93 Somalia and it has since lost some of its explanatory power. After all, for every 1992 Somalia, there was a 1994 Rwanda; for every 1999 Kosovo, there was a 1993 Sarajevo; for every 2011 Libya, there was a 2011 Syria. In other words, scholars and activists have discovered that media exposure of human rights atrocities does not necessarily lead the public to pressure governments to act (see Robinson 2002, Livingston 1997, and Strobel 1996 for critiques of the concept). Still, no one seems prepared to say that media coverage is irrelevant. Rather, the more complex argument made by most current scholars of the CNN Effect is that the media are a necessary but not sufficient variable for explaining state responses to other states' gross violations of human rights. Keenan sums up the sentiment best: 'Images, information, and knowledge will never guarantee any outcome, nor will they force or drive any action. They are, in that sense, like weapons or words: a condition, but not a sufficient one. Still the only thing more unwise than attributing the power of causation or of paralysis to images is to ignore them altogether' (Keenan 2002, 560). A direct causal effect, it turns out, is much too simple.

Part of the complexity is illustrated by David Kieran in his chapter 'Humanitarian intervention in the 1990s: cultural remembrance and the reading of Somalia as Vietnam' in which he argues that Americans' remembrance of Vietnam during the 1990s shaped the emerging legacy of the 1993 Somalia intervention. Specifically, while it has become common wisdom that the 'Somalia debacle' is a prime reason the US has been reticent about subsequent humanitarian forays in Africa, Kieran shows that it was in fact the way in which Americans were remembering Vietnam (not Somalia) in the 1990s, through recently published popular literature including memoirs of that war, that molded the Somalia legacy and defined that mission's place within broader debates about future US military commitments to humanitarian intervention. In other words, while the CNN Effect refers to some loose and ill-defined 'public opinion,' Kieran demonstrates that public opinion is not formed in a vacuum. It is, in part, filtered through cultural remembrances of other events. The cultural remembrances of Vietnam were again surfacing in contemporary bestselling popular literature at precisely the moment when Americans were beginning to doubt the Somalia intervention. Memories of a past conflict, in other words, can become culturally significant and reproduced in a current one. The deaths of American soldiers in Somalia were mediated by CNN but also by and through popular literature on Vietnam, with all of the painful cultural memories this brought back to life. Kieran argues that popular literature – both the literature on Vietnam and the emerging literature on Somalia – did more than simply compare the two conflicts (a trope the media were already employing). In addition, they contributed to the realist critiques of all future human-

CNN not the only driving factor, **8** Cultural remembrances also factor into public opinion.

itarian interventions by explicitly representing Somalia *as* Vietnam. In other words, fresh memories of Vietnam happened to intersect with Americans' anxieties about humanitarian intervention as a result of Somalia. A memorial discourse was created that blended the memories of Vietnam with those of Somalia, which then served to legitimize the critiques offered by opponents of humanitarian intervention in general. We can extrapolate from Kieran's conclusions that both the media and public opinion about future humanitarian interventions will be mediated through cultural remembrances, which are only now being created, of conflicts in Afghanistan and Iraq in the first decade of the twenty-first century – both of which were in part sold to the public as humanitarian missions. In sum, Kieran illustrates that the CNN Effect is far more complex than early theorizing of it held. In Somalia, media images played into a cultural memory that was inclined to push for withdrawal in the first place; the cultural memory of Vietnam made the images coming out of Somalia ripe for looking like a CNN Effect.

Ordinary people, the media, and distant suffering

While David Kieran's chapter reminds us that much more theorizing about the role of the media in state-level humanitarian interventions is warranted, we also need to look at how individuals respond to mediated atrocities. As Paul Slovic notes, 'behind every president who ignored mass murder were millions of citizens whose indifference allowed them to get away with it' (Slovic 2007, 80). Why are some individuals indifferent to mass suffering, turning the page on shocking images in the morning newspaper? Or, as Susan Moeller eloquently asks: 'Why, despite the haunting nature of many images – narrative images, photographic images, video images – do we seem to care less and less about the world around us?' (Moeller 1999, 4). Why do people respond emotionally to some images and with a shrug to others? Why do they act on that emotion in some cases and not in others? Individuals' psycho-emotional reactions to stimuli are, of course, highly complex, and all of the questions above are likely to have multiple and interrelated answers. At the same time, scholars have tried to theorize why individuals respond differently to information, either images or texts, about gross violations of human rights, and what role the media play in their varied responses. Three of the most common explanations will be examined here: psycho-physical numbing that makes it difficult to care about large-scale, distant suffering; the difficulty of effecting a cosmopolitan citizenry; and compassion fatigue. A brief overview

Once again, why public opion 9 varies on different events.

of each of the three explanations is provided below, followed by a summary of the core contribution of the book – how each of the remaining chapters responds to, interacts with, clarifies, and expounds upon some or all of the theories, and, most importantly, how each chapter contributes to a better understanding of the varying responses to media portrayals of human rights violations.

Psychic numbing Psychologist Paul Slovic examines why most people, despite the fact that they are caring and would make a great effort to help an individual in need, appear to be indifferent – indeed numb – when the number of those suffering is much larger. In bringing the question from the level of the state to that of the individual, Slovic asks: 'Why, over the past century, have good people repeatedly ignored mass murder and genocide?' (Slovic 2007, 79). He argues that at a psycho-physical level, people are unable to experience affect – the positive and negative feelings that combine with reasoned analysis to guide judgments, decisions, and actions – for large-scale suffering. Affect, he says, is the most basic form of feeling – the sense (not necessarily conscious) that something is good or bad, without which information lacks meaning and cannot be used in judgment (ibid., 82). Images are particularly important in affect. Affect is supplemented by other feelings such as empathy, sympathy, compassion, sadness, pity, and distress. Together, these feelings are critical for motivating people to help others. Quite simply, according to Slovic, people help others when they 'feel' for them, and humans are unable to fathom, to 'wrap our minds around,' or to feel for large-scale suffering. The incapacity to feel for large groups of people suffering far away is an evolutionary trait; humans evolved to protect their families or small communities from immediate danger, not to respond to distant mass murder. We are not hardwired to care about, to feel for, people suffering en masse far away: 'the circuitry of our brain is not up to this task' (ibid., 84).

Slovic's argument is one of both distance and scale. In terms of distance, the closer the victims are to us, the more we are likely to feel for them. This obviously has consequences for the types of mediated atrocities discussed in this book, such as the East African famine declared in 2011. In terms of scale, the larger the number of sufferers, the harder it is for us to care about them. Slovic argues that the sentiment of Nobel Prize-winning biochemist Albert Szent-Györgyi, who struggled with the probable outcome of nuclear war, sums up his theory nearly perfectly. Szent-Györgyi said, 'I am deeply moved if

R.M.

Psychic numbing, evolutionary trait, 10 can't experience affect for large scale suffering, looks at indiv., distance, scale

I see one man suffering and would risk my life for him. Then I talk impersonally about the possible pulverization of our big cities, with a hundred million dead. I am unable to multiply one man's suffering by a hundred million' (ibid.). Others have confirmed this inability. Slovic quotes Mother Teresa, who said, 'If I look at the mass I will never act. If I look at the one, I will' (ibid., 80). More notoriously, from her moral opposite, Josef Stalin once said, 'One death is a tragedy. One million deaths is a statistic' (Moeller 1999, 36).

The difficulty of comprehending large-scale deaths has consequences for how human rights advocates and news producers – editors and reporters – frame foreign crises to maximize audience reception of their message, an issue dealt with in Tristan Anne Borer's chapter, as will be described below. Before delving into that, however, two other explanations for what Slovic calls 'mass murder and genocide neglect' will be reviewed.

Impediments to cosmopolitanism As noted earlier, most encounters with human rights-related suffering by Western audiences occur through reading about them in newspapers or watching them on television or the Internet. The victims are mostly strangers, living far away. Unfortunately, argue several scholars (Kleinman and Kleinman 1996; Boltanski 1999; Chouliaraki 2006; Kyriakidou 2009), it has proven very difficult to create a global citizenry or a sense of cosmopolitan solidarity, despite popular-culture references to global villages and 'we are the world' pronouncements. Even in an increasingly globalized and interconnected world, Kyriakidou argues, the expected deterritorializing that would come with fading or erased borders has not yet happened. Indeed, nationalism is as strong an identifying force as ever, and it has proven quite difficult to 'imagine ourselves beyond the nation' (Kyriakidou 2009, 481). Even the mediated connections facilitated by twenty-four-hour, instantaneous news coverage – the same connections allegedly responsible for a CNN Effect – have been unable to negate other forms of identity and belonging, keeping nationalism as the focal point of community (ibid., 482). It is, in other words, very difficult to sustain commitment to humanity as a whole. Theorists of cosmopolitanism, which Kyriakidou defines as 'a sense of global belonging and commitment to distant others' (ibid., 487), naturally study the role of media, given their centrality in global interconnectedness. As Kyriakidou notes, 'for most people most of the time, "cosmopolitan" experience is restricted to media images and news; it is mostly through the media that they are confronted with and experience "otherness"' (ibid., 484). Lilie Chouliaraki is similarly interested in determining whether the media are able to create a global public – which she calls an ethically engaged cosmopolitan citizenry – with a sense of social responsibility toward the distant sufferer. She concludes that 'despite the instantaneous and global reach of visibility that [media] technologies have achieved, the optimistic celebration of our planet as a global village or the [audience] as a new cosmopolitan should be held in check' (Chouliaraki 2006, 4). While the media could theoretically 'cultivate a "beyond the nation" cultural resonance among Western audiences,' more often than not they simply reproduce a dichotomous 'us' versus 'them' sentiment (ibid., 12). Finally, a cosmopolitan ethic of care and action is difficult to achieve – despite instantaneous and continuous news of human rights violations around the world – because, Kyriakidou points out, 'the national, as collective history and memories, culture and political identities, forms the lens and the interpretative framework through which audiences around the world make sense of global events and distant suffering' (Kyriakidou 2009, 493). In sum, theorists of media and cosmopolitanism question the creation of global solidarities and subsequent mobilization; at the very least, they argue, nationalism remains a strong pull on peoples' identities, making it difficult to overcome apathy toward distant suffering.

It is precisely this question – what role the media can play in 'infiltrating people's everyday lives with emotionally engaging values that orient them toward geographically distant others,' as Kyriakidou puts it (ibid., 484), that Michael Galchinsky addresses in his chapter 'Framing a rights ethos: artistic media and the dream of a culture without borders.' In particular, Galchinsky is interested in how a universal human rights culture might be created, and how the media might help in its creation. After all, the idea of the existence of human rights needs to be firmly entrenched in people's minds before they can be receptive to the messages of the media. As Galchinsky states: 'Culture helps construct the civil society in which human rights can be meaningful ... Neither the UN nor a national government can simply compel people to respect each other's rights: people have to *want* to.' His chapter is about artistic media in general – with a specific focus on graphic novels – and how they produce and reflect that desire. Can artistic media ground the formal rights system in an informal rights ethos, and can they do it transnationally, helping audiences recognize 'those aspects of experience that ... transcend nationality, race, and ethnicity; gender and sexuality; religion and class'? What scholars of cosmopolitanism refer to as a global ethic of care, Galchinsky calls a universal structure of feeling – a 'socially constructed and sanctioned sympathy with others across identity differences' – and his chapter investigates whether human rights-related art, such as novels, biographies, films, and graphic novels, can cultivate rights-oriented 'habits of the heart' so that, when exposed to atrocities, audiences will take a stand against them. To make his case, he examines four artistic 'modes': protest (such as the film *Cry Freedom*), testimony (such as *The Diary of Anne Frank*), lament (such as the novel *Beloved*), and laughter (such as Kafka's *The Trial*). Galchinsky's most important contribution, however, is his case-study analysis of graphic novels and graphic reportage that explores how artistic media can foster cosmopolitanism, and the problems they encounter. Some obstacles are operational, such as figuring out how to translate idiomatic works into universally acceptable language and how to market them without potentially endangering the artists. Other problems stem from the lack of a borderless global citizenry. As he notes, artists are 'severely hampered by the absence of any global public to which they could appeal ... There really aren't any citizens of the world.' Like other cosmopolitanists, then, Galchinsky argues, drawing on the work of John Tomlinson, that the biggest obstacle facing artists is conceptual:

> The symbolic, emotional, and ideational links that make people everywhere feel they share a common destiny are thinner than the thinnest nationalism. Unlike national citizens, 'citizens of the world' lack common territory, ethnicity, language, ideology, and history – all the horizontal ties that bind imagined communities. In the absence of such ties, works of human rights culture could theoretically construct a system of shared symbols that might serve to form some bonds of common passion and understanding. To function in this way, however, such works would have to be taken out of their national habitat. To be globalized, they would have to become nomads, bound not to territory or local lore, but to shared values.

Galchinsky is not entirely pessimistic, however, concluding that artistic media can at times succeed in crafting and promoting a global ethos. While they may not result in immediate action in any given situation, in the long run they can produce 'a sense of sympathetic identification for the victims of abuse'; they 'fend off the numbness, voyeurism, and distance that are all too often the psychological effects of other mediated relations.'

Compassion fatigue A third, arguably best known, explanation for

13

apathetic responses to news of atrocities is the phenomenon of compassion fatigue, a counterintuitive phenomenon that states that the more suffering we see, the less we feel. Keith Tester (2001, 13) defines compassion fatigue as:

> becoming so used to the spectacle of dreadful events, misery or suffering that we stop noticing them. We are bored when we see one more tortured corpse on the television screen and we are left unmoved ... Compassion fatigue means being left exhausted and tired by those reports and ceasing to think that anything at all can be done to help ... Compassion fatigue means a certain fatalism. It leads to the conclusion that this is just the way things are and nothing can be done that will make a difference.

Kinnick et al. similarly describe the phenomenon as pertaining to a public that has 'grown weary of unrelenting media coverage of human tragedy and ubiquitous fund-raising appeals' (Kinnick et al. 1996, 687). Unlike Slovic's argument above, in which psychic numbness results from an inability to process the sheer number of victims, here people become numb to remote human suffering as a result of overexposure to it, a concept that Birgitta Höijer describes as 'distantiation from compassion' (Höijer 2004, 524). Some scholars are skeptical that compassion fatigue even exists. Tester argues, for example, that 'the whole debate about compassion fatigue has a number of significant logical problems,' and that theorists of compassion fatigue 'make a number of assumptions which are questionable at best and untenable at worst' (Tester 2001, 2 and 15). Tester makes an argument similar to Slovic's claim that humans are not naturally – in Slovic's argument not hardwired – to feel compassion; he rejects the implicit normative assumption of compassion fatigue that people are and will be compassionate toward one another. Rather, he says, 'compassion is not a natural, innate or inevitable ethic' (ibid., 20). Others see it as an inevitable, unavoidable – and very real – consequence of the way in which news is covered, which results in the repetitive use of language and images. Susan Moeller, for example, argues that the media, afraid to stray from what they think will 'sell,' cover what they think the audience wants, which results in repetition, which breeds indifference: 'Compassion fatigue is a consequence of rote journalism, and looking-over-your-shoulder reporting ... Newspapers, news magazines and television don't want to get beat by the competition – either in the stories they cover or in the packaging they come in. As a result, much of the media looks alike. The same news, the same pictures.

Compassion fatigue is becoming numb to overexposure of suffering.

What's the inevitable result much of the time? Compassio͏
(Moeller 1999, 32). Still others, like Höijer, aver that the proces͏
complex than either Tester or Moeller claim. Her findings ind͏
there is a gendered dimension to compassion, and that distantiation
(i.e. compassion fatigue) is more prevalent among men than women
(Höijer 2004, 525).

These three explanations for uneven responses or non-reaction to
news reports about distant suffering – psychological numbness, the
lack of a cosmopolitan citizenry, and compassion fatigue – are not
unrelated; indeed, they are quite interactive. Many scholars argue that
both compassion fatigue and the difficulty of fostering a cosmopolitan
ethos result in part from the process of news production. And, if people
are increasingly numb to distant suffering – because of either psychological barriers or compassion fatigue – then news producers and
human rights activists alike need to work harder and more creatively to
grab their audiences' attention, which is an audience reception issue.
The remaining chapters of this book examine either news production-
related issues or audience reception issues, and how they help make
sense of why knowledge does not always result in action.

News production – the first half of the equation

Scholars of both cosmopolitanism and compassion fatigue argue
that there is something about the way in which faraway atrocities are
covered in the news that makes it less likely that people will act to
end them; i.e. that the problem is, in part, a news production one. As
noted above, cosmopolitanism competes with nationalism as a pull on
individual identity. As Simon Cottle points out, news producers – both
editors and reporters – tend to reinforce the primacy of the national
over the global, especially through the framing of global crises 'in
ways consonant to national interests and identities' (Cottle 2009, 509).
For example, he notes, 'wars continue to be reported through blood-
tinted glasses colored by national interests and/or returning coffins
draped in the national flag. When reporting on distant disasters and
humanitarian emergencies, national news media continue to seek out
and populate stories with their own "nationals" – whether embodied
as victims, survivors, heroes, or concerned celebrities' (ibid.). As a
result, he argues, 'global news stagings are not destined to necessarily serve processes of "enforced enlightenment," much less promote
cosmopolitan solidarity' (ibid.).

Tester likewise argues that the *way* in which distant crises, specifically
those in Africa, are covered by the media makes the emergence of a

Three explanations linked. Media **15** doesn't promote globalism.
Cover global crisis on national glasses, e.g. flag covered coffin.

cosmopolitan citizenry less likely: 'Africa is invariably presented as a place of endemic and persistent pain and suffering. Therefore ... the message is that it is simply the way that things are. It becomes their unalterable fate' (Tester 2001, 7). This results in what historian Michael Ignatieff calls 'one of the dangerous cultural moods of our time, the belief that the world is so out of control and so terrible that all we can do is disengage from it' (Ignatieff 1998, 25).

While Cottle, Tester, and Ignatieff all argue that the process of news production impedes the creation of a cosmopolitan ethic, Moeller focuses on how the business of news production inevitably results in compassion fatigue. She argues that editors and producers do not assign stories and that correspondents do not cover events they believe will not appeal to their readers or viewers. As a result, the media present simplistic, formulaic coverage of international events; moreover, the coverage is highly repetitive, under the assumption that if it sold last time, it will sell this time. Thus, as Moeller states: 'If images of starving babies worked in the past to capture attention for a complex crisis of war, refugees and famine, then starving babies will headline the next difficult crisis' (Moeller 1999, 2). However, this constant repetition contributes to the result Tester and Ignatieff noted above – that Africa is hopeless and there is nothing that can be done. So, when the 1991 East African famine worsened into one of the most severe in recent memory, Moeller quotes a non-governmental organization (NGO) worker as saying, 'people worldwide must have the feeling of "African famine again?"' Another NGO worker agreed: 'Donors are tired of repetitious events, and Sudan and Ethiopia are repetitious. Every time there's a famine in Africa ... you can always count on somebody asking, "Hey didn't they just do that last year?"' (ibid., 8). News of African famine, in 1991 and twenty years later in 2011, evokes a 'been there, done that' attitude among Westerners, she argues. The result is that news consumers, 'weary of pouring money into crises that never seem to go away,' fall into 'a discouragingly contagious compassion fatigue' (ibid., 9). And the cause of this is the way in which the media cover crises.

Experiencing compassion fatigue despite viewing images of suffering seems particularly disconcerting to some. It is one thing to turn the page when reading about atrocities, the argument goes, but how can you see pictures of starving children or mutilated bodies and still not care? Moeller's explanation for the persistence of compassion fatigue in the face of horrifying images is remarkably similar to Slovic's argument about scale. 'Didactic images can overload the senses,' she argues. 'A

- News reports what will sell, after awhile though, shock value wears off. Brings 'this is the way things are attitude'.

single child at risk commands our attention and prompts our action. But one child, and then another, and another, and another and on and on and on is too much. A crowd of people in danger is faceless. Numbers alone can numb. All those starving brown babies over the years blur together' (ibid., 36). In the end, she argues, the sheer number of images, all seemingly presented in the same redundant manner, lead to what one journalist has referred to as the MEGO, or 'My Eyes Glaze Over,' syndrome (ibid.).

However, Moeller argues, compassion fatigue is not only a result of the way in which news is produced, it also influences news production. She provides an interesting cyclical model in which the way in which a story is covered leads to compassion fatigue, and the fact that audience members seem no longer to care about a story (i.e. they are fatigued by it) leads the media to cover it less and less: 'There is a reciprocal circularity in the treatment of [ongoing] crises; the droning, "same-as-it-ever-was" coverage in the media causes the public to lose interest, and the media's perception that their audience has lost interest causes them to downscale their coverage ...' (ibid., 12). This, then, is one of the 'most devastating effects of compassion fatigue: no attention, no interest, no story' (ibid.), a charge indeed leveled against the media during the 2011–12 Somalia famine.

What is clear from the above analysis is the fact that whether people respond to information about human rights violations has much to do with how those violations are portrayed – an issue generally referred to as 'framing.' A prior media production issue, however, is whether distant crises are even covered at all. After all, people cannot respond to something they know nothing about. The question of how human rights-related news stories are chosen is discussed by Ella McPherson in her chapter on Mexican newspapers, while the question of how these stories (once chosen for coverage) are framed is taken up by Dan Chong in his chapter on framing strategies.

Determining newsworthiness While compassion fatigue theorists argue that people become numb to suffering as a result of overexposure to it, others argue that distant mass atrocities are, in reality, underexposed by the media. For Steven Livingston, 'overall, the *lack* of media coverage of humanitarian emergencies is most striking' (Livingston 1997, 9; italics in original). Virgil Hawkins refers to this lack of coverage as 'the other side of the CNN factor,' and argues further that media coverage of international humanitarian crises is uneven, with some regions – perhaps not surprisingly Africa – being covered significantly less than other regions. He provides evidence of what he calls 'an almost insignificant amount of coverage' of ongoing conflicts in Angola, the Democratic Republic of Congo, Ethiopia, Eritrea, and Sierra Leone, during the same time as coverage in the run-up to the 1999 NATO intervention in Kosovo (Hawkins 2001).[1] At a very minimum, then, whether or not an audience responds to distant suffering depends on whether they are aware of it. And, since 'conflicts in distant countries have little bearing on the everyday lives of citizens, whether or not they are aware of the magnitude of a crisis, and whether or not they are concerned, is entirely dependent on the level of media coverage' (ibid.).

So, what factors determine whether a particular medium will cover international human rights crises? This is the subject of Ella McPherson's case studies of Mexican newspapers in her chapter 'How editors choose which human rights news to cover: a case study of Mexican newspapers.' While McPherson certainly agrees that 'a significant proportion of human rights information never reaches a public because it is not witnessed, it is not considered newsworthy, or because it contraindicates media's editorial line aims,' her interest lies in understanding the decisions behind those human rights news stories that *do* appear – decisions that are not made in a vacuum. Her chapter dissects all of the factors at play in whether people can pick up a newspaper and read stories about human rights violations – how, in her words, 'headlines are plucked from the informational ether of every news day.' She notes that 'in pursuit of their practice, members of the media are battered by a maelstrom of influences that determine not only what information they choose to report and how they report it, but also what information they choose to ignore.' Like Moeller, McPherson zeroes in on the business of news production, arguing that journalists, who in theory have no agenda other than reporting the news, actually must compete with such overt influences on journalism as economic considerations and political pressures. She describes, through an analysis of the relatively new phenomenon of Mexican newspapers having an established human rights beat, a news selection framework akin to a process of survival in which human rights news stories are 'winnowed' through their assessment against a series of criteria: first they must be considered generally newsworthy; then they need to be in line with the newspaper's editorial stance; then they need to be in line with the newspaper's economic (i.e. the advertisers') needs. In other words, even when an event is considered newsworthy, it will not necessarily become news. She concludes: 'Of that which is considered newsworthy, the more a particular piece of information is in line with a newspaper's journalistic, economic and political aims relative to other bits of information, the more likely it is to be published.' These criteria – newsworthiness, journalistic aims (i.e. whether the newspaper self-identifies as a watchdog civil society organization), economic aims (how reliant it is on advertising revenue), and political aims (generally speaking, its editorial position) – are not, however, always self-evident or easily definable.

Determining what makes one human rights crisis newsworthy while another is not is sometimes more art than science, and is an issue that has long interested media sociologists. Moeller quotes Carroll Bogert, a foreign correspondent for *Newsweek* (who is also a former acting foreign editor there), as saying that what was covered 'has to do with the predilections of the editors in New York.' How the decisions are made about what to cover is a 'fairly flukey thing ... I think it's just quirks of fate' (Moeller 1999, 23). One study of the gatekeeping function of editors – i.e. their power to choose which stories pass through the 'gate' to be consumed by readers and which get held back – revealed that editors' judgments are subjective and based on personal values (Kratzer and Kratzer 2003, 35). McPherson argues that it is not quite as random as this, although it is still impossible to apply a formula that spits out a 'newsworthiness' rating. Rather, she says, the determination of newsworthiness remains 'improvisational.' In general, in Mexico, the determination of the newsworthiness of human rights news came down to a combination of factors; the stories must contain violations and be novel, exclusive, impactful, representative, and timely.

If Slovic is correct that images play an important role in affect – the ability to feel compassion for others – and if Moeller is correct that images play a role in the ratcheting up of shock that leads to compassion fatigue (an issue that will be discussed in more detail below), then one interesting newsworthiness-related question is how editors decide what pictures to publish. Shahira Fahmy argues that images play an integral role in framing, arguing that 'visuals and text are distinct yet equally important parts of the news-making process' (Fahmy 2010, 3). Indeed, she argues, past studies have shown that image choices clearly influence how the audience perceives an event, and that 'competing media outlets portray events in different ways, carefully selecting particular images, as visuals are consistently used to present specific views to the audience' (ibid.). Höijer agrees; referring to 'the penetrative power of pictures,' she argues: 'Compassion is dependent on visuals... Pictures, or more precisely our interpretations of pictures, can make indelible impressions on our minds, and as a distant audience we become bearers of inner pictures of human suffering' (Höijer 2004, 520).

The question of image choice is especially fraught when the images are particularly graphic portrayals of atrocities. This was a poignant question in the aftermath of the 11 September 2001 terrorist attacks in the United States (see Kratzer and Kratzer 2003 and Zelizer 2010), and it remains an important one for trying to understand why audiences react in the way they do to news of foreign violence. Editors are forced to walk a line between news and sensationalism, between the journalistic imperative – the need to tell the story – and other considerations, such as the dignity of the victims (Dunlap 2009). Debbie Madsen argues, first, that most papers do not have a hard-and-fast policy about which pictures to publish because every picture tells a different story; second, that editors often do not see eye to eye when it comes to publishing graphic and shocking photographs; and, third, that most newspapers do not publish most of the shocking images they receive (Madsen 1991). The bottom line, says Barbara Cochran, former president of the Radio-Television News Directors Association, is that one of the great decision-making issues for any news organization is having to decide 'how much is too much?' (quoted in Sharkey 2003).

In sum, news about human rights atrocities doesn't just appear out of nowhere. Someone, or many people, makes a decision or many decisions – about newsworthiness or about whether a picture is too graphic to publish – for an audience to have access to it. In reality, the majority of human rights violations go uncovered by the media. For a variety of reasons, Moeller argues, certain disasters, especially the mid-level ones, are in effect rendered invisible (Moeller 1999, 20). The very first role, then, that the media play in affecting an audience's reaction to distant suffering is simply to cover that suffering. If an audience is not exposed to news of violence, it cannot act to stop it. Deciding a story is worth covering, however, is only the first step. The event being covered needs to be presented to the audience in a way that makes them believe that they can and should do something about it. The story needs, in other words, to be framed in a certain way.

Framing As the basic lenses through which we interpret reality, frames help select which aspects of reality are important and, once selected, help to define them in a certain way. Media framing of an issue is obviously important for how the audience will respond to it. There is nothing inherently positive or negative about framing, and the media can and have framed events in ways that portray victims of

- Deciding the picture long task, **20** editors don't always agree, how much is too much?

human rights in both lights – although arguably the negative aspect of the media's framing of events receives more critical and analytical attention than when victims are portrayed in a positive light. An example of an analysis of negative media framing is Peter Gale's study of Australian newspaper reporting on the refugee 'crisis' (the term itself is a frame) in late 2001. Gale argues that the media engaged in fearmongering embedded in postmodern racist portrayals of refugees, couched in such language as Iraqis (the majority of refugees seeking entrance to Australia at the time) representing a 'threat to Australian national culture,' and hence, implicitly, a 'threat to whiteness, and Western, core values or democracy itself' (Gale 2004, 322–3). Identifying three 'representational themes,' or frames, Gale argues that refugees, and the 'crisis' inherent in the number of people seeking refuge, were frequently framed – through the use of both language and images – as representing a threat to Australia's national security. In headline after headline, refugees were not referred to as such, but as 'boat people' trying to enter the country 'illegally.'

Ariella Pasackow, in an analysis of the *New York Times'* framing of victims in the aftermath of Hurricane Katrina in 2005 and the 2010 earthquake in Haiti, similarly argues that media framing can criminalize victims. In Haiti, 'exemplified in the repeated use of the word "looting" (including its derivatives loot, looted, and looters), *New York Times* journalists framed survivors of the earthquake as violent perpetrators carrying out inexcusable crimes' (Pasackow 2010, 3). The framing is evident when read in light of Jude Fernando's contention in his study of media reporting of disasters in general that 'what is called looting in news reports is often a desperate search for food and water by suffering disaster victims, but local law enforcement agencies often take these photo opportunities to transform a humanitarian crisis into a law-and-order crisis' (Fernando 2010, 4).

Framing is obviously an important part of the explanation of why some humanitarian crises receive attention while others do not. If victims are portrayed as 'criminals,' 'looters,' or 'illegal immigrants,' regardless of whether they are any of these, the situation being reported is less likely to provoke activism to help them. The power of the media is clear – nothing is more symbolic of this than the term 'looting,' which can transform desperate victims into violent criminals, and humanitarian emergencies into calls for increased law enforcement budgets. Pasackow sums it up best when she argues that 'the language employed by the media is far from neutral and powerless; on the contrary, biases and stereotypes, omissions and emphases, and

21

syntax and diction build a frame in which post-disaster narratives are presented. More than simply reporting, media outlets have the power to indirectly determine emergency responses and disaster priorities' (Pasackow 2010, 7). As a result, readers become desensitized to their plight – one more factor added to our growing list of reasons why distant crises elicit little more than a shrug.[2]

The discussion so far highlights the fact that, in much of the literature on framing, the media are doing the framing (as in 'The *New York Times* frames earthquake victims as looters,' or 'Australian newspapers frame refugees as illegals'). Dan Chong, in his chapter 'Framing strategies for economic and social rights in the United States,' takes a wholly different approach. Chong illustrates that the media do not have a monopoly on the use of framing techniques. Human rights advocates can also employ framing, and his chapter discusses the various strategies they have used to put economic and social rights on the human rights map in the United States.[3] In this case, rather than the media driving public opinion, human rights advocates are the ones doing the framing, presenting issues in a way to elicit policy responses by pushing public opinion and setting political agendas. In appropriating framing techniques, he argues, human rights advocates can drive media coverage of events. In the case of distant suffering, framing becomes important precisely because it is so difficult (as Slovic tells us) to connect to the suffering of others. Framing strategies can most successfully overcome this apathy, Chong argues, when issues are framed as universal moral claims, tailored to a specific audience, representative of a consistent message, and resonant with existing social practices and cultural assumptions. He states: 'Frames are successful when they *resonate* with people (i.e. when they have an immediate visceral appeal, or match up with existing personal/cultural beliefs) rather than when they try to *persuade* people of the logic of a position. Visual images, sensationalism, and personal stories tend to resonate more deeply than merely citing facts and statistics' (italics in original). As will become clear in Borer's chapter discussed below, this quote almost perfectly explains why Nicholas Kristof's op-eds in the *New York Times* are written as they are. While not using Chong's exact approach, Kristof has a clearly definable formula – a 'framing strategy' if you will – for grabbing his readers' attention for whatever human rights atrocity he is writing about at the moment.

Audience reception – the other half of the equation

The first half of the equation, then, for why people sometimes remain unmoved by reports of atrocities is that humanitarian crises first need to be reported before anyone can care about them, and framed in a way that makes it probable that the audience will respond to what they are seeing or reading. This is only part of the issue, however, because obviously many crises are reported and appropriately framed, and still people do not react. The explanation that there is a lack of actionable information simply does not hold in many instances; very few people can claim in this day and age that 'I didn't know.' Keith Tester (2001, 4–5) could just as well be referencing the 2011–12 Somali famine when he wrote in 2001, citing Alain Finkielkraut:

> when it comes to the problem of world hunger, we are in a different situation from our ancestors because we do not have the defense of ignorance. Whereas our ancestors could claim, probably in all good conscience, that they did nothing about famine in Africa or slaughter in Asia because they knew nothing about it, we cannot develop that kind of argument without lying to ourselves. We know, we know we know and everybody else knows that we know.

Thus, even in the face of sufficient information that is appropriately presented, some people still do not act for various reasons already discussed – a natural psychological numbing to large-scale atrocities, or an increasing desensitization due to compassion fatigue, for example. When this happens, human rights advocates and people in the business of selling news need to become ever more creative in capturing the attention of their audience. The flip side of the media production literature, therefore, is the field of study known as 'audience reception,' which Sonia Livingstone defines as 'the interactive link between text, audience and context,' and is primarily concerned with how audiences interpret texts in different ways, a highly complex and context-dependent phenomenon (Livingstone 1998). For our purposes, given the reality of compassion fatigue, given the obstacles to the creation of a truly cosmopolitan sense of compassion, and given that we are not hardwired to care about distant mass suffering, human rights advocates and media producers have a hard row to hoe in getting an audience to consume their news and to care about the suffering they see or read about. Simply put, how do the media and human rights advocates grab the attention of their audience, and prompt them to act? Three approaches are detailed in this book: the use of shock media, the use of celebrity advocates, and the use of social media.

23

Shock media If Moeller and Slovic are right that audiences become inured and numbed to pictures of suffering, then it will take more and more dramatic coverage to elicit the same level of sympathy as in the past. Moeller points out that compassion fatigue ratchets up the criteria for stories that get coverage: 'To forestall the I've-seen-it-before syndrome, journalists reject events that aren't more dramatic or more lethal than their predecessors. Or, through a choice of language and images, the newest event is represented as being more extreme or deadly or risky than a similar past situation' (Moeller 1999, 2). Another way of saying this is that journalists and editors try to shock their audiences into paying attention, which is the subject of Tristan Anne Borer's chapter '"Fresh, wet tears": shock media and human rights awareness campaigns.' She defines shock media as 'the use of graphic and disturbing images and prose to try to shock readers into taking action on a particular human rights issue.' The chapter focuses in particular on the use of shocking language in petitions and op-eds, such as those by Nicholas Kristof of the *New York Times*, as well as the use of shocking photographs, such as *TIME Magazine*'s 2010 cover portrait of a mutilated Afghan woman with her nose and ears sliced off. As noted earlier, images are an especially important mechanism for shock; Madsen (1991) notes: 'Pictures shock where words cannot. Facts and figures can be forgotten, but images are difficult to erase from the mind. Pictures act like a chisel on the brain, etching images into long-term memory.'

Borer draws on literature in the advertising field, where shock ads have long been used, especially in health-related public safety campaigns. Do such shock tactics work? Findings from the field of 'shockvertising' indicate that shock ads – such as images of diseased mouths meant to encourage people to stop smoking – *do* often work to change personal behavior, and suggest that Kristof and others may be on the right track in using shock to try to affect personal behavior in terms of taking action to stop human rights abuses. However, Borer argues that there are also some significant negative consequences that should give pause to those considering using such tactics.

In her analysis of Kristof's gender-based op-eds (in which he focuses on such gender-based violations as acid burnings, female genital cutting, and punishments for sexual transgressions grounded in sharia law, including floggings and stonings), Borer draws on both feminist literature and the literature of cosmopolitanism cited above to argue that his use of shocking words and images so exoticizes these women that, rather than effecting a cosmopolitan response, his columns result

24

in the exact opposite – an inability of his Western readers to relate to the women or their experiences. Rather than forging closer ties – and thus presumably a desire to help these women – shock media increase the distance between the sufferer and the spectator, thus making the audience less rather than more likely to act. In other words, shock media may well undermine their own purposes, doing more harm than good by reinforcing anti-cosmopolitan, pro-national sentiments. Borer draws on Chouliaraki to argue that the use of shock media, rather than fostering empathy for those who are not like us, instead creates a dichotomous 'we' who live in a zone of safety and whose lifestyle must be preserved, versus an 'other' who live in a zone of danger and who must be kept out of our zone (Chouliaraki 2006, 10). Birgitta Höijer describes the sentiment thus: 'Why bother about people who are primitive and uncivilized and not like us, civilized citizens in democracies?' (Höijer 2004, 525).

A second drawback is that there is every reason to believe that today's shocking photograph will leave tomorrow's news consumer unfazed. In other words, given Moeller's theory of compassion fatigue, it is not clear whether there will ever be an end to the 'ratcheting up' of shock; can the spiral of ever more necessary shock end, and, if so, how?

Although he is aware of these critiques, Kristof is quite clear about his methodology, employing exactly the sort of framing strategies that Chong describes in his chapter. Taking Slovic's (whom he frequently cites as having influenced him) argument that statistics fail to convey the meaning of atrocities, Kristof quite deliberately uses shock in the form of visual images, sensationalism, and personal stories – three of Chong's framing strategies.

Celebrities as news mediators A second way in which human rights advocates try to grab the attention of news consumers is through the use of celebrities. James Traub points out that 'an entire industry has sprung up around the recruitment of celebrities to good works' (Traub 2008), and some issues are closely affiliated with particular celebrities: Bono and foreign aid, Angelina Jolie and refugees, George Clooney and Darfur, the late Princess Diana and the anti-landmine campaign, to mention the best known. As Traub notes: 'Hollywood celebrities have become central players on deeply political issues ...' (ibid.). What do we make of this? Are they successful in bringing attention to – and action to stop – human rights crises? These questions are the subject of much debate among human rights scholars and advocates. Those

25

who believe that celebrity activism works and should be used argue that celebrities do produce results. Their primary success is at garnering attention; however, sometimes they go beyond this to actually influencing policy outcomes. In terms of the first category – bringing attention to an issue – one journalist describes the process thus: 'Each of the initiatives hinges on the same strategy: using [the celebrity's] face to illuminate a problematic part of the world we might normally remain in the dark about. It's like surfing to TMZ.com and then having UNICEF.org hijack your browser' (Dittrich 2009, 125). Some celebrities do more than just highlight a cause – they influence policy at the highest levels. One journalist claims, for example, that Bob Geldof 'was instrumental in getting the [UK] government to commit to the UN target to give 0.7 per cent of national income to global aid' (Vallely 2009). In another example: 'George Bush wouldn't meet the heads of aid agencies, but he [would] see Bono and Bob [and] Angela Merkel wants to know from Bono what Nicolas Sarkozy really thinks' (ibid.).

Those who argue that celebrity activism is a good thing say that stars 'exercise a ludicrous influence over the public consciousness' (Traub 2008), and, because of this, 'like it or not, we're more likely to listen to a plea about landmines in Darfur from Don Cheadle than from a one-legged Darfuri' (Dittrich 2009, 122). Celebrities, because they are not elected representatives of any nation-state, are quite literally cosmopolitans. Bob Geldof himself described this position as 'inhabiting this bizarre thin space between the pieties of the NGOs and the politics of government' (Vallely 2009). However, even their proponents concede that celebrities cannot do everything. Apart from calling for boycotts, they have less influence on the private sector than on government officials, and they have more leverage in the West than in other parts of the world. (Vallely points out that African leaders have not been particularly moved by George Clooney's work on behalf of Darfur.) It is obviously easier, Traub points out, to raise money and consciousness than to influence policy and change a country's behavior, and yet some have managed to do so (Traub 2008).

Not everyone is as sanguine about celebrity involvement in human rights-related work, and there are some vociferous critics of the phenomenon, with a couple of academic bloggers in particular devoting much attention to it. Laura Seay, in a blog entitled *Texas in Africa*, and William Easterly, in the blog *Aid Watch*, refer to the phenomenon as 'badvocacy,' which Seay defines as 'a good catch-all term to describe advocacy that begins with great intentions to help those who are suffering, but that at best accomplishes nothing or at worst actually

. More likely to listen to celebrity. 26 But they can also affect
the results of policy. Too much power?

makes the problem even more difficult to solve' (Seay 2009). One cause of 'badvocacy,' she argues, is 'a focus on celebrities and trendiness rather than intelligent analysis,' and she describes the problem thus: 'Everybody opposes genocide, of course, and the suffering of innocents is something we should all be committed to ending wherever it happens in the world. The problem, however, is that when people who are trained as actors and musicians start traipsing around war zones without having done any homework independent of the organization supporting their visits, we tend to get a narrative that isn't exactly representative of the facts' (ibid.). Heribert Dieter and Rajiv Kumar add to these warnings about oversimplification, noting that in the world of celebrity activism 'the world is painted in black and white and good is pitted against evil. Nuance is inevitably lost' (Dieter and Kumar 2008, 260). Easterly has taken a more tongue-in-cheek approach, writing blog entries with such titles as 'Supermodel vows to stay naked till USAID funds reach starving children' (Easterly 2009a) and 'African leaders advise Bono on reform of U2' (Easterly 2009b).

Other critiques of celebrity activism are that high-powered Western celebrities drown out alternative voices from the global South and the anti-globalization voices from the North. Moreover, critics on the left say that 'they defuse, drain or stifle more radical forms of protest and political mobilization' (Vallely 2009). Dieter and Kumar level two specific, strongly worded charges against celebrity diplomacy. First, celebrities can be incompetent, and Dieter and Kumar go so far as saying that 'Bono and his fellow celebrity activists might in fact be doing major harm to the people of Africa. Their well-meaning interventions probably prolong the tragedy instead of ending it' (Dieter and Kumar 2008, 261). Second, they question the representative legitimacy of celebrities, noting that 'people like to listen to the music of Bono and Geldof, but these stars are not democratically elected to public office. Charisma as well as their wallets may give them power, but in most cases celebrities are self-appointed' (ibid., 262).

Andrew Cooper responds directly to these critics, arguing that their lumping together of all celebrities is misleading, and that while there are many 'amateur enthusiasts,' there are also those who really know their stuff. Bono rises to the level of a diplomat whose approach 'has as many traits commonly associated with Henry Kissinger as it does with Audrey Hepburn' (Cooper 2008, 268). Cooper concludes that it is wrong to take a one-image-fits-all approach to celebrity diplomacy, something he claims most critics are guilty of (ibid., 269). In their chapter 'Celebrity diplomats as mobilizers? Celebrities and activism in a hypermediated time,' Andrew Cooper and Joseph Turcotte expound on the debate over celebrity activism, especially in the current era of new and faster communication technologies and social media. Media technologies such as the Internet, Twitter, Facebook, and YouTube have afforded activist movements in general new forms of outreach and coordination (an issue covered by Sarah Kessler, discussed in more detail below), and celebrity activists are no exception. Cooper and Turcotte argue that in our current celebrity-obsessed and celebrity-driven culture, celebrities have become – in part as a result of new media forms – the new gatekeepers who disseminate and direct the narrative of the day: 'In a hypermediated time ... celebrities remain prominent forces for capturing attention and initiating action.' Given the networked nature of our culture, in which individuals can become easily mobilized, and given their privileged position in the world of social media, 'celebrities are often arbiters and drivers of the topics of conversation,' they argue, and in many humanitarian crises 'celebrities have become active participants in the dialogues surrounding these events as well as in efforts to engage and respond in the front lines.' Their equation is clear: a celebrity-obsessed culture combined with online social networking tools equals a tremendous amount of salutary attention to human rights causes. The result, they argue, is that 'in a culture dominated by mass as well as emerging media forms, the ability of the celebrity to frame discussions is profound.'

The linchpin of Cooper and Turcotte's analysis of the power of celebrity activists is the emerging networked society. There is something about the explosion of new communications technology in a globalized world that means that, in this hypermediated time, 'celebrity culture and the structures of globalization and the media industry offer avenues for connecting with the public that cannot be matched by very many others in distant positions.' Social networking and web-based platforms 'enhance the opportunities for disseminating messages and further the connections between celebrities and members of the public by presenting the feeling of increased intimacy and interaction.' Celebrity activism, then, is highly interrelated with the third method of grabbing an audience's attention: social media.

Social media and human rights activism In addition to traditional forms of news media – radio, television, and newspapers – which disseminate media in a hierarchical and one-to-many way, a number of new tools for media dissemination and consumption have exploded in popularity in the twenty-first century. These tools, which include blogs, social network platforms such as Facebook and Twitter, and photo- and video-sharing sites such as Flickr and YouTube, allow anyone to distribute content on the Internet. In addition to media distribution and consumption, these tools allow people at great distances to become connected or networked. The social media phenomenon has led to an active debate in the human rights field over whether the digital activism that has arisen as a result has any real impact in ameliorating human rights abuses, or whether such activism is better thought of as mere 'slacktivism,' which Wikipedia defines as 'a pejorative term that describes "feel-good" measures, in support of an issue or social cause, that have little or no practical effect other than to make the person doing it feel satisfaction' (cited in Naidoo 2010). The debate is nicely summed up by journalist Aneshree Naidoo, who notes: 'The social and connected nature of the web today has made activism easy. But is it possibly too easy? Is it a good thing that you can feel you are changing the world one click at a time?' (Naidoo 2010). Is clicking a 'join' link, signing an online petition, or joining a Facebook group really activism, tantamount to citizen mobilization? Does it make a difference?

Like the question of celebrity activism, strongly held opinions can be found on both sides of the debate.[4] Perhaps the most widely read critic of the idea that the use of these tools will lead to any real change is Malcolm Gladwell, who wrote an article in *The New Yorker* called 'Small change: why the revolution will not be tweeted' (Gladwell 2010). Gladwell first states the hypothesis of those who *do* believe that new social media will increase social activism – 'with Facebook, Twitter and the like, the traditional relationship between political authority and popular will has been upended, making it easier for the powerless to collaborate, coordinate, and give voice to their concerns' – before quickly and condescendingly rejecting it. The crux of his argument is that this was not the way that civil rights activism occurred in the 1960s in the United States, the era of lunch-counter sit-ins, bus boycotts, and mass marches. 'The civil-rights wars that engulfed the South happened without email, texting, Facebook, or Twitter ... Fifty years after one of the most extraordinary episodes of social upheaval in American history, we seem to have forgotten what activism is,' he laments (ibid.). And the reason why online activism will never amount to anything more than 'small change,' he says, is because the activism of the 1960s was built on strong ties – highly personal connections among activists. On the other hand, the kind of activism associated with social media is built around weak ties, where activists are 'connected' to people they have never met. 'Weak ties,' he says, 'seldom lead to high-risk activism,' because 'the only way you can get someone you don't really know to do something on your behalf [is] by not asking too much of them.' So, 'Facebook activism succeeds not by motivating people to make a real sacrifice but by motivating them to do the things that people do when they are not motivated enough to make a real sacrifice' (ibid.). Secondly, social media cannot effect significant change, he argues, because they are not hierarchically organized, and if you want to take on a powerful, organized establishment, you need to be part of a hierarchy. He concludes his critique by again invoking the 'high-risk' strategies of the non-violent protests of the 1960s and arguing sneeringly that they could not be replicated with the tools of social media: 'Enthusiasts for social media would no doubt have us believe that King's task in Birmingham would have been made infinitely easier had he been able to communicate with his followers through Facebook, and contented himself with tweets from a Birmingham jail ... If Martin Luther King, Jr. had tried to do a wiki-boycott in Montgomery, he would have been steamrollered by the white power structure' (ibid.). In making his 'modern-day-activism-isn't-really-activism' argument, Gladwell echoes *New York Times* op-ed columnist Thomas Friedman's dismay with his daughter and her friends. Friedman (2007) writes, in relation to the policy issues facing the 'twenty-something' generation:

> they can't e-mail [activism] in, and an online petition or a mouse click for carbon neutrality won't cut it. They have to get organized in a way that will force politicians to pay attention rather than just patronize them. Martin Luther King and Bobby Kennedy didn't change the world by asking people to join their Facebook crusades or to download their platforms. Activism can only be uploaded, the old-fashioned way – by young voters speaking truth to power, face to face, in big numbers, on campuses or the Washington Mall. Virtual politics is just that – virtual.

One wonders what Gladwell and Friedman would make of the Occupy Wall Street (OWS) movement in late 2011, which began in New York and quickly spread across the country, and in some cases the globe. The OWS movement seems to be grounded in exactly the sort of 'strong ties,' high-risk, impossible-in-the-age-of-social-media approach that Gladwell claims typified the successful actions of 1960s US civil rights activists. At the same time, the movement was characterized by an *Economist*-affiliated blog as 'the world's first genuine social media uprising' (G.L. 2011). The role that social media tools played in organizing and sustaining the movement seems indisputable, as is the fact that, for many, it has constituted a very high-risk form of activism indeed (see Cherkis 2011, for an example).

In her chapter 'Amplifying individual impact: social media's emerging role in activism,' Sarah Kessler responds to Gladwell and other critics, arguing that they are overly pessimistic and insufficiently clear on how social media can make a difference – too narrowly focused 'on the clichés of slacktivism.' She argues that while social media cannot cause revolutions, they certainly have begun to revolutionize the way in which activists approach them. What social media have done, she argues, is shift the world of activism from one in which organizations and centralized movements are the agents of change to one in which individuals or decentralized groups of people are equally effective or more effective change agents. There are three reasons for this. First, social media make it easier for users to publicly align themselves with a cause and to access their weak ties (the same weak interpersonal ties that are seen as a detriment for Gladwell are a positive thing for Kessler). And because it is easier to publicly align with an issue, it is easier for that issue to transfer from private to public discourse without actions that at one time had to be coordinated centrally. Elsewhere, Kessler has referred to the fact that social media make it easier for individuals to publicly state their alliance with a cause as 'the power of one' (Kessler 2010). The ability of social media to quickly connect single individuals with a global cause makes it easier for invested people to create change without the need for a bureaucracy. So, the first advantage of social media is that they present only a minimal barrier to public alignment with a cause and they allow for easy access to weak ties.

These characteristics of social media lead to the second advantage – they can be used to coordinate collective actions, or what Kessler refers to elsewhere as 'the power of 1 million' (ibid.). Low-cost collaborative actions such as online petitions increase participation in movements, which increases the number of people who are engaged with a cause. She notes: 'While 100,000 people ranting on Twitter might not be worth anything, organizing those 100,000 people in a simultaneous action can have significant impact.'

Kessler's third argument for why critics should not dismiss social media's activism-promoting abilities is that online activism can be the first step on the ladder of engagement. Even if so-called 'five-minute activism' is immediately useless (as the critics would claim), it can eventually be valuable because 'small actions might eventually lead to bigger ones.' Kessler concludes that 'the more people who casually engage with a cause, the more opportunities there are to engage individuals past that first step. Accumulating piles of so-called "slacktivists" isn't necessarily a wasted effort if there are steps they can take to deepen their minimal commitment. Unremarkable actions such as signing an online petition can, in theory, be a "gateway drug" for deeper engagement.'

In sum, will social media alone end distant mass atrocities? No. Are they increasingly becoming a necessary, albeit not sufficient, tool for activists who want to end distant suffering? In arguing in the affirmative, Kessler likens social media tools to the revolutionary role of the printing press, of which it has been said: 'Two things are true about the remaking of the European intellectual landscape during the Protestant Reformation: first, it was not caused by the invention of movable type, and second, it was possible only after the invention of movable type.' Nicholas Kristof agrees with Kessler – he has suggested to his readers that they download humanitarian logos, embed them in email signature files, and make them clickable as a useful way to spread awareness of specific human rights campaigns (Kristof 2009) – thus pitting himself against Friedman, his op-ed colleague at the *New York Times*.

Critiques

Thus far this chapter has focused on two broad questions. First, why do people sometimes act to stop human rights abuses when they learn of them while at other times they respond with apathy? Second, what can news producers – journalists and editors – and human rights advocates do to grab the attention of the audience, especially given psychic numbing, the difficulties of achieving a post-national cosmopolitan sense of empathy, and compassion fatigue? The questions not yet addressed here surround the downsides of mediating atrocities. What are the negative consequences of using shock media to bring violence to an audience's attention? What are the ethical issues involved in viewing the mutilation and death of people we will never meet and whose stories we will likely soon forget? Several scholars have voiced strong criticisms of how atrocities are mediated, in particular about the use of shocking images of suffering, especially when those images are commodified for the sake of raising funds (in addition to raising awareness), and the offensive, exoticized, one-dimensional portrayal in the Western media of 'others' – especially Africans. The critical perspective is expressed by Joel Pruce in his chapter 'The spectacle of suffering and humanitarian intervention in Somalia.' One aspect of the 'spectacle' has to do with how suffering, especially the suffering of Africans, is portrayed; these portrayals have been referred to by several critics as 'disaster pornography' (Omaar and de Waal 1993) or 'death pornography' (Warah 2010). Writing at the time of the 1992 intervention in Somalia, Rakiya Omaar and Alex de Waal (1993) of the human rights NGO Africa Watch opined that:

> now we will see more of the familiar pictures of grotesque human degradation, with foreign angels of mercy ministering to starving children, juxtaposed with images of trigger-happy teenage looters ... The camera can't lie, we are told. But anyone who has watched a Western film crew in an African famine will know just how much effort it takes to compose the 'right' image. Photogenic starving children are hard to find, even in Somalia ... Film crews in hospitals rush through crowded corridors, leaping over stretchers, dashing to film the agony before it passes. They hold bedside vigils to record the moment of death ... This is disaster pornography. Reduced to nameless extras in the shadows behind Western aid workers or disaster tourists, the grieving, hurting and humiliated human beings are not asked if they want to be portrayed in this degrading way.

Likewise, Keith Tester, referring to a 1998 report by former BBC Africa correspondent George Alagiah from a famine zone in Sudan, remarks, 'personally I cannot recall ... Alagiah's [report], but I am happy to wager that [it] included babies suckling at the empty breasts of their mothers, toddlers with flies around their eyes and, quite probably, a picture of two naked children aged about eight or nine walking along a dusty track. The report probably included as well pictures of the overwhelmed famine relief facilities' (Tester 2001, 9).

Howard French, a former senior writer for the *New York Times* and current journalism professor, argues that Western media portrayals of Africa are in part a function of news production values. It is the least-covered continent and also the continent 'where inexperienced reporters have been historically sent for their first overseas assignments, on the theory that if they screw up in Africa, it won't be much noticed.' It is also the continent where news producers 'figured out that they could get away with a single bureau to cover all of the "black" part.' Finally, he argues, 'it is the continent where editors have always stretched credulity and good sense to speak commonly of events or trends taking place "in Africa". This, on the theory that something short of a major catastrophe happening in any given African country was too insignificant to warrant the commission of precious column inches' (French 2011). One person's 'disaster pornography' is another person's well-honed methodology: Nicholas Kristof, in his deliberate use of shock, has written many op-eds, some accompanied by graphic images, that could be described in almost exactly the manner derided by Omaar and de Waal, Warah, and others.

Pruce asks what the effect on the audience is when the spectacle of suffering is mediated through television news, a platform he suggests is 'thoroughly fraught with levity and commercialism.' Is the audience's witnessing of this spectacle more likely to translate into political action for intervention? He thinks not, for reasons related to the argument made earlier – that while in theory the media could act as a force for cosmopolitan empathy, in reality they do not. And, Pruce argues, one reason for this is the demands of capitalism in a globalized world. The rise of the twenty-four-hour news cycle and the collapsing of space and time (i.e. globalization) *could* have led to a sense of cosmopolitanism but did not. He notes a trend in television and cable news in favor of content of a light nature instead of pressing crises, and traces that trend directly to the medium's commercial demands. Television was never intended, he argues, to cultivate cosmopolitan human rights defenders, but rather spectators and consumers who consume as much advertising as they do news content. The demands of television in twenty-first-century globalized capitalism results in news production that traffics heavily in images of suffering that are 'rote, repetitive, and predictable.' Suffering becomes spectacle, all in the name of profit. And that spectacle has an impact on whether the news consumer will act to end it. He argues that:

> Night after night, and story after story, repetition of imagery of suffering becomes so familiar to the audience so as to affect how this news and information is absorbed and processed, and how the reaction is induced. Western audiences become attuned to coverage of children, women and the elderly fleeing war zones and natural disasters. At what point does the endlessness of ghastly, brutal imagery transform both the subject and object, and how? Is the audience able to separate the difficult reality of events from the otherwise light content on television? Is there a point at which human rights become mere human interest? Can the audience distinguish between coverage of a humanitarian intervention and that of the rescue of a cat stuck in a tree?

In terms of images as framing devices, Pruce illustrates what he calls an 'iconography of famine,' in which African famines – across various cases – are framed in certain ways in the Western media. Women and children are often the subjects of photographs portraying them as innocent victims, reflecting traditional gendered assumptions of female and child passivity. Starvation itself is portrayed in simple terms, more akin to natural disasters such as earthquakes than as a calculated political strategy. (Because food is almost always used as a weapon of war to punish civilians, famine is usually at least partly the result of policy choices.) While such photographs certainly seem to spur public outcry and financial contributions to aid agencies – and in that sense might be deemed successful, someone like Kristof might argue – at the same time they are likely also to be a testament to Tester's sentiment, noted earlier, that Africa is consistently presented as a place of endemic and persistent pain and suffering; it is simply the way things are in Africa, and there is nothing to be done about it. It is 'their unalterable fate' (Tester 2001, 7). While audiences are temporarily shocked (at least through their dinner hour), Pruce argues, they are not surprised. The spectacle of suffering, therefore, inhibits rather than contributes to the audience's desire to learn more about the causes of famine and other forms of distant suffering. And this disengagement, or distantiation, goes on and on as the image of 'the starving African child' has reached near ubiquity through its repeated use in print advertisements and television commercials for human rights causes. As a result, 'instead of witnesses, in the traditional sense, the spectacle of suffering produces spectators: those audiences that watch without engaging, willfully detached from reality.'

Kleinman and Kleinman echo Pruce's critique of spectacle in the age of globalization. They are concerned about how Westerners benefit from images of distant suffering: they have become a highly tradable commodity on the international media market and they provide a source of profit and, sometimes, photographic prizes for photographers and newspapers. Most damning, they argue, the message that results from these images and their framing is that 'for all the havoc in Western society, we are somehow better than this African society. We gain in moral status and some of our organizations gain financially and politically, while those whom we represent, or appropriate, remain where they are, moribund, surrounded by vultures' (Kleinman and Kleinman 1996, 8).

They conclude their critique of the spectacle of suffering by again invoking the analogy to pornography: 'Ultimately, we will have to engage the more ominous aspects of globalization, such as the commercialization of suffering, the commodification of experiences of atrocity and abuse, and the pornographic uses of degradation' (ibid., 19). The frequent analogy to pornography ('war pornography,' 'disaster pornography,' and 'death pornography') is befitting, Pruce argues, as the spectacle of suffering shares much in common with pornography: 'atrocity photography and pornography [both suggest] a certain self-indulgence in observing others in vulnerable, intimate and sensitive positions, while also injecting a power dynamic that connects the subject and object.'

Conclusion

What should be clear from this introduction and from all the chapters which follow is that we cannot talk about human rights atrocities and action (or inaction) to stop them without also talking about how they are mediated – by the traditional media of television and newspapers, but also through less traditional forms such as social media, literature, and artistic works. Of television, Michael Ignatieff has written: 'Whether it wishes or not, television has become the principal mediation between the suffering of strangers and the consciences of those in the world's few remaining zones of safety ... It [is] not merely the means through which we see each other, but the means by which we shoulder each other's fate' (Ignatieff 1998, 33). The question, however, is whether all of this watching makes a difference in the lives of those strangers. Common wisdom states that it must. The 2011–12 Somali famine suggests otherwise. Months of real-time coverage, replete with images of emaciated children and pleas from the UN Secretary-General did not prevent the UN from warning that it expected the crisis to worsen in 2012. This affirms one of Pruce's conclusions, that 'graphic news coverage of atrocity may be a necessary condition for awareness, but awareness is not a sufficient condition for action.'

What *is* sufficient? The answer is not simple, despite the widely held view that: 'If only people knew, they would do something.' There is nothing automatic about the link between information and action, between 'the report or the representation and the perceptions and feelings of the audience' (Tester 2001, 102). As Keith Tester says: 'It is impossible to predict in advance whether, how or which journalistic production will be or become morally compelling. Social action is actually much too complex to allow for prediction' (ibid., 71). Or, as Joel Pruce concludes: 'The relationship between seeing and acting is neither natural nor linear.' Sometimes all of the pieces *are* in the right place at the right time: an editor decides to run a particular photograph, a story is framed in exactly the right way, a viewer always tunes in when George Clooney is on TV, someone read a novel about a similar issue which moved her, a person heard about the issue from a Facebook friend – and money is given, a rally is attended, a political representative is contacted. At other times, the news is too depressing and the television channel is changed or the newspaper's page is turned. Why is action taken in one case and not the other? How do we escape the double-edged sword of the spectacle of mediated atrocities – if we look, we are little better than voyeurs; if we look away, we remain uninformed? Together, the chapters in this book help answer these questions. Given the tragic reality of suffering in the world today, never has finding answers been more imperative.

Notes

1 The Kosovo conflict averaged 14 percent of total international coverage in the *New York Times* during this three-month period, for example, while the Sierra Leone conflict averaged a mere 0.8 percent of coverage in the same paper. Other scholars provide similar quantitative data regarding the amount of media resources such as time and money devoted to distant humanitarian disasters. See, for example, Moeller 1999, especially chapter two.

2 It should be noted that not everyone is so negative. Simon Cottle argues, for example, that although the media tend to reinforce the strong pull of nationalism, they can at times, through their framing (or in his words 'staging'), also contribute to an emergent global cosmopolitan outlook. This is especially true with the form of news staging he calls 'global-focusing events' (Cottle 2009, 502–6).

3 While at first glance a chapter about social and economic rights in the United States might not appear to belong in a book whose focus is primarily on foreign atrocities, this chapter in fact has much to teach us about mobilizing to help distant victims of human rights violations, in addition to the important theorizing about human rights advocates' appropriation of framing techniques usually associated with the media, discussed earlier in this chapter. As Chong points out, while economic and social rights have achieved mainstream legitimacy throughout Europe and most of the developing world, in the United States they have not attained a similar level of legitimacy. Indeed, in the US, 'official policy for decades was to consider these rights un-American, collectivist and "alien in spirit and philosophy to the principles of a free economy."' The fact, then, that they are not seen as 'real' human rights by the majority of Americans, and their absence is not seen as a violation of those rights, means that the consequences of these violations – which include grinding poverty, or wide-scale lack of access to adequate health care, food, or shelter by some portion of the population – are frequently met with the same apathy as more 'traditional' violations of civil and political rights in faraway countries. In other words, one could argue that the indifference to violations of social and economic rights in the United States is not that dissimilar to the absence of a cosmopolitan ethic of care for victims

of distant atrocities. It is not too much of an exaggeration to say that most Americans feel as far removed from the idea that there are victims of social and economic rights violations in the US as they do from the actual victims of genocide in Darfur. In this sense, as much as violations of refugee rights need to be framed as such in Australia, violations of the right to minimum health care need to be framed as such in the United States. Much of this chapter and book indicate how hard it is to get people to care about and mobilize around human rights violations that are acknowledged as such but that occur at a distance. This chapter shows how equally difficult it is to get people to care about human rights abuses when the violations are not even seen as such. Carefully chosen framing strategies by human rights advocates are imperative in both cases.

4 Much of the recent analysis on the impact of new social media relates to their use in the 'Arab Spring' uprisings in Middle Eastern authoritarian regimes in 2010 and 2011. While fascinating, they are not the focus of the debate analyzed in this chapter and in this book. Our focus is on Western-based activism and the use of social media tools to effect an end to distant atrocities – i.e. how shock pundits, celebrities, and social media can get people to care about human rights abuses of people they will never meet. One would be hard pressed to refer to those who used social media tools in the middle of uprisings in Iran, Tunisia, Egypt, or Syria as 'slacktivists.'

References

Allen, Tim, and Jean Seaton, eds. 1999. *The Media of Conflict: War Reporting and Representations of Ethnic Violence.* London: Zed Books.

Ashdown, Paddy. 2011. 'Somalia's "children's famine" has been ignored.' *Guardian*, 21 July. www. guardian.co.uk/commentisfree/ 2011/jul/20/somalia-childrens-famine-media.

Bahador, Babak. 2007. *The CNN Effect in Action: How the News Media Pushed the West Toward War in Kosovo.* New York: Palgrave Macmillan.

Ban, Ki-moon. 2011. 'U.N. Chief Ban Ki-moon's plea: we can't allow Somalia to starve.' *Los Angeles Times*, 22 July.

BBC News. 2011. 'UN declares Somalia famine in Bakool and Lower Shabelle.' 20 July. www.bbc.co.uk/ news/world-africa-14211905.

Boltanski, Luc. 1999. *Distant Suffering: Morality, Media and Politics.* New York: Cambridge University Press.

Brookings Institution. 2002. '"The CNN Effect": How 24-hour news coverage affects government decisions and public opinion' (transcript). Brookings/ Harvard Forum: Press Coverage and the War on Terrorism, 23 January. www.brookings. edu/events/2002/0123media_ journalism.aspx.

Cherkis, Jason. 2011. 'UC Davis police pepper-spray seated students in Occupy dispute.' *Huffington Post*, 19 November. www.huffingtonpost.com/ 2011/11/19/uc-davis-police-pepper-spray-students_n_1102728.html.

Chouliaraki, Lilie. 2006. *The Spectatorship of Suffering.* London: Sage Publications.

Cooper, Andrew. 2008. 'Beyond one image fits all: Bono and the complexity of celebrity diplomats.' *Global Governance* 14(3): 265–72.

Cottle, Simon. 2009. 'Global crises in the news: Staging new wars, disasters, and climate change.' *International Journal of Communication* 3: 494–516.

Dieter, Heribert, and Rajiv Kumar. 2008. 'The downside of celebrity diplomacy: The neglected complexity of development.' *Global Governance* 14(3): 259–64.

Dittrich, Luke. 2009. 'The celebrity shall save you.' *Esquire*, October: 118–25.

Dunlap, David W. 2009. 'Behind the scenes: To publish or not?' *Lens* (*New York Times* blog), 4 September. http://lens.blogs.nytimes. com/2009/09/04/behind-13/.

Easterly, William. 2009a. 'Supermodel vows to stay naked till USAID funds reach starving children.' *Aid Watch* (blog), 8 September. http://aidwatchers. com/2009/09/supermodel-vows-to-stay-naked-till-usaid-funds-reach-starving-children/.

Easterly, William. 2009b. 'African leaders advise Bono on reform of U2.' *Aid Watch* (blog), 23 November. http://aidwatchers. com/2009/11/african-leaders-advise-bono-on-reform-of-u2/.

Fahmy, Shahira. 2010. 'Guest editor's note. Special issue: Images of war.' *Media, War & Conflict* 3(1): 3–5.

Fernando, Jude. 2010. 'Media in disaster vs. media disasters.' *Anthropology News* 51(4): 4.

French, Howard. 2011. 'How Africa gets covered (or doesn't).' *A Glimpse of the World* (blog), 5 December. www.howardw french.com/2011/12/american-journalism-is-failing-africa/.

Friedman, Thomas L. 2007. 'Generation Q.' *New York Times*, 10 October. www. nytimes.com/2007/10/10/ opinion/10friedman.html.

Gale, Peter. 2004. 'The refugee crisis and fear: Populist politics and media discourse.' *Journal of Sociology* 40(4): 321–40.

Gettleman, Jeffrey. 2011. 'U.N. officials say famine is widening in Somalia.' *New York Times*, 6 September.

G.L. 2011. '#Occupytheweb.' *Democracy in America* (*Economist* blog), 11 October. www.economist.com/ node/21532071.

Gladwell, Malcolm. 2010. 'Small change: Why the revolution will not be tweeted.' *The New Yorker*, 4 October. www.newyorker.com/ reporting/2010/10/04/101004fa_ fact_gladwell.

Hawkins, Virgil. 2001. 'The price of inaction: Intervention and the media.' *Journal of Humanitarian Assistance*, May 14. http://sites. tufts.edu/jha/archives/1504.

Hoffmann, Stanley, Robert C. Johansen, James P. Sterba, and Raimo Vayrynen. 1996. *The Ethics and Politics of Humanitarian Intervention*. Notre Dame, IN: University of Notre Dame Press.

Höijer, Birgitta. 2004. 'The discourse of global compassion: The audience and media reporting of human suffering.' *Media, Culture, and Society* 26(4): 513–31.

Ignatieff, Michael. 1998. *The Warrior's Honor: Ethnic War and the Modern Conscience*. New York: Henry Holt and Company.

International Commission on Intervention and State Sovereignty. 2001. *The Responsibility to Protect*. Ottawa: International Development Research Centre.

Jardin, Xeni. 2011. 'Atrocity exhibition.' *Guardian*, 4 April. www.

guardian.co.uk/commentisfree/
cifamerica/2011/apr/04/digital-
media-xeni-jardin.

Keenan, Thomas. 2002. 'Publicity
and indifference: Media,
surveillance, "humanitarian
intervention."' In *CTRL [SPACE]:
Rhetorics of Surveillance from
Bentham to Big Brother*, edited
by Thomas Y. Levin, Ursula
Frohne, and Peter Weibel, 544–61.
Cambridge, MA: MIT Press.

Keenan, Thomas. 2004. 'Mobilizing
shame.' *South Atlantic Quarterly*
103(2/3): 435–49.

Kessler, Sarah. 2010. 'Why social
media is reinventing activism.'
Mashable, 9 October. http://
mashable.com/2010/10/09/social-
media-activism/.

Kinnick, Katherine N., Dean M.
Krugman, and Glen T. Cameron.
1996. 'Compassion fatigue: Communication and burnout toward
social problems.' *Journalism &
Mass Communication Quarterly*
73(3): 687–707.

Kleinman, Arthur, and Joan
Kleinman. 1996. 'The appeal of
experience; the dismay of images:
Cultural appropriations of suffering in our times.' *Daedalus* 125(1):
1–23.

Kratzer, Renee Martin, and Brian
Kratzer. 2003. 'How newspapers
decided to run disturbing 9/11
photos.' *Newspaper Research
Journal* 24(1): 34–47.

Kristof, Nicholas. 2009. 'Social media
and activism.' *On the Ground*
(*New York Times* blog), 6 October.
http://kristof.blogs.nytimes.
com/2009/10/06/social-media-and-
activism/.

Kyriakidou, Maria. 2009. 'Imagining
ourselves beyond the nation?
Exploring cosmopolitanism in
relation to media coverage of distant suffering.' *Studies in Ethnicity
and Nationalism* 9(3): 481–96.

Lang, Jr., Anthony. 2003. *Just
Intervention*. Washington, DC:
Georgetown University Press.

Levitz, David, and Zulfikar Abbany.
2011. 'Horn of Africa needs more
money, says UN.' *Deutsche Welle*,
28 July. www.dw-world.de/dw/
article/0,,15272890,00.html.

Livingston, Steven. 1997. 'Clarifying
the CNN Effect: An examination
of media effects according to
type of military intervention.'
Research Paper R-18. The Joan
Shorenstein Center on the Press,
Politics, and Public Policy,
Harvard University. http://tamil-
nation.co/media/CNNeffect.pdf.

Livingstone, Sonia. 1998. 'Relationships between media and
audiences: Prospects for future
audience reception studies.' In
*Media, Ritual and Identity: Essays
in Honor of Elihu Katz*, edited by
Tamar Liebes and James Curran,
237–55. London: Routledge.

Madsen, Debbie. 1991. 'Indecent
exposure?' *Ryerson Review of
Journalism*, Spring. www.rrj.ca/
m3662/.

Moeller, Susan D. 1999. *Compassion
Fatigue: How the Media Sell
Disease, Famine, War, and Death*.
New York: Routledge.

Naidoo, Aneshree. 2010. 'Activism or
slacktivism: Is the web making
it too easy?' *Memeburn*, 14 July.
http://memeburn.com/2010/07/
activism-or-slacktivism-is-the-
web-making-it-too-easy/.

Omaar, Rakiya, and Alex de Waal.
1993. 'Disaster pornography from
Somalia.' *Media and Values* 61:
13–14.

ONE. 2011. 'ONE launches provocative PSA to fight famine in
Horn of Africa.' Press release,

4 October. www.one.org/c/us/
pressrelease/4065/.

Pasackow, Ariella. 2010. 'The
criminalization of victims post
disaster: A study of the *New York
Times'* framing of Haitians following the January earthquake.'
Unpublished manuscript.

Power, Samantha. 2007. *'A Problem
from Hell': America and the Age
of Genocide.* New York: Harper
Perennial.

Reuters. 2011. 'U.N. calls emergency
meeting on East Africa famine.'
Reuters, 21 July. www.reuters.com/
article/2011/07/21/us-somalia-fam-
ine-fao-idUSTRE76K2B120110721.

Rhoads, Christopher, and
Mustafa Haji Abdi. 2011. 'Somalia
militants bedevil famine-relief
efforts.' *Wall Street Journal*, 29
July. http://online.wsj.com/article/
SB10001424053111904888304576474
322145109838.html.

Richardson, Paul. 2011. 'United
Nations declares famine in
Southern Somalia amid drought,
conflict.' *Bloomberg*, 20 July.

Robinson, Piers. 2002. *The CNN
Effect: The Myth of News Media,
Foreign Policy, and Intervention.*
London & New York: Routledge.

Seay, Laura. 2009. 'What causes
badvocacy.' *Texas in Africa* (blog),
20 May. http://texasinafrica.
blogspot.com/2009/05/what-
causes-badvocacy.html.

Sharkey, Jacqueline E. 1993. 'When
pictures drive foreign policy.'
American Journalism Review,
December. www.ajr.org/Article.
asp?id=1579.

Sharkey, Jacqueline E. 2003. 'Airing
graphic footage.' *American
Journalism Review*, May. www.ajr.
org/article.asp?id=2989.

Slovic, Paul. 2007. '"If I look at the
mass I will never act": Psychic
numbing and genocide.' *Judgment
and Decision Making* 2(2): 79–95.

Soderlund, Walter G., E. Donald
Briggs, Kai Hildebrandt, and
Abdel Salam Sidahmed. 2008.
*Humanitarian Crises and Interven-
tion: Reassessing the Impact of
Mass Media.* Sterling, VA: Kumar-
ian Press.

Sontag, Susan. 2003. *Regarding the
Pain of Others.* New York: Picador.

Strobel, Warren P. 1996. 'The CNN
Effect.' *American Journalism
Review*, May. www.ajr.org/Article.
asp?id=3572.

Tester, Keith. 2001. *Compassion,
Morality, and the Media.* Philadelphia, PA: Open University Press.

Traub, James. 2008. 'The Celebrity
Solution.' *New York Times Magazine*, 9 March.

Vallely, Paul. 2009. 'From A-lister to
aid worker: Does celebrity diplomacy really work?' *Independent*,
17 January. www.independent.
co.uk/news/people/profiles/
from-alister-to-aid-worker-does-
celebrity-diplomacy-really-
work-1365946.html.

Warah, Rasna. 2010. 'Images of
the "Dying African" border
on pornography.' *The Citizen*,
8 July. www.thecitizen.co.tz/
editorial-analysis/19-editorial-
comments/2856-images-of-
the-dying-african-border-on-
pornography.html.

Weiss, Thomas G. 2007. *Humanitarian Intervention.* Malden, MA:
Polity.

Winter, Roger. 2000. 'The year in
review.' In *World Refugee Survey*,
14–25. Arlington, VA: United
States Committee for Refugees
and Immigrants.

Zelizer, Barbie. 2010. *About to Die:
How News Images Move the Public.*
New York: Oxford University Press.

1 | Humanitarian intervention in the 1990s: cultural remembrance and the reading of Somalia as Vietnam

DAVID KIERAN

On 24 March 1999, President Bill Clinton told Americans that the United States had begun bombing Kosovo. 'Ending this tragedy is a moral imperative,' he argued. 'It is also important to America's national interest' (Clinton 1999, 451). Clinton's determination came after months of contentious debate over whether a potential US intervention in the former Yugoslav republic constituted a national interest, could be militarily successful, or was worth the risk to American lives. For Clinton, clearly, it did, it could, and it was. His opponents, meanwhile, identified a different moral imperative: protecting US troops from dying in unnecessary wars for unachievable goals (Boot 2002, 327–8). 'America risks a debacle,' commentator Pat Buchanan opined, portending that 'US troops may have to go marching into the Big Muddy' while superciliously complaining that 'such are the fruits of Utopian crusades for global democracy' (Buchanan 1999, A21). This anxiety about what endangered troops could accomplish, Buchanan makes clear, was rooted in remembrance of the original 'Big Muddy' – Vietnam.

Clinton's speech and Buchanan's rejoinder are reminders that between the end of the Cold War and 11 September 2001 a central debate in US foreign policy was not whether the nation could win a long-term ideological struggle but whether it was morally and politically obligated to intervene in humanitarian crises. 'Clinton-era liberals,' Peter Beinart (2010, 277) writes, 'were more confident than their Cold War predecessors that human rights were achievable everywhere, soon. And militarily, they were more confident that America could defend those rights at the point of a gun.' Four years earlier, in 1995, Clinton had made similar claims before sending troops to Bosnia. But both speeches echoed Clinton's predecessor, who in 1992 told Americans that meeting the nation's interests and obligations required sending troops to end a famine on the Horn of Africa, a deployment that ended with perhaps one of the most infamous US military disasters of the post-Vietnam era, the 3 October 1993 raid in which eighteen American soldiers died and Somalis mutilated American bodies in the streets. Within days, newspapers around the country and politicians from both parties were referencing Vietnam. In the *Chicago Tribune*, the Vietnam-veteran father of one of the soldiers killed in Somalia wondered: 'What are we doing there? This is how we got into Vietnam, isn't it?' (McWhirter 1993, 10). Two days later, Anna Quindlen (1993, A14) marveled: 'We were as naïve about Aidid as we were about his ancestor, Ho Chi Minh. We learned a quarter-century ago that people can be inspired to fight tooth and nail for the sovereignty of their own small country, where they know the turf and we do not.' 'Just as we were flummoxed' in Vietnam, she concluded, 'we are flummoxed by how to be humanitarian in tanks.'

Such comparisons continued as Americans contemplated deployments to Bosnia in 1995 and Kosovo in 1999. Although interventionists argued that the nation had become unnecessarily gun-shy and could define a workable strategy for humanitarian missions, realists and isolationists insisted that Somalia made evident their folly (Shattuck 2003, 25–6; Boot 2002, 323–4; Power 2007, 261 and 283). Instead, they demanded adherence to the Powell Doctrine, the strict criteria for military action that Colin Powell and Caspar Weinberger had outlined in the 1980s to address what conservatives believed had been the root causes of the defeat in Vietnam and that envisioned 'an all-or-nothing approach to warfare, with the ideal war being one in which the US wins with overwhelming force, suffers few casualties, and leaves immediately' (Boot 2002, 323 and 319; Power 2007, 261–2; Shattuck 2003, 123).

But as Quindlen demonstrates, the doctrine was invoked somewhat differently than it had been a few years earlier. When Bush declared that the Gulf War '[would] not be another Vietnam,' he promised troops 'the support they need to get the job done, get it done quickly, and with as little loss of life as possible' (Bush 1992a, 61).[1] Emphasizing former Secretary of Defense Caspar Weinberger's dictum that if the US does commit troops, 'we should do so wholeheartedly, and with the clear intention of winning,' he continued earlier remembrances of Vietnam as a mismanaged, unsupported war (Boot 2002, 319). In only two of the eight speeches in which Bush dismissed the Vietnam analogy did he construe it as an error of intervention rather than prosecution (Bush 1992b, 72; Bush 1992c, 379).

For Quindlen, however, Vietnam was not a war the United States could have won: it had been 'flummoxed.' For her and others, the doctrine's other demands – that there be a compelling 'national interest,' that 'the commitment of US forces to combat should be a last resort' and, most importantly, that 'the relationship between ends and means "must be continually reassessed and adjusted if necessary"' – were more central (Boot 2002, 319). In shifting attention from fighting wars effectively to arguing that there were wars that the United States could fight but should not, the significance of Vietnam changed, too. No longer a noble cause poorly managed, it became the wrong war fought for the wrong reasons, and that remembrance, persistently linked to Somalia, informed opposition to humanitarian interventions.

This chapter examines how Americans' remembrance of Vietnam during the 1990s shaped the emerging legacy of the 1993 Somalia intervention and defined its significance within debates about US commitments to humanitarian intervention. I am hardly the first to note the persistent comparisons of such missions to Vietnam throughout the 1990s (Power 2007, 284; Shattuck 2003, 163 and 198). I am interested, however, in how the precise contours of Americans' remembrance of Vietnam at this moment contributed to critical conversations about and representations of humanitarian intervention.

My use of the word 'remembrance' embraces Jay Winter's (2006, 5) conception of 'what groups of people try to do when they act in public to conjure up the past.' Moreover, as Marita Sturken (1998, 9) argues, the process of remembering engages 'questions of political intent' and reveals 'the stakes held by individuals and institutions in attributing meaning to the past.' Put another way, as Fitzhugh Brundage (2000, 11) contends: 'The depth and tenacity of a historical memory within a society may serve as one measure of who exerts social power there.' Remembrance is thus politically significant; Americans' remembrance of Vietnam and their remembrance of Somalia in similar terms contributed significantly to the dominance of a discourse opposed to humanitarian intervention.

Brundage (ibid., 5) also points out that 'in order for a historical narrative to acquire cultural authority, it must appear believable to its audience.' Building on this premise, my project moves beyond simply tracing references to Vietnam in media coverage, editorials, and congressional debates about humanitarian intervention during the 1990s. I am interested, rather, in examining how such claims and the political positions that they undergirded became interpreted and reinterpreted. I thus interrogate the popular literature of the Somalia intervention, arguing that during a decade in which Americans routinely encountered opposition to human rights wars that persistently yoked Somalia and Vietnam together – as well-intentioned interventions marred by unrealizable goals and which had unnecessarily killed US troops – they also read important and bestselling popular texts about both the Vietnam War and the Somalia intervention, and that the popular literature about Somalia appropriated and redeployed the tropes and dominant discourses of the Vietnam texts that had preceded it a few years earlier. In so doing, these texts portrayed Somalia as precisely replicating the American soldiers' experiences and American leaders' errors during Vietnam's early years, thereby contributing to, buttressing, and legitimizing a discourse evident in both the media and political rhetoric that aligned Somalia with Vietnam to oppose US military commitments to humanitarian efforts. Because popular texts insistently portrayed the Somalia mission by mobilizing language and literary tropes nearly identical to those that dominated equally popular and roughly contemporaneous accounts of the Vietnam War, the frequent critique that humanitarian interventions might become 'another Vietnam' became, in Brundage's word, 'believable.'

I develop this argument in three parts, moving chronologically through the 1990s and early 2000s. I begin by analyzing a shift in the remembrance of Vietnam in popular literature during the early and mid-1990s. Concurrent with the evolving emphasis on the Powell Doctrine that I highlighted above was the increasing articulation of Vietnam as having been a strategic error from the outset. In 1992, retired Lieutenant General Harold Moore and journalist Joseph Galloway published *We Were Soldiers Once ... and Young: Ia Drang – The Battle That Changed the War in Vietnam*, which described American soldiers' first major clash with the North Vietnamese army. The book became a *New York Times* bestseller. Two years later, in the bestselling *In Retrospect: The Tragedies and Lessons of Vietnam*, former Secretary of Defense Robert McNamara famously admitted that intervening in Vietnam had been an error. Invoking, combining and also revising existing discourses of Vietnam memory – the celebration of the soldier and the vilification of his enemy, which were central to early and mid-1980s representations of Vietnam, and images of the soldiers' suffering familiar from the texts of the late 1980s – as well as representations of the 1991 Gulf War, these texts present American soldiers as consummate professionals while explicitly criticizing a misguided policy that led to an unnecessary, unwinnable war.[2] Particularly significant to this discourse is Moore and Galloway's multivalent deployment of the bodies of US soldiers, which simultaneously confirms American tenacity, Vietnamese brutality, and American suffering, and each text's explicit condemnation of policymakers who knowingly pursued a doomed war.

As readers were encountering Moore and Galloway's and McNamara's accounts of Vietnam, politicians and pundits were invoking that war as they condemned the 1993 Somalia intervention and warned against peacekeeping deployments to the former Yugoslavia in 1995 and 1999. The chapter's second section examines those debates, arguing that although realist politicians certainly opposed humanitarian missions on the grounds that they were outside US national interests, they also insistently emphasized the dangers that such missions posed to US troops by invoking Vietnam in language consistent with popular culture representations and declared Somalia a replication of Vietnam's errors.

I last analyze the popular culture of the Somalia intervention. At the end of a decade awash with critiques of humanitarian intervention that relied upon the rhetorical yoking together of Somalia and Vietnam, Americans began reading popular accounts of that intervention, particularly Mark Bowden's *Black Hawk Down: A Story of Modern War*, a book for which one editorialist suggested an important audience: 'Before Americans go [to Kosovo], the Clinton White House ought to talk to Mark Bowden' (Pinkerton 1999, A15). Another reviewer made a similar point and a significant comparison, writing that the text 'recalls the epic Vietnam narrative *We Were Soldiers Once ... and Young*.' before suggesting that '[Bowden's] book may join [Moore and Galloway's] as required reading for military officers. For the rest of us, hungering to understand the world of one superpower and the forces swirling around it, it might also be required' (Moniz 1999, 20).

Black Hawk Down and several memoirs that followed – Mike Durant's *In the Company of Heroes*, Martin Stanton's *Somalia on Five Dollars a Day*, and Dan Schilling and Matt Eversmann's *The Battle of Mogadishu* – did more, however, than simply compare the two conflicts. Rather, they contributed to the realist critiques that posited humanitarian interventions as *like* Vietnam by explicitly representing Somalia *as* Vietnam.

These texts explicitly appropriate and redeploy the discourses and tropes through which Moore and Galloway and McNamara portrayed Vietnam and with which American readers were already familiar, reaching identical conclusions, often in nearly identical language. Like the contemporary Vietnam literature, the Somalia texts describe exceptional soldiers sent to fight sadistic enemies in an unnecessary, inappropriate war. In both, the wounded American body is similarly an unstable signifier simultaneously enabling the soldier's valorization and the mission's condemnation, and policymakers likewise receive explicit condemnation for pursuing well-intentioned but misguided interventions that tragically lead to American deaths. Through this appropriation and redeployment, these texts cautioned against humanitarian intervention by casting the Somalia intervention as repeating Vietnam's errors and suffering. In so doing, they contributed to, amplified, and legitimated realist assertions that the United States should adhere to the Powell Doctrine by eschewing military commitments to humanitarian crises.

'We were wrong, terribly wrong': Vietnam in the 1990s

When Robert McNamara's *In Retrospect* appeared in April 1996, reviews of the war's planning and prosecution were scathing.[3] The planners had been 'bumblers of the worst sort,' one editorialist fumed, men 'contemptuous and ignorant of the land and people they sought to save, preoccupied in the most irrational of ways with global games, using the cloak of national security to mask a paucity of logical thought' (Scheer 1995, 7b). Another (Kaplan 1995, B11) suggested that they 'seem never to have stopped to ask themselves whether these evaluations might be flawed,' and a *St. Louis Post-Dispatch* editorial (19 April 1995, 6b) fumed that they 'were unable to understand that no compelling national interest was at stake.' Eighteen months after the Somalia debacle, these reviews in fact critiqued McNamara's admissions that the United States had been 'terribly wrong' in Vietnam (McNamara and VanDeMark 1996). *In Retrospect*, along with Moore and Galloway's *We Were Soldiers Once*, revised the dominant remembrance of Vietnam, celebrating tactical success while emphatically condemning the intervention as an unnecessary and avoidable failure of political vision.

This remembrance, constructed both in these popular texts and in the political discourse of those opposed to humanitarian interventions, recalled and revised earlier memorial discourses. Popular culture of the early 1980s presented idealized soldiers fighting a savagely inhumane enemy and a dysfunctional bureaucracy that, famously, refused to let them win (Jeffords 1989, 8–12; Studlar and Desser 1997, 101–12). In contrast, later texts such as *Platoon* and *The Things They Carried* construed the war as a theater for redemptive narratives in which the victimized soldiers endure in an incomprehensible setting (Aufderheide 1990, 84; Sturken 1998, 101–10; Klien 2005, 429; Haines 1997, 94–6; Kaplan 1993, 46; Robinson 1999, 258–9). These texts, Aufderheide (1990, 87) has argued, 'show boldly that we ... don't know why we were in Vietnam and are no longer afraid to admit it. Nor are we interested in finding out, in a political sense.'

The Vietnam literature of the 1990s built upon, but significantly adapted, these discourses as well as the discourse that dominated the 1991 Gulf War, which celebrated the Powell Doctrine and prized soldiers for their 'education, training ... willingness to subordinate themselves to the country's good, and the absolute nature of their commitment' (Kendrick 1994, 71). As *In Retrospect*'s reviews reveal, Vietnam in the 1990s was no longer Bush's or Reagan's Vietnam, yet neither was it Oliver Stone's. A war fought by men 'preoccupied ... with global games' was not one that could have been won had bureaucrats not hamstrung soldiers, nor was it one about which political questions were inconsequential. In the 1990s, Vietnam became a failed war not because of policymakers' reluctance, but because of their exuberance.

This remembrance combined elements of those earlier memorial discourses, matching portrayals of soldiers who were simultaneously the exceptionally competent, dedicated, and moral figures of the early 1980s and the Gulf War and the vulnerable victims of the intervening years, while recasting Vietnamese enemies as uncomplicated, bestial villains, and policymakers as problematic not for their timidity but for their eagerness in pursuing a war that was, from the outset, a strategic mistake.

'Those who survived would never forget the savagery': remembering combat in Vietnam in the 1990s The revised discourse of the 1990s is most clearly articulated in 1992's *We Were Soldiers Once*, which repudiates earlier descriptions of soldiers' ambivalence about and mere endurance of the war. Portraits of the troops' skill, commitment, and patriotism fully redeem Vietnam-era soldiers by replacing images of frustration and fear. Moore's (Moore and Galloway 1992, 21 and 22) praise for his officers as 'simply superb' and 'exceptionally competent' replaces critiques of incompetent careerists; the enlisted men's courage and commitment explicitly counters remembrances of fearful, insubordinate draftees. Moore (ibid., 143) finds that 'morale among the men was high' even after nearly three dozen Americans were killed: 'I heard weary soldiers say things like: "We'll get 'em, sir" and "They won't get through us, sir." Their fighting spirit had not dimmed.'

In spite of Moore and Galloway's occasional praise of the enemy's bravery and inclusion of a North Vietnamese perspective, enemy soldiers appear as near savages. Moore (ibid., 248) describes the campaign's final battle, in fact, as 'the most savage one-day battle of the Vietnam War' and writes that 'those who survived would never forget the savagery, the brutality, the butchery.' This butchery, it seems, is entirely one-sided; a captured North Vietnamese soldier reports that his colleagues 'want very much to kill Americans,' an indicator of Vietnamese barbarity that Moore (68 and 123) later reinforces by commenting that 'they were eager to kill us ... they hungered for our deaths.' Over a dozen portrayals of Vietnamese soldiers executing Americans substantiate this portrayal. One soldier describes 'at least a couple of hundred of them walking around for three or four minutes ... shooting and machine gunning our wounded and laughing and giggling'; another reports Vietnamese who 'would beat [Americans] to death, bayonet them, or machete them' (ibid., 171 and 310). The Vietnamese executioners' vaguely feminized glee and apparent brutality undermine descriptions elsewhere of their professionalism.

American soldiers, in contrast, are never described committing such acts. The Vietnamese body is almost entirely absent, and American killing is described as though Vietnamese soldiers were vegetation or refuse – North Vietnamese soldiers are 'cut down,' 'cleaned up,' and 'got[ten] rid of' (ibid., 87, 93 and 133; Scarry 1985, 66 and 74). Elsewhere, killing is a display of steely courage and skill, as when a soldier 'calmly dropped to one knee and methodically shot fifteen enemy before help arrived' (ibid., 174). Another soldier's description of shooting a Vietnamese soldier hidden behind a tree makes the body a prop that reveals American professionalism: 'I took a shooting-range stance and ... kept shooting this pop-up target. I fired ten more times, methodical single shots until the pop-up target range closed down' (ibid. 1992, 164).

American bodies receive more complicated treatment, at times appearing unfazed by injury and at others enduring devastating wounds. The contrast between painstaking accounts of American 'precariousness' and descriptions of inconsequential wounds reflects the text's simultaneous embrace of tropes from heretofore competing remembrances of Vietnam – the spectacle of gruesome injury that dominates texts critical of the war and the image of impervious bodies central to earlier texts (Butler 2009, 34; Jeffords 1989, 8–12).

Seemingly serious wounds seem hardly to impinge on American soldiers' fighting ability. In one skirmish, 'Specialist Clarence Jackson took a round clean through his left hand, shifted his rifle to his right, and continued firing until he was hit a second time,' while 'Sergeant Ruben Thompson was struck by a bullet above his heart that exited under his left arm; bleeding heavily, he grabbed a rifle and fought on' (Moore and Galloway 1992, 96–7). Men's bodies are hardly impermeable, but their ability to suffer grievous wounds and carry on fighting certifies their tenacity and commitment.

Just as frequently, however, Moore and Galloway emphasize American precariousness. 'They were shockingly wounded, terrible sight to see,' Moore (ibid., 107) recalls. 'Lefebvre's right arm and dangling hand were both mangled and shattered, with bones protruding'; while 'One of Taboada's legs was a gaping, raw, bloody mess from hip to foot.' Particularly striking are their nearly clinical descriptions of American wounds. One lieutenant 'was shot in the throat and the round had ricocheted down and came out his left side' (ibid., 85). Another soldier describes a bullet that 'went in my leg above the ankle, traveled up, came back out, then went into my groin and ended up in my back close to my spine' (ibid., 166). Such detailed accounts of bullets' paths transform the reader into Michel Foucault's 'medical eye,' demanding empathy with the soldier body by making evident 'the evolution of a whole morbid series' of events related to neither neat nor painless wounds (Foucault 1994, 136 and 143; Noble 1997, 303). The stark juxtaposition of bodily trauma with earlier accounts of soldiers' endurance enables American bodies to simultaneously signify American commitment and precariousness. These concerns lie at the heart of Moore and Galloway's broader conclusion that soldiers acquit themselves well but suffer grievously in an unnecessary war.

'Although we sought to do the right thing ... hindsight proves us wrong': political critique of the Vietnam War in the 1990s Unlike both the depoliticized texts about the Vietnam War that preceded them and earlier texts that described the war as having been winnable, both Moore and Galloway and Robert McNamara remember a war escalated by planners fully aware of its futility. Implicitly invoking Powell's command to re-evaluate 'the relationship between ends and means,' Moore and Galloway write that McNamara 'now knew that the Vietnam War had just exploded into ... a cause that he was beginning to suspect would be difficult to win' and notes that McNamara argued that increased troop levels 'will not guarantee success' (Boot 2002, 319; Moore and Galloway 1992, 368). Moore and Galloway (ibid., 370) recount, however, a 1965 White House meeting in which 'McNamara's option number one – get the hell out of Vietnam now, while the getting is good – was never seriously considered,' while 'the huge build-up of American combat and support troops – was readily approved by all.' Moore and Galloway thus condemn policymakers and military leaders for escalating the war despite fully recognizing the likelihood

of failure, ultimately contrasting soldiers' success and suffering against policymakers' refusal to recognize the impending disaster. Chiding General William Westmoreland for 'learn[ing], too late, that ... the American people didn't see a kill ratio of 10–1 or even 20–1 as any kind of bargain,' Moore (ibid., 374) concludes that 'we could stand against the finest light infantry troops in the world and hold our ground' and that the war 'had validated both the principle and the practice of airmobile warfare' but, more importantly, that 'some of us learned that Clausewitz had it right 150 years earlier when he wrote these words: "No one starts a war – or rather no one in his senses ought to do so – without first being clear in his mind what he intends to achieve by that war and how he intends to conduct it."' Vietnam's tragedy thus lies in McNamara's knowing silence, Westmoreland's miscalculations, and overall ignorance regarding a fundamental principle of warfare consistent with Powell's dictums.

The most profound contribution to this discourse, however, came from McNamara himself. He repeatedly suggests that the United States was well intentioned but went to war based on faulty assumptions about both Vietnam's strategic importance and the United States' chances of effectively prosecuting the conflict. Most infamously, McNamara (McNamara amd VanDeMark 1996) writes that policymakers 'acted according to what we thought were the principles and traditions of this nation' but had been 'wrong, terribly wrong.' Throughout the memoir, he declares that 'ill-founded judgments were accepted without debate,' 'show[ing] how limited and shallow our analysis and discussion of the alternatives' were (ibid., 33 and 107). His chief lesson, one that reviewers applied to contemporary politics, cautions against overestimating the United States' potential to influence another nation's affairs: 'It became clear then, and I believe it is clear today, that military force – especially when wielded by an outside power – just cannot bring order to a country that cannot govern itself' (ibid., 261). For him, too, the war is a well-intentioned failure of imagination.

Yet, McNamara (ibid., 333), like Moore and Galloway, declares above reproach the men he sent to Vietnam: 'Does the unwisdom of our intervention nullify their effort and their loss? I think not. They did not make the decisions. They answered their nation's call to service. They went in harm's way on its behalf. And they gave their lives for their country and its ideals. That our effort in Vietnam proved un-wise does not make their sacrifice less noble.' The soldier is here again victimized by a foolhardy, not a reluctant, bureaucracy. Notably, these soldiers are implicitly Moore's patriotic volunteers, not the many draftees or reluctant volunteers who served in Vietnam. Carefully forgetting the inequalities of Vietnam-era service (see Appy 1993, 44–85 and especially 32–3), McNamara, too, valorizes soldiers' exceptionalism while condemning the policy. This remembrance of Vietnam demands adherence to the Powell Doctrine's stipulations that interventions serve only national security interests and that leaders evaluate and re-evaluate the likelihood of success, a logic that likewise dominated media coverage and political rhetoric about humanitarian intervention throughout the decade.

'We saw it ... in Vietnam. We saw it in Somalia': debating humanitarian intervention in the 1990s

'A quagmire all too reminiscent of Vietnam': the 1993 Somalia intervention Humanitarian intervention became a matter of public debate in December 1992, when George H. W. Bush announced that he was sending troops to famine-stricken Somalia. 'When we see Somalia's children starving, all of America hurts,' he maintained (1993, 2175–6), asserting that 'some crises in the world cannot be resolved without American involvement' before reprising language from his Gulf War speeches asserting that the troops 'will have our full support to get the job done.'

The initial public support – the Atlanta Journal and Constitution (29 November 1992) bluntly declared that 'to fail to act in cases where mass starvation is being applied as a military tactic would be the worst form of indifference' – quickly dissipated. By the summer of 1993, the New York Times encouraged a strategy first proposed about Vietnam – 'Declare victory, hand off, slip out, cross fingers' – while musing, 'so simple from afar, Somalia demonstrates how intractable the problems that demand the rescue by foreign armies can be' (Schmeo 1993). This attitude worsened after the disastrous 3 October 1993 raid in which eighteen American soldiers were killed, one was taken captive, and two Black Hawk helicopters were shot down. Newspapers brimmed with comparisons between Somalia and Vietnam, but it matters precisely how Vietnam was invoked, for the 'Vietnam' that critics conjured recalled We Were Soldiers Once and anticipated In Retrospect.

On the US Senate floor, Democrat Frank Lautenberg opined 'we went over there to be of help, not to sacrifice our youngsters' and that 'this evokes all kinds of recollections of what Vietnam looks like' before concluding that 'we did what we had to. The rest has to be up to them.' In the House of Representatives, Republican Rick Lazio fumed that 'we find American troops in a quagmire all too reminiscent of

[Vietnam] ... If we had withdrawn from Vietnam in 1962, over 50,000 young Americans would have been spared' (Cong. Rec. 1993, S13077-8 and H7521). For both, arguing that Somalia was not the United States' battle to fight turned upon invoking Vietnam as a war from which the United States should have immediately extricated itself, remembrances that echoed Moore and Galloway's and foreshadowed McNamara's.

'Let us hope that McNamaraism does not strike us': the debate over sending troops to Bosnia If what became known as the 'Somalia syndrome' negated subsequent humanitarian interventions, most notably in Rwanda in 1994, the extent to which Somalia remained fused to the dominant remembrance of Vietnam in the 1990s was most evident among opponents of Balkan peacekeeping missions, first in Bosnia in 1995 and, in 1999, to Kosovo (Shattuck 2003, 286–7; Lacy 2003, 618; Beinart 2010, 274). Certainly, some opposition to such deployments stemmed from an ideology that identified humanitarian crises as outside the United States' national interests. As Samantha Power (2007, 261, 282 and 259) argues, many felt that 'the United States did not have the most powerful military in the history of the world in order to undertake squishy, humanitarian "social work"'; that genocide resulted from 'hatreds that had raged for centuries'; and that the region was Europe's problem. When the Senate debated the Bosnia peacekeeping mission in December 1995, Colorado's Hank Brown dismissed the notion that 'these people, with American troops' presence, will suddenly honor their peace commitments that they have never honored in 500 years' (Cong. Rec. 1995, S18407). Senator Russell Feingold asked: 'What is the ultimate physical threat to the United States that requires the sacrifice of American lives in this case? ... Is it just the pictures on CNN? I will show you pictures from Liberia, Angola, and East Timor and they are the same or worse' (ibid., S18459). Other senators responded similarly; the violence was deplorable, but the intervention was not in the national interest and was doomed to fail (Power 2007, 262).

What is particularly noteworthy, though, is that, even as they invoked these ideas, senators voiced their opposition in language that relied upon the tropes that simultaneously dominated Vietnam's popular remembrance. In November, even before President Clinton announced the deployment, Robert McNamara's shadow loomed over Bosnia. '"McNamaranism" ... is when you pursue a policy which you know is substantially wrong but you pursue it because of the political need,' Senator Judd Gregg asserted, hoping that it 'does not strike us in Bosnia' (Cong. Rec. 1995, S17517). In the House, Robert Dornan quoted an article calling the administration's claims 'the same guff that McNamara tossed off during Vietnam' (ibid., H13791).

This rhetoric reached its apogee in December, when senators repeatedly conflated Somalia and Vietnam. Veterans Hank Brown and Bob Smith invoked Vietnam not as a righteous cause poorly prosecuted but as a debacle whose potential success had been insufficiently interrogated. 'I volunteered to serve in Vietnam and I did because I believed ... we were there to defend freedom worldwide,' Brown declared, lamenting that 'our political leaders did not believe that' and 'were not willing to establish a clear military mission' (ibid., S18406). Brown thus conflates an earlier argument – that the United States had not made a sufficient effort to win – with another argument, that 'the political leaders did not believe in the cause'; ultimately, Brown connects Vietnam and Somalia, inveighing against both as essentially purposeless and stating that 'the line is drawn when you ask Americans to give their lives for nothing' (ibid., S18407). 'I believe it is morally wrong, to have Americans give their lives in Somalia when you do not have a clear military mission and you will not stand behind them,' he thundered. 'It is wrong to ask them to do it for nothing, and that is what we did in Somalia ... It is wrong to ask them to do it for nothing in Vietnam, when our very leaders would not stand behind the men' (ibid.). For Brown, both interventions were fought over 'nothing.'

Smith likewise remembered Vietnam not as a war that should have been avoided but, like Lautenberg had, as a peacekeeping mission. Recalling 'the McNamara charts and the pointers, how if we could just ... secure the peace, everything would be alright,' he laments that '58,000 lives later, we gave it back to the North Vietnamese' (ibid., S18418). Smith's Vietnam was futile from the outset, and he justifies his many questions by asserting that: 'If we had asked them in the Vietnam War we would not have lost 58,000 people' (ibid., S18420). And for Smith, too, Vietnam and Somalia were identical failures: 'We saw it in Somalia, if you do not like the Vietnamese example' (ibid.).

The most powerful conflations, however, came from Senators James Inhofe and Kay Bailey Hutchison, who cast Somalia as a continuation of the government's errors in Vietnam by recalling conversations with Vietnam-veteran fathers of soldiers killed in Somalia. Hutchison combines discourses of Vietnam veterans' stalwart patriotism and the war's inexplicability to condemn peacekeeping missions. 'I went to Vietnam twice. I am a military man. And now my only son, on his very first mission as a Ranger, is not coming home,' Larry Joyce tells her before asking, 'Senator, I would just like to know why' (ibid., S18405).

This demand paraphrases one familiar within Vietnam's legacy, and yet Joyce is hardly anti-war; rather, he is a 'military man,' a dedicated patriot who nonetheless recalls a remembrance of Vietnam as disastrous. Hutchison applies this construction to Somalia, similarly celebrating the younger Joyce while disparaging the mission and insisting that she 'would never vote to send our troops into harm's way if I could not give the mother or father a good answer about why' and that 'sending our troops into Bosnia under these circumstances is not meeting the test' (ibid., S18405). Despite sympathy toward Bosnian suffering, then, congressional opposition to intervention relied upon the discourse of Vietnam remembrance defined in *We Were Soldiers Once* and *In Retrospect* – Vietnam, though fought valiantly, had been an ill-conceived tragedy.

'The lessons learned six years ago in Somalia should not be forgotten': debating peacekeeping in Kosovo American troops were sent to Bosnia, and the intervention was widely seen as successful (Beinart 2010, 284; Power 2007, 443; Shattuck 2003, 288). Yet this apparent satisfaction did not produce support for peacekeeping in Kosovo. Anxieties about casualties and opposition rooted in the Powell Doctrine remained dominant (Boot 2002, 326–37; Beinart 2010, 87; Power 2007, 454–5). Legislators repeated familiar points from the Bosnia debate. During a lengthy House debate on a resolution disapproving of a peacekeeping deployment, North Carolina's Howard Coble asserted that 'Bosnia and Kosovo are European problems' (Cong. Rec. 1999, H1183). Colorado's Scott McInnis contested that 'those kinds of tragedies are going on throughout the entire world. This country cannot be the world's police officer' and that 'we do not have the capability to take hundreds of years of battle and hundreds of years of rock-solid feelings and force them into a peace agreement' (ibid., H1184).

Alongside those relatively abstract arguments, however, were speeches that revived the imprecations of Vietnam and Somalia in terms familiar from popular culture and the Bosnia debates. In that same debate, Senator Mark Sanford invoked Henry Kissinger, who 'believed that we were in trouble in Vietnam because our predecessors had launched the US into an enterprise in a distant region for worthy causes but without adequately assessing the national interest and the likely cost,' before declaring that 'Clifford Clark was sent by Lyndon Johnson to see our SEATO allies in Southeast Asia ... [They] said, no, we do not think this will grow into a giant conflict in Southeast Asia. We choose not to go into South Vietnam or North Vietnam. We ignored their advice and, as a result, 50,000 American boys died' (ibid., H1200). Despite transposing Clifford's name, Sanford does invoke the decade's dominant remembrance of Vietnam – that it was an ill-founded war prosecuted with full knowledge that it was both unnecessary and unwinnable. His colleague Senator Lindsey Graham similarly invoked Kissinger before asking: 'How many more young men and women are going to go in faraway places to get in the middle of civil wars where there is a dubious reason to be there to start with and no way home?' (ibid., H1203). Georgia's Nathan Deal was perhaps most concise: 'Let us not forget the lessons of Vietnam, which ... include that of non-intervention in the internal affairs of another Nation' (ibid., H1236). And, unsurprisingly, Vietnam was linked to Somalia. 'This brings back haunting memories of Korea, Vietnam, and Somalia,' Nebraska's Doug Bereuter reflected. 'As history has shown, peace-enforcement does not lend itself to an exit strategy. Police presence is rarely a temporary situation' (ibid., H1218). As in the Bosnia debate four years earlier, Vietnam inexplicably became a peacekeeping mission.

In the Senate, Robert Smith reprised his Bosnia speech: 'When presidents use force in a way that they do not or cannot explain to the American people, and for a cause that the American people do not in their gut support, that policy collapses. We saw it by the end of the war in Vietnam. We saw it in Somalia' (ibid., S3702). Senator John Ashcroft suggested that: 'As we consider a possible deployment to Kosovo, the lessons learned six years ago in Somalia should not be forgotten. The American people will not support a Kosovo deployment that costs American lives when America's vital security interests are not at stake. Yet American casualties are a very real prospect in Kosovo' (ibid., S3071). Senator Larry Craig called Vietnam 'a quagmire that we finally simply had to drop because we could no longer sustain it politically and we could no longer justify that another one, two, or three American lives should be lost' (ibid., S3067). As they had three years earlier, conservative senators remembered Vietnam not as a war that should have been won, but one that was intractable from the outset, could never be sufficiently 'explained,' and unnecessarily killed Americans.

Throughout the 1990s, members of Congress responded to the Somalia mission and debated the Bosnia and Kosovo deployments by mobilizing and contributing to the remembrance of Vietnam that was simultaneously dominating the war's depiction in popular culture. For legislators, as for McNamara and Moore and Galloway, Vietnam was not a good war gone wrong but one that the United States should have known to avoid. Soldiers died because policymakers failed to heed obvious warnings, and Somalia was an identical failure. As these discussions played out on Capitol Hill, Americans began encountering popular literature about the Somalia intervention, texts that drew upon the tropes and discourses central to Moore and Galloway and McNamara to construct a remembrance of the 1993 intervention that contributed to legitimizing the critiques offered by opponents to humanitarian intervention.

'We should have said no': Vietnam's legacy and popular culture of the Somalia intervention

It was in the realm of popular culture that Americans contemplated how the soldier and the nation would experience humanitarian interventions. They began to do so in early 1999, when *Black Hawk Down* reintroduced the events of 3 October 1993. Over the next four years, the bestseller was joined by captured pilot Mike Durant's bestselling *In the Company of Heroes*, Martin Stanton's *Somalia on Five Dollars a Day*, and Matt Eversmann and Dan Schilling's *The Battle of Mogadishu*. These texts are culturally and politically significant because, in a moment in which Somalia and Vietnam were frequently invoked in opposition to humanitarian deployments, the texts' critical portrayals of the intervention drew upon the tropes, discourses, imagery, and, at times, the particular language of contemporary Vietnam literature, establishing Somalia as an identical experience for American troops created by an identical failure of political leaders.

Few scholars have interrogated these texts. Klien's analysis of Ridley Scott's 2001 film as a 'pro-soldier, anti-war' film is to some extent true of the book as well (Klien 2005, 428). Yet his persuasive reading of the film's emphasis on and defense of soldiers' character even amid 'wars fought for questionable purposes under poorly planned conditions,' finds only 'sporadic critique of Washington's Somalia policy'; this, he argues, ultimately contributes to pro-war discourse (ibid., 436, 434, 444 and 432). Lacy, noting that 'we achieve proximity only to the deaths of Americans' but 'do not get to see the deaths of Somalis with any moral proximity,' posits that 'the movie suggests that it is best to leave the irrational savages to themselves' and that 'it is unacceptable to place young US troops in [such] environments' (Lacy 2003, 620–1). These points are likewise largely valid for the book, but Lacy concludes that such depictions truncate considerations of policy (ibid., 624). Most importantly, neither Klien nor Lacy notes the film's indebtedness to contemporary tropes of Vietnam remembrance.

The Somalia literature hardly absolves readers from condemning policy decisions, and it constructs this critique by appropriating and re-deploying the tropes, strategies, and occasionally the language through which Moore and Galloway and McNamara remember Vietnam, forging a discursive connection between the remembrance of Somalia and the contemporary remembrance of that war. Vietnam receives little mention, but for readers familiar with this Vietnam literature and public debates that persistently compared Vietnam with humanitarian missions in this language, the Battle of Mogadishu appeared very much akin to the Battle of the Ia Drang Valley.

'The most highly motivated young soldiers of their generation': remembering combat in Somalia As in Moore and Galloway's description of air mobility as uniquely suited to Cold War interventions in the developing world, the Somalia literature describes units essentially suited to contemporary foreign policy goals. As idealized warriors of Beinart's (2010, 283) 'new liberalism' of the 1990s (a liberalism that was 'idealistic about ends, but somewhat brutal about means' and 'confident that vanquishing evil and extending American dominance were usually one and the same'), Bowden's Delta Force (2002, 37–8) 'allowed the dreamers and the politicians to have it both ways ... They did America's most important work, but they shunned recognition, fame, and fortune.' Durant and Stanton likewise echo Moore. Durant's (2004, 146) elite corps of helicopter pilots emerges from an awareness that 'America was entering an era of unconventional warfare, yet we did not have dedicated unconventional capabilities.' Stanton (2001, 4) nearly paraphrases Moore: 'We, of course, had to maintain heavy forces to face our potential adversaries in Europe and Korea. But we also had to have forces ready to deploy swiftly to conduct operations on the lower end of the spectrum.'

The soldiers who populate these specialized units similarly recall Moore and Galloway's idealized cavalry. The Rangers, Bowden (2002, 9) writes, 'were the cream, the most highly motivated young soldiers of their generation,' 'achingly earnest, patriotic, and idealistic' men who 'held themselves to a higher standard than normal soldiers.' Delta operators are even more glamorous, 'allowed a degree of personal freedom and initiative unheard of in the military' and 'trained to think and act for themselves' (ibid., 38 and 183). Other writers follow suit. The Rangers, were 'a different breed of men, a different caliber of soldier,' Matt Eversmann (Eversmann and Schilling 2005, 6) writes: 'They were *expected* to perform difficult and dangerous things' and

58

'were given a lot of responsibility and taught to be problem solvers.' Durant's (2004, 149) unit similarly required 'patience, perseverance, determination, and nerve' and was populated by men 'constantly honing [their] skills, improving, improvising.' And Stanton (2001, 17, 18 and 11), once again, clearly echoes Moore: 'The soldiers were motivated. The NCOs and officers were competent and professional,' and 'everyone had a common sense of mission'; his leader is 'absolutely competent,' and the enlisted men are 'pure gold.' Unlike the draftee grunt who previously dominated the American remembrance of Vietnam – and, more importantly, like Moore's troopers – professionalism defines the contemporary military.

This rhetoric continues in descriptions of battle. Like their predecessors, whose 'fighting spirit had not dimmed,' soldiers fighting in Mogadishu remain undiscouraged by the battle's violence and continually risk their lives to achieve a tactical victory. One soldier recalls that 'if he was afraid, he simply filed the emotion away' (Bowden 2002, 267). Another, returning to the city to rescue the trapped Rangers, reflects: 'if he was going to die today, so be it. The pull of loyalty felt stronger in him than the will to survive' (ibid., 325). Tim Wilkinson (2005, 156), meanwhile, demurs that he was 'only holding up my end of the deal, like everyone else.' Even when faced with combat's gruesome realities, these men's commitment remains undiminished.

The Somalis, in spite of Bowden's – like Moore and Galloway's – efforts to include an enemy perspective, share none of these traits. They are, throughout this literature, dehumanized sadists who, like the North Vietnamese, perversely enjoy killing people, particularly injured Americans. Just as Moore (1992, 115) realizes that 'if the air bridge failed,' the Americans 'would be ... butchered to the last man,' one Somali militiaman 'believed if the Rangers didn't have the helicopters ... he and his men would surround and kill them with ease, with their bare hands' (Bowden 2002, 216). Beyond the parallel language, it is notable that Somalis, too, can hardly refrain from killing Americans. After his helicopter crashed, Durant (2004, 40) believed that 'they were going to chop me to pieces' because 'that's what they did to *everybody*.' If such accounts are extreme versions of the 'laughing and giggling' North Vietnamese referenced earlier in this chapter, Bowden (2002, 127 and 278) paraphrases accounts of Vietnamese enthusiasm: 'It was as if "Kill-an-American Day" had been declared' and 'everybody in the city wanted suddenly to help kill Americans.'

While Somalis share the North Vietnamese bloodlust, American bodies receive the multifaceted treatment central to *We Were Soldiers*

Once. Bowden's Rangers and Delta operators, like Moore's troops, are alternately brutally victimized and strangely unaffected in combat, and here as well these juxtapositions assert simultaneously the soldier's heroism and vulnerability while preserving his integrity and questioning the wisdom of the deployment itself.

Throughout *Black Hawk Down* (ibid., 190 and 151), heads are cut open to reveal men's brains, and men hear 'the awful slap of bullets into flesh and heard the screams and saw the insides of men's bodies spill out.' One soldier 'hold[s] his entrails in his hands' after 'the whole back of his pelvis had been blown off' and another is 'torn in half' with 'his insides ... lying next to him on a gurney' and a limb 'twisted off the side of the stretcher, swinging, attached to the trunk by a hunk of meat' (ibid., 277 and 187). Like Moore's Lefebvre and Taboada, gruesome American wounds receive graphic descriptions. In particular, Bowden appropriates Moore and Galloway's explicit delineations of bullets' paths through American bodies, as in his description of Jamie Smith's death (ibid., 257):

> [The bullet] had entered Smith's thigh and traveled up into his pelvis
> ... The aorta splits low in the abdomen, forming the left and right iliac
> arteries. As the iliac artery emerges from the pelvis it branches into
> the exterior and deep femoral arteries, the primary avenues for blood
> to the lower half of the body. The bullet had clearly pierced one of the
> femoral vessels.

Other injuries receive similarly wrenching descriptions. One 'bullet had exploded [a soldier's] shinbone and traveled on down his leg and exited at his ankle, shredding the foot'; another Ranger is 'hit by a round that entered his buttock and bored straight through his pelvis, blowing off one testicle as it exited through his upper thigh' (ibid., 224 and 267). As in *We Were Soldiers Once*, this trope demands readers' empathetic recognition of American precariousness.

However, the wounded body also signifies, as it often does in *We Were Soldiers Once*, the soldier's tenacity. After one assault, a soldier 'felt no pain, just some numbness in his hand ... The shrapnel had fractured a bone in his left forearm, severed a tendon, and broken a bone in his hand. It wasn't bleeding much and he could still shoot' (ibid., 138). Here, pathological description renders the soldier's body a marvel. A later account (ibid., 332) is even more incredible:

> He had a trickle of blood running down his face and a neat hole, a
> small one, right in the middle of his forehead ... Doctors would later

determine that a piece of shrapnel had lodged between the frontal lobes of his brain, missing vital tissues by fractions of an inch in either direction. He was alright. It felt like he had just banged his head.

Here, a potentially fatal wound is merely a nuisance. As in Moore and Galloway, merging antithetical representations of wounded bodies allows soldiers to occupy simultaneously the opposing roles of invincible heroes and vulnerable victims. Just as these competing representations allowed *We Were Soldiers Once* to emphasize Vietnam-era soldiers' heroism and commitment while at the same time foreshadowing the trauma that followed policymakers' refusal to escalate the war, Bowden's appropriations of these discourses similarly enable the argument that, although American soldiers fight valiantly, the gruesome suffering that they will endure makes untenable their deployment in human rights wars.

The soldiers' professionalism is further established through the appropriation of Moore and Galloway's contrasting of enemy brutality with Americans' trauma-free precision. Somali deaths are instantaneous and painless, and Somali bodies rarely receive sustained attention. Like North Vietnamese soldiers at the Ia Drang Valley, Somalis simply die, as when 'the Somali just fell forward ... without even getting off a shot' or 'just fell over sideways' (ibid., 201 and 202). Echoing Moore and Galloway, Bowden (ibid., 204, 262 and 78) deploys language of inanimacy and refuse: Somalis are 'dropped' or 'flattened' by American bullets or, after being shot, 'lay in a rumpled heap.' Sometimes they simply disappear. 'One moment the Somali's head was there, and the next moment he was gone,' Durant (2004, 37) writes of a man he shoots. One soldier echoes the account in *We Were Soldiers Once* of the 'pop-up target range': killing Somalis was 'just like target practice, only cooler' (Bowden 2002, 75).

Implicitly and explicitly, the literature of the Somalia intervention draws upon the tropes and language central to *We Were Soldiers Once*, establishing combat Somalia as a repetition of the United States' first battle in Vietnam. In so doing, they contributed to and buttressed a political discourse fearful that humanitarian interventions would reprise the Vietnam War.

'*A noble decision ... but the wrong one*': political critique of the Somalia intervention These texts likewise echo Moore and Galloway's and McNamara's critiques of the policies that underlay Vietnam, also carefully distinguishing between tactical success and strategic failure and arguing that, in spite of the disaster that Somalia became, the soldiers were beyond reproach. Recalling Moore and Galloway's conclusion that validating air mobility was a sufficiently satisfactory outcome, nearly every writer emphasizes tactical success over strategic failure. 'The Battle of the Black Sea was perceived outside the special operations community as a failure,' Bowden (ibid., 408) writes. 'It was not, at least in strictly military terms ... Against overwhelming odds, the mission was accomplished.' Stanton (2001, 258) concurs that although 'the whole Somalia mission was a disorganized mess ... no matter what happened or what task we were given, we would do it well. This in and of itself was all that mattered.' Dan Schilling (Eversmann and Schilling 2005, 201), recalling Moore's claims that Americans 'could stand against the finest light infantry troops in the world and hold our ground,' writes that 'we'd accomplished our mission' and 'had dished out more than we took against people who liked to dish it out.'

These texts, like the Vietnam literature of the moment, shield soldiers from the condemnation that policymakers apparently deserve. This is most pronounced in Bowden's (2002, 422) epilogue, which echoes McNamara's defense of the soldier: 'No matter how critically history records the policy decisions that led up to this fight, nothing can diminish the professionalism and dedication of the Rangers and Special Forces units who fought there that day.' The implication, of course, is that those calculations warrant severe critique, which Stanton (2001, xi) provides: 'The soldiers, sailors, Marines, and airmen did all that was asked of them. More's the pity the policymakers were not asking for the right things.'

The wrong things are precisely those that Moore and Galloway and McNamara condemn about Vietnam, the failure to realize that the mission met no national interest and was unwinnable. Although some soldiers resent being withdrawn, they complain most vigorously about being sent at all. These writers forcefully echo McNamara's sentiment that the United States had benevolent but misguided intentions, insisting that the Somalia mission emerged from the faulty conviction that the United States should right the world's wrongs. 'Bush believed that going to Somalia to end the suffering there was the moral thing to do,' Stanton (ibid., 69) explains, nearly paraphrasing McNamara: 'It was a noble decision – motivated by thoroughly decent impulses – but the wrong one.' Bowden (2002, 409) similarly paraphrases McNamara, writing that Somalia has come to represent 'the futility of trying to resolve local animosity with international muscle.' This is a concept to which he returns (ibid., 427): 'The foreign policy lesson I take from this story is like the old prayer, "Lord, grant me the strength to change the things I can, to accept the things I can't, and the wisdom to know the difference." Learning what America's power can and can't accomplish is a major challenge in the post-Cold War world.' Ultimately, he concludes about Somalia what Moore and Galloway, as well as McNamara, admitted about Vietnam, that 'it would have been hard for the United States not to go after Aidid, but it would have been better not to try ... We should have said no' (ibid., 427–8). Bowden's assessment that the United States' misplaced confidence in its ability to shape world affairs rearticulates the foreign policy lessons of Vietnam that Robert McNamara defined in 1996 about the events of 1965, and he and Stanton likewise conclude that moral commitments should not lead to military ones.

Here, again, the parallels are explicit. In a moment in which they encountered political critiques that compared peacekeeping missions to Somalia and Vietnam, readers of American war literature in the 1990s consumed portrayals of the United States' mission in Somalia that relied heavily upon the tropes through which Vietnam had been imagined just a few years earlier. In recalling and replaying those tropes, this literature contributed to the widespread public sentiment that Somalia, and thus all peacekeeping missions, were, in fact, 'another Vietnam.'

Conclusion

Throughout the 1990s, political leaders and the public questioned whether the United States had an interest or obligation in humanitarian missions and peace enforcement. Interventionists viewed the matter as one from which the United States could hardly abstain without abdicating global leadership. Others, however, argued that such missions met no national security goals and were likely to succeed only in killing American soldiers. For these opponents, Vietnam remained a potent analogy, and Somalia was a persistent analogue to the policymaking errors of the 1960s. As Americans debated humanitarian missions, these opponents echoed – and sometimes invoked – Moore and Galloway's account of the First Cavalry's gallant fighting, the Johnson Administration's failure to heed the battle's lessons, and Robert McNamara's admission of his errors, and declared themselves, as Senator Robert Smith did, to be asking about peace missions the questions that should have been asked about Vietnam.

As this debate raged at the turn of the century, Americans also began reading accounts of the Somalia intervention, the only peacekeeping mission about which there is a substantial body of literature. In these texts, they discovered representations of American combat experiences that replicated the simultaneously dominant remembrance of the American experience in Indochina as it condemned that mission as similarly futile and misguided. These texts are thus not politically neutral, nor do they simply compare Somalia with Vietnam. In crafting Somalia's remembrance by appropriating the tropes that were also central to remembering the United States' most divisive war, this literature contributes to a discourse opposed to humanitarian deployments by enabling an audience anxious about such interventions to conceptualize very graphic and specific portrayals of how a peacekeeping mission might, in fact, actually be 'another Vietnam.' In so doing, the popular culture regarding Somalia reveals that the evolving contours of Vietnam's legacy remained a defining touchstone for US foreign policy between the end of the Cold War and the beginning of the 'War on Terror.'

Notes

1 On the Gulf War as antithetical to the Vietnam War, see Boot 2002, 319, among many others.

2 This discourse is thus more complicated than the 'pro-soldier, anti-war movie' that Klien (2005, 429) identifies as emerging after Vietnam, in that it offers a more nuanced portrayal of the soldiers' experiences and a more explicit policy critique.

3 For an overview of *In Retrospect*'s reception, see Hendrickson 1996, 378–80.

References

Appy, Christian G. 1993. *Working-Class War: American Combat Soldiers and Vietnam*. Chapel Hill, NC: University of North Carolina Press.

Atlanta Journal and Constitution. 1992. 'Just Cause in Somalia.' Editorial. *The Atlanta Journal and Constitution*. 29 November.

Aufderheide, Pat. 1990. 'Good soldiers.' In *Seeing Through the Movies*, edited by Mark Crispin Miller, 83–111. New York: Pantheon Books.

Beinart, Peter. 2010. *The Icarus Syndrome: A History of American Hubris*. New York: HarperCollins.

Boot, Max. 2002. *The Savage Wars of Peace: Small Wars and the Rise of American Power*. New York: Basic Books.

Bowden, Mark. 2002. *Black Hawk Down: A Story of Modern War*. New York: Signet.

Brundage, W. Fitzhugh. 2000. *Where These Memories Grow: History, Memory, and Southern Identity*. Chapel Hill, NC: University of North Carolina Press.

Buchanan, Pat. 1999. 'The mess they've made.' *Washington Post*, 13 April: A21.

Bush, George H. W. 1992a. 'Remarks to the Reserve Officers Association, January 23, 1991.' *Public Papers of the Presidents: George H. W. Bush* 1: 60–2. Washington, DC: Government Printing Office.

Bush, George H. W. 1992b. 'Remarks

at Annual Convention of National Religious Broadcasters, January 28, 1991.' *Public Papers of the Presidents: George H. W. Bush* 1: 70–2. Washington, DC: Government Printing Office.

Bush, George H. W. 1992c. 'Remarks on assistance for Iraqi refugees and a news conference, April 16, 1991.' *Public Papers of the Presidents: George H. W. Bush* 1: 378–85. Washington, DC: Government Printing Office.

Bush, George H. W. 1993. 'Address to the nation on Somalia, December 4, 1992.' *Public Papers of the Presidents: George H. W. Bush* 2: 2174–6. Washington, DC: Government Printing Office.

Butler, Judith. 2009. *Frames of War: When Is Life Grievable?* Brooklyn, NY: Verso.

Clinton, William J. 1999. 'Address to the nation on airstrikes against Serbian targets in the Federal Republic of Yugoslavia (Serbia and Montenegro), March 24, 1999.' *Public Papers of the Presidents: William Jefferson Clinton* 1: 452–3. Washington, DC: Government Printing Office.

Congressional Record. 1993. 103rd Congress, 1st Session.

Congressional Record. 1995. 104th Congress, 1st Session.

Congressional Record. 1999. 106th Congress, 1st Session.

Durant Michael J., with Steven Hartov. 2004. *In the Company of Heroes*. New York: New American Library.

Eversmann, Matt, and Dan Schilling (editors). 2005. *The Battle of Mogadishu: Firsthand Accounts from the Men of Task Force Ranger.* New York: Ballantine Books.

Foucault, Michel. 1994. *The Birth of the Clinic: An Archaeology of Medical Perception*. New York: Vintage Books.

Haines, Harry W. 1997. '"They were called and they went": The political rehabilitation of the Vietnam veteran.' In *From Hanoi to Hollywood: The Vietnam War in American Film*, edited by Linda Dittmar and Gene Michaud, 81–100. New Brunswick, NJ: Rutgers University Press.

Hendrickson, Paul. 1996. *The Living and the Dead – Robert McNamara and Five Lives of a Lost War.* New York: Knopf.

Jeffords, Susan. 1989. *The Remasculinization of America: Gender and the Vietnam War.* Indianapolis: Indiana University Press.

Kaplan, B. D. 1995. 'Is McNamara still blanked?' *Cleveland Plain Dealer*, 17 April: B11.

Kaplan, Steven. 1993. 'The undying uncertainty of the narrator in Tim O'Brien's *The Things They Carried.' Critique* 35(1): 43–52.

Kendrick, Michelle. 1994. 'Kicking the Vietnam Syndrome: CNN's and CBS's video narratives of the Persian Gulf War.' In *Seeing Through the Media: The Persian Gulf War*, edited by Susan Jeffords and Lauren Rabinovitz, 59–76. New Brunswick, NJ: Rutgers University Press.

Klien, Stephen A. 2005. 'Public character and the simulacrum: The construction of the soldier patriot and citizen agency in *Black Hawk Down.' Critical Studies in Media Communication* 22(5): 427–49.

Lacy, Mark J. 2003. 'War, cinema, and moral anxiety.' *Alternatives* 28: 611–36.

McNamara, Robert S., and Brian VanDeMark. 1996. *In Retrospect: The Tragedy and Lessons of Vietnam*. New York: Vintage Books.

McWhirter, Cameron. 1993. 'Grieving vet asks: "Why are we there?"' *Chicago Tribune*, 6 October: 10.

Moniz, Dave. 1999. 'A peacekeeping mission gone wrong.' Review of *Black Hawk Down* by Mark Bowden. *Christian Science Monitor*, 11 March: 20.

Moore, Harold G., and Joseph L. Galloway. 1992. *We Were Soldiers Once ... And Young: Ia Drang – The Battle That Changed the War in Vietnam*. New York: Presidio Press.

Noble, Marianne. 1997. 'The ecstasies of sentimental wounding in *Uncle Tom's Cabin*.' *Yale Journal of Criticism* 10(2): 295–320.

Pinkerton, James P. 1999. 'Beware of our good intentions in Kosovo.' *Albany Times Union*, 14 April: A15.

Power, Samantha. 2007. *'A Problem from Hell': America and the Age of Genocide*. New York: Harper Perennial.

Quindlen, Anna. 1993. 'It's time to say so long, Somalia – We're outta here.' *Seattle Post-Intelligencer*, 8 October: A14.

Robinson, Daniel. 1999. 'Getting it right: The short fiction of Tim O'Brien.' *Critique* 40(3): 257–64.

Scarry, Elaine. 1985. *The Body in Pain: The Making and Unmaking of the World*. New York: Oxford University Press.

Scheer, Robert. 1995. 'Imagine how many lives could have been saved in 1967 if McNamara had released a warning; nation paid for bumbling and secrecy.' *San Jose Mercury News*, 14 April: 7b.

Schmeo, Diana Jean. 1993. 'Declare victory, hand off, slip out, cross fingers.' *New York Times*, 2 May, section 4: 1.

Shattuck, John. 2003. *Freedom on Fire: Human Rights Wars and America's Response*. Cambridge, MA: Harvard University Press.

Stanton, Martin. 2001. *Somalia on Five Dollars a Day: A Soldier's Story*. Novato, CA: Presidio Press.

Studlar, Gaylyn, and David Desser. 1997. 'Never having to say you're sorry: Rambo's rewriting of the Vietnam war.' In *From Hanoi to Hollywood: The Vietnam War in American Film*, edited by Linda Dittmar and Gene Michaud, 101–12. New Brunswick, NJ: Rutgers University Press.

Sturken, Maria. 1998. *Tangled Memories: The Vietnam War, the AIDS Epidemic, and the Politics of Remembering*. Berkeley: University of California Press.

Wilkinson, Tim. 2005. 'Be careful what you wish for.' In *The Battle of Mogadishu: Firsthand Accounts from the Men of Task Force Ranger*, edited by Matt Eversmann and Dan Schilling, 127–56. New York: Ballantine Books.

Winter, Jay M. 2006. *Remembering War: The Great War Between Memory and History in the Twentieth Century*. New Haven, CT: Yale University Press.

2 | Framing a rights ethos: artistic media and the dream of a culture without borders

MICHAEL GALCHINSKY

Human rights culture has many tasks to perform. In literature, film, and the visual and performing arts, works of human rights culture seek to reflect, and do reflect *on*, our fundamental dignity, equality, and freedom. Human rights culture draws on the theory of natural rights first declared during the American and French revolutions, and later institutionalized in the Universal Declaration of Human Rights (UDHR) and the complex array of treaties, monitoring bodies, and courts that followed. At the same time, human rights artists draw on the universalistic strains within their own particular religious, cultural, and ethnic traditions.

Human rights *culture* shares civic and ethical functions with human rights *law*, but while the orientation of the law is vertical, reaching down from government bodies to individuals, the orientation of rights culture tends to be horizontal, with the artist appealing as a human being directly to his or her fellows. In this way, works of human rights culture participate in the public sphere, in Habermas's sense (Habermas 1998; Slaughter 2007). Along with the work of non-governmental organizations (NGOs), news media, and *new* media, culture helps construct the civil society in which human rights can be meaningful. The human rights artist assumes that neither the United Nations (UN) nor a national government can simply compel people to respect each other's rights: people have to *want* to. The artist seeks to produce and reflect that desire to a national or global citizenry, striving to ground the formal rights system in an informal rights ethos.

Only rarely does a work of human rights culture produce a direct outcome – the change in a policy or law, the release of a prisoner, or the overthrow of a regime. Its work is generally more subtle, indirect, and long term: it helps to produce what cultural sociologists call a 'structure of feeling,' a socially constructed and sanctioned sympathy with others across identity differences (see, for example, Williams 1997 and Alexander 2007). In other words, human rights art seeks to cultivate rights-oriented 'habits of the heart' before abuses start, so that when they do, a rights discourse will already be in place to stand against the discourse of the violators (Durkheim 1972, 1992 and 1995; Hunt 2007; Mill 1989; Sontag 2003; Tocqueville 1969).

In *Inventing Human Rights*, historian Lynn Hunt provides a demonstration of how literature produced a rights-oriented structure of feeling in the rights revolution in eighteenth-century France. Novels such as Samuel Richardson's *Pamela* modeled empathy across social lines. As Hunt (2007, 40) tells us:

> In the eighteenth century, readers of novels learned to extend their purview of empathy ... across traditional social boundaries ... As a consequence, they came to see others – people they did not know personally – as like them, as having the same kinds of inner emotions. Without this learning process, 'equality' could have no deep meaning, and in particular no political consequence.

By promoting identification with the interior lives of people who had been considered unequal, novels prepared 'the seedbed' of the French revolution's declaration of human rights (ibid., 58). Critics have made similar arguments about the role of fiction in helping build support for the American civil rights movement, among other cases.

Human rights culture performs its many tasks by addressing multiple audiences. Most rights works are directed to their national audiences and speak to national crises in a global dialect. A small proportion of these – in addition to addressing their national audience – also reach out to a global public. At the national level, we can split the audience into three parts: the abused, the witnesses and allies, and the perpetrators. The artist's fellow sufferers look to the work for voice, protest, satire, and commiseration. The witnesses and allies look to it for information, history, inspiration, and a focal point for grief. To the perpetrators the work is directed as testimony and protest. Addressing all three audiences simultaneously can be a difficult task, so artists sometimes limit the work's distribution to *one* of the audiences: for example, protest songs and poems passed hand to hand among dissidents or distributed via selective listservs create solidarity and build resistance.

Those works of human rights culture that reach for the global public aim to inspire international outrage and intervention. Here special difficulties arise, because, for reasons to be explored in this chapter, it is not clear that a global public exists. But the fantasy of a global audience provides many artists – under conditions of censorship and threat of punishment at home – a lifeline beyond the national frame.

We could say that the dream of broadcasting rights works to the world is the dream of a 'culture without borders' – a yearning to tap into a universal structure of feeling.

Purposes

Human rights culture raises many questions: beyond the general aim of establishing an ethos among their multiple audiences, to what more specific purposes do human rights artists set themselves? What aesthetic modes – or formal approaches – have they adopted to fulfill their purposes? And what problems have they, their distributors, critics, and audiences faced in creating a human rights culture?

Apart from the general task of engendering sympathy beyond identity, human rights artists set themselves a variety of more specific tasks. They seek to clarify or dispute historical narratives, protest current practices, foment resistance, promote reconciliation, express solidarity, inspire others, and mourn. With so many purposes, it is no wonder that works in this field are so difficult to analyze as a class. To begin to make some analytical headway, cultural critics have recognized the need to adjust their habits of reception.

The readjustment has, in the past several years, been increasingly led by the new field of human rights literary criticism. Human rights literature has had its own special topic section in *PMLA*, the journal of the Modern Language Association of America. Important sole-authored works of criticism such as Joseph Slaughter's *Human Rights, Inc.* (2007) have emerged. Sophia McClennen and Slaughter (2009) have edited a special-topic issue of *Comparative Literature Studies*, and Routledge is set to publish a volume of articles edited by Elizabeth Swanson Goldberg and Alexandra Schultheis on theoretical frameworks for approaching human rights literature.

In the short time since its 2007 publication, Slaughter's path-making book has become a kind of founding document. He offers an ambitious argument about the parallelism between legal discourse on human rights and the narrative form of the coming-of-age novel: both value the individual's development, socialization, and incorporation into the larger community. Both take for granted a plot trajectory of progress – or document the obstructions to such progress – a plot that finds its source in Enlightenment thinking about the modern subject and has increasingly found a foothold in postcolonial thinking as well. The coming-of-age novel, Slaughter says, is the 'novelistic wing of human rights' (Slaughter 2007, 25); indeed, for him it is the exemplary type of such literature.

Useful as Slaughter's thesis is, I think it is too soon to a make a claim that any particular genre is exemplary. That could be established only after the slow accumulation and synthesis of numerous empirical studies of individual texts and genres. Slaughter himself suggests that 'other cultural forms ... may make imaginable alternative visions of human rights' (ibid., 4), mentioning other novel subgenres such as the picaresque, romance, epistolary, and sentimental. Curiously, he discounts the human rights potential of non-narrative forms such as poetry and plays (ibid., 41–2).

I suggest a different yet still preliminary approach that I hope is able to account for a larger variety of texts. The temptation is to proceed with an expanded socio-historical investigation of genres. But while that kind of study is necessary, human rights literature seems to me, at least initially, to demand a different kind of analysis – not of genre, but of mode. Genres are historically evolving forms of writing, their features contingent on the time and place in which they are put to use. By contrast, modes are major forms of writing that persist in many times and places. A genre contains a spectrum of possibilities activated contingently in relation to a specific historical context. As Franco Morretti has shown, genres have a life cycle: they are born, mature, evolve, die off, and may be born again, perhaps amalgamated with features from another genre. By contrast, a mode remains the same no matter where or when it is produced. Modes are trans-spatial and trans-historical, because they are logically derived rather than historically conceived. Aristotle famously identified three major modes: lyric (a single voice), drama (multiple voices), and narrative (multiple voices organized by an overarching teller). Later critics and historians, such as Northrop Frye (2007) and Hayden White (1975), have elaborated the modal concept. The idea of modes seems suited to human rights, which scholars characterize as similarly rationally derived, trans-spatial, and trans-historical.

In the last thirty years the movement in the arts and criticism has been toward multiculturalism – the exploration and celebration of cultural diversity and difference. There have been, of course, good reasons for this approach. Yet a human rights art asks audiences to follow the pendulum as it swings in the other direction. It asks audiences to balance multiculturalism with a kind of humanism – and this time not an exclusively Western-oriented humanism. While recognizing the uniqueness of a given community's experience (as per the multicultural model), it asks audiences to recognize those aspects of the experience that can be communicated across social divides. It challenges critics to adopt concepts that are independent of local or national context, of historical period or artistic genre. It asks them to imagine an aesthetic that transcends nationality, race, and ethnicity; gender and sexuality; religion and class.

Modes

The difficulties here are manifold, but we can reduce them if we recognize that literary reactions to human rights situations share certain stable structures no matter where or when they were produced and they share a common cast of characters – the victim, the violator, the witness, and the judge. I break down human rights culture into four modes, which I claim are non-contingent and universal. I call them protest, testimony, lament, and laughter. Although these modes often appear in combination, each has special features.

Protest My first mode is the literature of protest. From revolutionary political pamphlets to slave narratives to prison memoirs to blogs, polemics have participated in horizontal protests among citizens. (For examples of the literature of protest, see the bibliography.) Protest encourages the public to shame abusive governments and appeal to what Emile Durkheim called 'the conscience of the world' and what the preamble of the UDHR calls 'the conscience of mankind.' It wears its cause on its sleeve, reading as a manifesto or prophetic indictment. Works such as Richard Attenborough's film *Cry Freedom* (1987), which dramatizes the South African government's killing of Steve Biko, a leader in the anti-apartheid movement, represent collective indignity through the eyes of one. Aleksandr Solzhenitsyn's brief and moving novel *One Day in the Life of Ivan Denisovich* (2000) tells the story of the Siberian gulag through a single prisoner's experience. The narrator's freedom to travel inside the protagonist's head shows us the world of violations through the experience of the one who suffers them. Narrative interiority – the view from the inside – evokes the reader's sympathetic identification in a way that no exterior reportage can do. Simply by allowing readers *in* and permitting them to see that a character in an oppressive regime can still think for himself, a protest novel effectively represents a zone of freedom that eludes a regime's best efforts at social control.

Because its purpose is to provoke public outrage, protest is drawn to represent the most extreme forms of suffering – mass graves, summary executions, starvation, medical experiments, and so on. This tendency to gravitate toward extreme violence can prevent it from depicting more ordinary, banal forms of evil, like the bureaucratic terror found in less direct, more ironic works such as Kafka's *The Trial* or Orwell's *Nineteen Eighty-Four*.

One of protest's most pervasive fictional genres is the *Bildungsroman*, the novel of development. Joseph Slaughter has shown that this form is congruent with the UDHR's assertion that everyone has the right to 'the full development of the human personality' (see UDHR Articles 22, 26(2) and 29). *Bildungsromane* from the nineteenth century, but especially those written after the UDHR was proclaimed, perfectly capture the changing emphasis in international law from an arena restricted to relations between states to an arena in which the individual human person is a subject of increasing concern. They represent protests against the efforts of violator states to restrict human potential.

Ironically, however, in making the protagonist undergo abuses typical of the crisis, protest runs the risk of abstracting the individual into a type – that is, the type of the human being in extremis, the one who represents many, the survivor who silences his own voice in order to give voice to the dead. In the process of abstraction the unique personhood that human rights are meant to protect may sometimes be lost. Protest's romance may produce unintended ethical and aesthetic consequences.

· deals with the individual

Testimony Like protest literature, the literature of testimony focuses a reader's attention on a single case rather than on general reportage. In this way it appeals to the reader's narrative greed. Even if, as in *The Diary of Anne Frank* (Frank 2002), we already know the ending in advance, the individualized focus enables the reader to *feel* what she already *knows*. In *Hotel Rwanda* (directed by Terry George in 2004), as we follow the plight of Paul Rusesabagina, we witness the genocide next to him: we are there on the ground, sharing what he knows and what he does not know.

While protest calls for present action against continuing injustices, testimony seeks to establish what happened in the past for future generations. Because its central theme is bearing witness, testimony often takes the form of memoir or oral history, or fictionalized versions of these. (For examples, see the bibliography.) Poets have also acted as witnesses to the brutality they suffered. Anyone who has watched or read the fascinating proceedings of the South African Truth and Reconciliation Commission will recognize that testimony raises the question of how we can know the truth about the past: the reliability of the testifier is always at issue because of the possible distortions of memory, the desire to touch up or omit details, the urge for exoneration or expiation, or the use of the past to justify a present course of action. Hence, while protest tends to be political and prospective, testimony tends to be psychological and retrospective. It focuses on the uncertainty of our knowledge and causes us to meditate on the relation between history and memory.

· Feel sorry about something

Lament Closely allied with testimony is lament, the literature of mourning. As in testimony, lament focuses on memory, but here the effort is less on establishing the truth than on memorializing the victims. Lament has a ritualistic quality and indeed plays a part in rituals of remembrance such as memorials, museums, monuments and prayers, which is why there are fewer literary examples than in the other categories. (For examples, see the bibliography.) While testimony focuses on establishing what happened, lament's focus is on helping people in the present exorcise their pain, anger, and loss. While protest and testimony address themselves to the experience of one, lament tends to tell its story through the experiences of many. In lament, massive numbers of victims can take on a talismanic quality: the number 6 million in relation to the Jewish victims of the Holocaust has been given artistic significance in many cases, as when a group of schoolchildren from the town of Whitwell, Tennessee collected 6 million paper clips and housed them in a cattle car. Toni Morrison's great novel *Beloved* (2006) is dedicated to 'Sixty million and more' – an estimate of the number of people subjected to slavery. Her novel makes clear that lament is always a ghost story, a means of apprehending past violations that still haunt the present, and a way to perform and assuage grief. As literature that performs a public ritual function, lament's natural forms are poetry and oratory rather than prose fiction.

Laughter My final mode – laughter – would seem out of place in a discussion so sobering and wrenching as human rights abuse. In fact, however, laughter has been a significant, even indispensable, thread in the human rights canon. I am thinking of the kind of laughter described by Mikhail Bakhtin in his book on Rabelais (Bakhtin 1984). For Bakhtin, laughter is a kind of novelistic language that arises from folk tales, from common speech, from carnival. This sort of language laughs from below at the pretensions of the mighty, refusing to recognize the legitimacy of authority. Laughter imagines raucous reversals, reminding its readers that totalitarian leaders have bodies that are subject to the same misfortunes and humiliations as anyone else's. (For examples, see the bibliography.)

Laughter often points to the absurd in closed societies. It recognizes that the world depicted in narratives is full of languages – not only the official language of those in charge but the unofficial speech found in dialects, jargons, slang, and earthy humor – the unofficial speech that undermines leaders' claims that they have imposed a single order on a heterogeneous mass. Mikhail Zoshchenko's satire on Communist ideology, 'Nervous people' (1924), involves a fight that breaks out among the comrades living in a small housing cooperative. Ivan Stepanovich, one of the residents, objects to the use of his bottle-brushes by what he calls, in a parody of Soviet bureaucratic lingo, 'unauthorized outside personnel.' Punches fly, everyone gets hit, including a one-legged war veteran, until 'in comes the law,' threatening to open fire, which makes 'people come to themselves a tad' and wonder: 'What the heck were we fighting about, fellow citizens?' The communal order is restored, but only for the time being, and only 'a tad.' The Communist ideology of cooperation runs up against uncooperative human nature. As the cultural sociologist Raymond Williams argues, there is a gap between 'official' and 'practical' consciousness, which laughter exploits.

As Zoshchenko's story illustrates, laughter insists that no order is final, or finalizable: existing forms of authority are open-ended and mutable. Laughter's forms – parody, satire, absurdist art – are gestures toward freedom – if not of action then of thought, conscience, belief, and speech. Laughter raises its middle finger and bares its ass.

Case studies

To see how a modal approach makes possible a particular kind of cultural criticism, I offer case studies of cultural productions that work to represent human rights issues with respect to each of the modes, demonstrating at the same time that texts most often combine multiple modes. To make the analysis easier, I have chosen to study texts that share a common set of aesthetic techniques: graphic novels and graphic reportage. Choosing formally similar texts offers several advantages. For one thing, although it would be possible to compare the way in which many different types of cultural production employ human rights modes, comparing texts from a similar genre enables the use of a common formal and stylistic vocabulary. The texts analyzed here share a sophisticated use of verbal and visual cues, a combination that has profound effects on the way in which they put human rights modes to use. Moreover, the choice of texts for this analysis relies on the, perhaps surprising, fact that the graphic text has become a major genre in the developing human rights canon. This originated, in part, because many graphic novelists, journalists, and memoirists, from many different places, were inspired by Art Spiegelman's graphic memoir about the Holocaust, *Maus*, and the more entries into the field there are, the more that are produced. What Spiegelman discovered is that the graphic text's surface artifice places readers at a productive distance from the events depicted in the text: ironically, rather than disconnecting readers from the atrocities and tragedies represented, the less realistic images require the reader to take an imaginative leap into the world of the characters, producing a kind of deep engagement. In this way, iconic representation avoids the kind of desensitization response that often results from viewers' exposure to more realistic images, as Susan Sontag has argued in *Regarding the Pain of Others*.

The texts studied come from different geographical regions, were originally written in diverse languages, and have been translated into English. (At the end of the chapter, I will have something to say about the unique problems of translation faced by human rights writers.) They were produced by survivors and/or witnesses. They are Marjane Satrapi's *Persepolis* (2004), Joe Sacco's *Safe Area: Goražde* (2002), Jean-Philippe Stassen's *Deogratias: A Tale of Rwanda* (2000), and Guy Delisle's *Burma Chronicles* (2008).

To begin with, we will want to explore the texts not just as windows into a time or an issue but as artistically composed works. Paying attention to several concrete elements of the graphic genre helps us understand how the visual elements in the comics combine with the verbal elements to address a human rights theme or create a feeling. The artists use the formal features as means of protesting, testifying, lamenting, and laughing.

Protest: frame sequencing and iconography Marjane Satrapi's graphic novel *Persepolis* (2004) tells the first-person story of a young girl growing up in revolutionary Iran. Her parents are secular and oppose the new regime's theological dogmatism, censorship, and restrictions on the rights of women. Taking up her parents' cause, Marji seeks her own forms of protest. Satrapi uses the technique of frame sequencing as a subtle artistic method with which to represent Marji's form of protest. Figure 2.1 shows a page with two panels. The first is a visual representation of a bomb exploding in the Iran–Iraq war, killing soldiers – young boys from poor families who are gripping the plastic keys they have been told will get them into paradise. Note the sharp triangular white shapes that seem to cut through the boys like knives. The following frame, so different in visual style, has a different kind

THE KEY TO PARADISE WAS FOR POOR PEOPLE. THOUSANDS OF YOUNG KIDS, PROMISED A BETTER LIFE, EXPLODED ON THE MINEFIELDS WITH THEIR KEYS AROUND THEIR NECKS.

MRS. NASRINE'S SON MANAGED TO AVOID THAT FATE, BUT LOTS OF OTHER KIDS FROM HIS NEIGHBORHOOD DIDN'T.

MEANWHILE, I GOT TO GO TO MY FIRST PARTY. NOT ONLY DID MY MOM LET ME GO, SHE ALSO KNITTED ME A SWEATER FULL OF HOLES AND MADE ME A NECKLACE WITH CHAINS AND NAILS. PUNK ROCK WAS IN.

I WAS LOOKING SHARP.

2.1 Satrapi uses frame sequencing as a method of ironic juxtaposition. Reproduced by permission from Marjane Satrapi, *Persepolis: The Story of a Childhood* (New York: Pantheon, 2004).

of sharpness. The narrator tells us: 'Meanwhile, I got to go to my first party. Not only did my mom let me go, she also knitted me a sweater full of holes and made me a necklace with chains and nails. Punk rock was in.' The moment of defiance is nailed down by the frame's final pointed comment in the bottom right-hand corner: 'I was looking sharp.'

The plastic keys in the first frame point to another important feature of protest in the graphic genres: iconographic representation. As Scott McCloud, one of the most prominent comics critics, has observed, comics artists interweave several aesthetics, sometimes in a single frame, ranging from the more realistic to the more iconographic. The latter form of representation radically simplifies the object so that it is stripped of everything but the essence of the idea it represents. In other words, iconic representation is ideational (McCloud 1993). This reductive aesthetic works well for protest writers because it communicates a concrete (usually vehement) idea in a rapid, easily comprehensible, visual shorthand. An early example is Art Spiegelman's *Maus* (1986), a graphic memoir about those who survived the Holocaust and those who survived the survivors, which depicts Jews as mice and Nazis as cats, reducing the two groups to ideas: prey and predators. Guy Delisle puts iconographic representation to powerful use in *Burma Chronicles* (2008), his memoir of a year spent in Myanmar, where he traveled with his wife Nadège, a physician with Doctors Without Borders. At one point he discusses the close relationship between the governing junta and Total, a gas and oil company, pointing out the West's complicity with the regime. The first frame is entirely iconographic: Total is the devil (Figure 2.2), tearing down villages and displacing people on a massive scale. In subsequent frames, he complicates this icon by pointing to the social programs – schools, orphanages, hospices, and hospitals – that Total has built in the country (Figure 2.3). But he ends the discussion with a cynical observation that when the United Kingdom pulled its oil company out of the country, Malaysia's oil company came in and

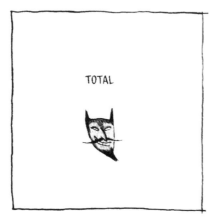

2.2 Delisle uses iconography to reduce an oil and gas company to its essence. Reproduced by permission from Guy Delisle, *Burma Chronicles*, trans. Helga Dascher (Montreal: Drawn and Quarterly, 2008), p. 191.

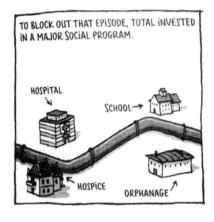

2.3 Delisle uses the iconic representation of institutions to indicate a complex social program in a visual shorthand. Reproduced by permission from Guy Delisle, *Burma Chronicles*, trans. Helga Dascher (Montreal: Drawn and Quarterly, 2008), p. 192.

kept all the same employees (Delisle 2008, 192). Perhaps the initial image of the devil is not so far off, but he suggests that it cannot be identified solely with the West.

One of the most interesting examples of protest iconography from these texts is quite subtle. Joe Sacco's *Safe Area: Goražde* (2002) is a piece of graphic journalism that recounts the war in Bosnia from 1992 to 1995 using a generally realistic mode of representation. The landscapes, bridges, buildings, and interiors are rendered in detail and the interviewees are individualized. But at key moments of heightened emotion and protest, Sacco moves in the direction of iconography. At one point, he is harangued by a man who has been separated from

2.4 Sacco uses iconographic reduction in an otherwise realist setting, distilling F.'s essence to his enraged mouth. Reproduced by permission from Joe Sacco, *Safe Area: Goražde: The War in Eastern Bosnia, 1992–1995* (Seattle, WA: Fantagraphics, 2002), pp. 191–2.

his wife for years because she is in Sarajevo and Serbs do not permit passage from Goražde. As the man (known here only as F.) becomes more agitated, the frames focus in higher and higher resolution on his grimace and his teeth: it is clear he is consumed with anger until a ferocious rage has become his essence (Figure 2.4). Just as interesting in these frames is the difference between F.'s glasses, which are transparent, and Sacco's, which are rendered as opaque. The artist adopts the opaqueness in his self-presentation throughout, turning his persona into an icon of the detached observer, whose justification for being in Goražde is here being called into question by F.

Testimony: visual metaphors and gaps between panels When it comes to the mode of testimony, graphic writers often use two comics techniques – visual metaphors and the strategic use of gaps between frames to control the pace of the testimony. Like so many comics techniques, the use of striking visual metaphors as a testimonial technique was developed by Spiegelman in *Maus*. In one frame, the protagonists Anja and Vladek are attempting to escape from their town, which has become unsafe for Jews, but when they set out on the road they don't know 'where to go' (Spiegelman 1986, 125). In fact, the roads are rendered as a swastika, implying that no matter where they go, they are in Nazi territory (Figure 2.5). In *Persepolis*, visual metaphors

2.5 Spiegelman uses visual metaphor to testify to his father's experience of being trapped. Reproduced by permission from Art Spiegelman, *Maus: A Survivor's Tale* (New York: Vintage, 2007), p. 125.

2.6 Satrapi juxtaposes visual metaphors of modernity and the West with Persian culture. Reproduced by permission from Marjane Satrapi, *Persepolis: The Story of a Childhood* (New York: Pantheon, 2004).

help convey Marji's confused and terrified emotional state as Iran is gripped by revolution. As shown in Figure 2.6, the young girl is confused about what to believe about the revolution's clearest symbol of change for women, the veil. 'I really didn't know what to think about the veil,' the narrator tells us. 'Deep down I was very religious, but as a family we were very modern and avant-garde.' The illustration helps underscore the words: on the left, a series of machine gears representing modernity and the West; on the right, Persian arabesques and Marji dressed in the veil. Sometimes the visual metaphors not only match the verbal content but intensify it. Figure 2.7 shows the climactic

2.7 Satrapi recasts Edvard Munch's iconic image of *The Scream* as an Iranian girl's horror of the revolution. Reproduced by permission from Marjane Satrapi, *Persepolis: The Story of a Childhood* (New York: Pantheon, 2004).

frame in a sequence in which Marji is stopped on the street by one of the Guardians of the Revolution, a moral force with the power to detain anyone indefinitely for infractions against Islam. Marji has just purchased a tape of Western rock music, a piece of contraband that could land her in detention. So, to escape the Guardian, she pretends to be terrified of punishment at her mother's hands: 'She'll make my father put me in an orphanage!' As Marji becomes more distressed, her speech bubble becomes more jagged, in line with the contortions of her face, which increasingly resemble the iconic image from Edvard Munch's *The Scream*. The visual metaphor of terror and alienation in the face of modernity ironically underscores the feelings of a young Iranian girl in the face of a movement intent on retreat from modernity.

A more disturbing use of visual metaphor appears in *Deogratias*, a fictional testimony about a traumatized young Hutu man living in the aftermath of the Rwandan genocide. At night, when he has gotten drunk on the local banana beer, Deogratias believes he is a dog (Figure 2.8). Bosco, a soldier in the Tutsi-led Rwandan Patriotic Front, trenchantly and sympathetically remarks that in the aftermath of the genocide 'all that's left are corpses, madmen, and dogs' (Stassen 2000, 76). Given that earlier in the narrative Deogratias has told a French army sergeant cryptically, 'The dogs ... They're eating the corpses' (ibid., 5), Deogratias' nightly hallucination potentially aligns him with the perpetrators of atrocities. At a critical point he experiences his dog hallucination for the first time during daylight, and he worries that there are 'No bellies to open, to eat ...' (ibid., 52). A few frames later he has transformed back into a human but now he cannot get the traumatic images he has suppressed out of his mind. His face streaked red like blood, the narrator reports his subjective experience:

2.8 Stassen uses the dog metaphor to indicate Deogratias' self-image. Reproduced by permission from Jean-Philippe Stassen, *Deogratias: A Tale of Rwanda*, trans. Alexis Siegel (New York: First Second, 2000).

2.9 Satrapi makes use of the gaps between panels to slow down the pace of the action. Reproduced by permission from Marjane Satrapi, *Persepolis: The Story of a Childhood* (New York: Pantheon, 2004).

'My head's spilling out into the day: the insides of bellies are blending into the inside of my head ... and sharp, sharp blades plunge into women's genitals' (ibid., 53). This disturbing graphic memory makes us wonder whether he is the one who plunged those blades. It later turns out that he was compelled at machete point by Julius, a Hutu militia leader, to rape and murder Venetia, the Tutsi mother of the woman he loves. He was then forced to rape and murder his lover, Apollinaria. It is no surprise that after these atrocities 'The dogs were there' (ibid., 74), only this time they are literal dogs eating the corpses. We are left to assume that this experience was the origin of Deogratias' hallucination. Stassen uses the visual metaphor of Deogratias as dog to indicate that genocide is a dehumanizing experience, even for the ones who commit it.

If visual metaphors help orient readers toward a particular take on the action, the pacing between panels helps convey the characters' subjective experience. Satrapi repeatedly uses the gaps between panels to testify to Marji's subjective experience of the pace of the action (Figure 2.9). On this page, Marji and her mother return to her neighborhood after it has been shelled, only to find that the home of her friend Neda has been destroyed. When Marji sees Neda's bracelet in the wreckage, 'still attached to … I don't know what,' we get two frames of what in film criticism would be called reaction shots, followed by an entirely black frame. The reaction shots are used to slow the pace of the action, miming the stages that Marji goes through in recognizing that her friend has been killed. The black frame simultaneously closes the curtain on the scene and conveys the grief, anger, and fear Marji experiences.

The gaps between frames permit the artist to speed or slow time, but also to jump forward or backward in time. In *Deogratias*, Stassen uses non-linear narrative to reproduce the protagonist's disorientation. Time jumps happen between frames and are, in addition, indicated graphically through the use of color 'filters' to distinguish past from present, even when the narrator leaves the time frame unspecified. The time cues are left to these formal techniques rather than stated explicitly in the narrative, resulting in a narrative logic that resembles a dream state. This technique enables Stassen to hint at Deogratias' status as perpetrator but, by withholding the exact sequence of events, to delay the reader's fully fledged recognition of that fact, a ploy that makes it possible for the reader to set aside judgment and sympathize with the character's pain. By focusing on Deogratias' subjective experience of the events, the narrative also calls into question his reliability as a testifier.

Lament: chiaroscuro and the sublime Human rights texts generally provide numerous moments of lament – pauses in the text that permit readers to stay with the feeling of loss and grief. Of the many such moments in *Persepolis*, perhaps none is as moving as the text's final frame, which takes up two-thirds of the last page (Figure 2.10). Marji has been sent to Vienna to get a Western education and escape the revolution, while her parents remain behind. At the airport, she watches through the glass while her father carries her mother away in a swoon. The father is swallowed up in darkness, contrasting with the mother's paleness. The chiaroscuro pattern intensifies the sense that a great shadow has fallen over all their lives, just as it does in the third frame of Figure 2.9, when Marji covers her face with her hands.

Images of darkness, night, and the sublime natural landscape are common tropes for lament. After Deogratias has confessed his crimes

2.10 Satrapi employs chiaroscuro to represent lament. Reproduced by permission from Marjane Satrapi, *Persepolis: The Story of a Childhood* (New York: Pantheon, 2004).

to Brother Philip, a well-meaning white missionary, he reverts to his dog persona and Brother Philip covers his face with his hands, saying, 'Deogratias. Poor Deogratias ...' (Stassen 2000, 76). His grief is palpable, for the destruction both of Deogratias' victims and of Deogratias himself. With great sympathy for the Rwandan man but horror at his deeds, Brother Philip pronounces an uncertain moral judgment: 'He was a creature of God' (ibid., 78). The uncertainty, the grief, and the horror all give way to the text's final image, a night sky full of stars, as if to say that some experiences are so terrible that only the God of the darkest night would know how to make sense of them. In the history of aesthetics, vastness and might in nature have been associated with sublimity, an experience that touches on divine power. In human rights works, there is a carnage so vast, the consequence of so much abused might, that atrocity itself reaches toward sublimity: it is the traditional sublime's dark double. On the image of the night with its thousands of stars the narrative ends, and we are left to look there, pause at the thought of all the human lights that have gone out, and mourn.

Laughter: parody, detachment, understatement, carnival If a slow pace can be a significant means of testimony, a quick pace can aid the graphic novelist in representing laughter. At one point in her narrative, Marji recalls the explicit official propaganda fed to the girls in her school about the torture of Iranian war martyrs (Figure 2.11). But she remarks, 'After a little while, no one took the torture sessions seriously any more. As for me, I immediately started making fun of them.' Then she gives us a series of examples from different moments, covering an extended period of weeks in just a few panels. Mockingly, she moans 'The martyrs! The martyrs!' in the first panel and 'Kill me!' in the second panel, with other girls laughing along. In the third panel, when confronted by the teacher asking her what she's doing on the ground, she replies with a sly smile, 'I'm suffering, can't you see?' Her laughter riles her teacher and provokes a week's suspension from school for all the girls.

Satrapi's example suggests that laughter in human rights work depends on parody in the face of danger and deprivation. Sacco explores the psychological importance of performance in two chapters entitled 'Silly Girls.' These chapters represent breaks from the horror of the Serbs' ethnic cleansing campaign. In one, the 'cowboys' – i.e. the North Atlantic Treaty Organization soldiers – have managed to deliver flour and sugar, and Joe and his friends have a rare chance to eat dessert. This causes Riki, a hardened veteran of the war, to romance Kimeta with loud drunken choruses of Paul Simon's 'The Sound of Silence.' Sacco is somewhat nonplussed by the frivolity: 'Amusing? One could say. But I had my obligations, you understand, and let me add that I wasn't getting paid to sample Kimeta's desserts or listen to Riki sing, either' (Sacco 2002, 151). As shown in Figure 2.12, he tries to get one of the girls, Sabina, to stop messing around by questioning her about her wartime experiences, but he reports that she 'grinned about the time the cannon fired at her while she hung the wash ... and giggled about how bad posture saved her and Kimeta from shrapnel' (ibid., 151). Here the joke seems to be on the foreign reporter, who does not

2.11 Laughing at the curriculum on torture. Reproduced by permission from Marjane Satrapi, *Persepolis: The Story of a Childhood* (New York: Pantheon, 2004).

2.12 Sacco's reporter fails to understand that laughter *is* the story. Reproduced by permission from Joe Sacco, *Safe Area: Goražde: The War in Eastern Bosnia, 1992–1995* (Seattle, WA: Fantagraphics, 2002), p. 151.

understand that the distance laughter creates between a victim and her monstrous experience *is* the story – the story of how this young woman has coped with her endangerment, the story of how, surrounded by death, she has chosen life. The self-critical view is part of a larger effort by Sacco to deromanticize war reporting. In the aftermath of the siege of Goražde, reporters stream into the town to tell the stories of the horrors. They tell Riki that they 'want to see some damaged buildings,' and Riki points behind them and says, 'LOOK! There is a hole in that wall! There are damaged buildings everywhere' (ibid., 217). The rather superficial, self-glorifying, and mercenary attitudes of war journalists come in for a skewering.

In *Burma Chronicles*, Delisle calls attention to a parallel dynamic, not with respect to the victims of human rights disasters or the journalists who report on them, but with respect to human rights defenders. While his wife, Nadège, is one of the Doctors Without Borders, he and their baby have just come along for the ride and he has no official role to play in the romantic 'Struggle to Defend Burmese Rights.' He has an ironic detachment, both about the military junta ruling the country and about the NGO world. While Nadège is off in the 'field,' navigating dangerous country and various militias to deliver medical aid to the Burmese in the hinterland, he and the baby remain in a rented house in Rangoon. But it is precisely because he is not a front-line human rights defender that Delisle is able to record the everyday experiences of living under tyranny. He lives around the corner from Aung San Suu Kyi, the Nobel Prize-winning dissident kept under house arrest by the regime. He drives himself crazy trying to find the right kind of ink for his comics in a country where products are rationed and censored. He lives with the uncertainty of when the next power outage will take place. Still, he has the feeling that he is missing the 'real' struggle because he has not gone on one of Nadège's missions. When finally he convinces her to take him with her, it is not a heroic event: he is itchy and cold, can't sleep well, comes down with malaria, and

2.13 Delisle presents the annual Water Festival as Burmese carnival. Reproduced by permission from Guy Delisle, *Burma Chronicles*, trans. Helga Dascher (Montreal: Drawn and Quarterly, 2008), p. 117.

can't wait to get back to Rangoon. The joke is on the myth of the romantic nature of the human rights struggle. Sitting at an endless dinner with NGO workers whining about how they can get permits and visas, someone asks him a question and he responds: 'Uh, I don't really know' (Delisle 2008, 102).

Even the drawing style here is nothing to crow about. Simplistic and cartoony, Delisle's drawings bring the whole drama of the human rights struggle down to earth. Because he has taken the time to build up a picture of the ordinary, daily deprivation that the Burmese experience through mundane artistic means, the text's extended moment of laughter works as a huge release. He gives a detailed account of the annual four-day Water Festival that precedes the hot season and celebrates the Buddhist new year. Because it is yoked to religious tradition, the festival has protection from state censorship. As seen in Figure 2.13, the narrator remarks, it is 'one of the few times a year when the Burmese are allowed to gather in groups and celebrate' (ibid., 117). He notes laconically, 'In principle, you're not supposed to spray monks and cops,' but the panel's illustration shows a police officer's hat being knocked off by water streaming from a fire hose. A terrific example of Bakhtinian carnival, the festival implicitly raises the question of the legitimacy of the junta's authority, and in a moment of pathos the narrator realizes that 'the Lady' – Aung San Suu Kyi – lives nearby and might be able to hear the noise 'alone in her home' (ibid.).

There are, of course, some experiences that laughter cannot touch. There is no laughter in *Deogratias*.

Problems

Having surveyed the purposes and modes of human rights culture, we can now turn to problems of production, distribution, and reception.

Institutional challenges To start with the institutional obstacles, at the national level artists' efforts to communicate with their audiences can encounter a host of restrictions, from state censorship to social ostracism to imprisonment. As a general rule, these obstacles will increase at the same rate as the increase in violations.

At the global level, artists' publication efforts are severely hampered by the absence of any global public to whom they could appeal. It is true that human rights culture has its own international organization, the United Nations Educational, Scientific and Cultural Organization

(UNESCO). Certain human rights NGOs run their own cultural promotion and education arms, such as Human Rights Watch, which mounts its own ongoing mobile film festival. But these efforts generally lack resources because most of the NGOs' budgets go to monitoring and advocacy. While UNESCO tries to exercise authority over governments, protect world heritage, promote cultural education, and fund new global art, the question is, for whom? There really aren't any citizens of the world. There is no universal suffrage. The world order is still largely set up to give voice and vote to states, not individuals. The absence of global media – CNN, BBC, and Al Jazeera notwithstanding – means that arts reviews carry a national or regional, not global, stamp. While states pursue their national conflicts, they have little incentive to support the formation of a horizontally oriented, global public sphere, without which works of human rights art at the global level have no one to address.

Some globalization theorists have contended that the Internet is a powerful distribution network for human rights artists, particularly those under the constraints of censorship. It would be hard to argue otherwise. However, the web's diffuseness fragments the potential global public into niche publics, limiting the artist's reach. Authoritarian governments have shown themselves quite capable of censoring the Internet, and the unequal access to it enjoyed by individuals in democratic and authoritarian countries – the so-called 'digital divide' – may limit its promise.

Theoretical challenges The question of whether a global public exists goes beyond a weak institutional infrastructure, however, to the way in which we conceptualize it. The symbolic, emotional and ideational links that make people everywhere feel they share a common destiny are thinner than the thinnest nationalism. Unlike national citizens, 'citizens of the world' lack common territory, ethnicity, language, ideology, and history – all the horizontal ties that bind imagined communities. In the absence of such ties, works of human rights culture could theoretically construct a system of shared symbols that might serve to form some bonds of common passion and understanding. To function in this way, however, such works would have to be taken out of their national habitat. To be globalized, they would have to become nomads, bound not to territory or local lore but to shared values (Tomlinson 2007).

But are such nomadic works possible? Globalization theorists including Diana Crane and Jurgen Habermas are skeptical, and they question whether the dissemination of such works can be fair and effective. In the most common model, that of cultural imperialism, theorists such as Frederic Jameson have tended to focus on the asymmetrical relationship between hegemonic culture producers (primarily the United States) and the global recipients of their products (Jameson and Miyoshi 1998; Crane 2002, 'Introduction'). This theory maintains that culture is largely disseminated globally by media conglomerates based in the West, whose aim is to effect homogenization and American cultural control.

On this model, the universalism expressed in human rights works is itself an attempt to spread Western values to non-Western nations. While there is some truth to this view, the theory of cultural imperialism can overstate its claims. Many human rights artists ground their work not in the West's secular liberal humanism but in the universalism they find in a particular cultural tradition – in the Koran, the Torah, the Gospels, the Vedas. Each of these traditions has *within* it its own universalistic impulses. For example, artists in Sudan and the Netherlands might both resist the violation of free speech rights, but the former are likely to locate free speech not in the secular Western tradition associated with John Locke but in the progressive Islamic tradition associated with Sudanese theologian Mahmoud Mohamed Taha. These distinctions are examples of what Jack Donnelly calls 'relative universality' – the artists appeal to internationally recognized norms using a local language (Donnelly 2003; Appiah 2000).

The idea of a culture without borders *can* sound overly optimistic, but the cultural imperialism model sometimes has the opposite problem. Art as an expression of historical and spatial hegemony needs to be balanced against art as an expression of trans-historical, trans-spatial ethics.

The latter notion of ethics is a fundamental departure from the post-structuralist strains of humanities criticism of the past forty years, which emphasize contingency and epistemological uncertainty. Human rights theory cannot depend on situational ethics because rights are conceived as natural, essential and 'self-evident.' Moreover, a right has to be codified as a law or constitutional provision in order to be meaningful, and the law requires certainty. More congenial to human rights is the school of criticism that grows out of the ethics of Emmanuel Levinas, because here ethics are based in the universal fact of death. Human rights theory does make some provision for cultural and national difference through its principle of the 'margin of negotiation,' a small window on either side of the absolute right that enables states to administer it in accordance with their local traditions and circumstances.

Operational challenges Finally, along with institutional and theoretical problems, there are operational challenges that must be overcome to bring a work of human rights culture to a global public. The dissemination of human rights art to a global public (or at least to multiple national publics) requires artists and their distributors to figure out how to translate their works from a particular idiom into one that is more universally accessible.

If the work is translated into a number of languages, the various translations will inevitably reflect the biases and constraints – aesthetic, ideological, legal, and bureaucratic – of their production context. For translators of human rights art such biases and constraints pose challenges that are distinct from other translations, in that they carry potentially grave political risks for everyone involved (for example, see *Two Women*, directed by Tamineh Milani, 2002). Public reception of these works is shaped by the audience's awareness of how much it cost the artist to defy her government and bring the work to the global stage. In fact, publishers and exhibitors often exploit these difficulties as part of the work's marketing campaign. Writers such as Salman Rushdie and Ayaan Hirsi Ali will always be figures once marked for death, and in that sense their aura will always precede their work (Rushdie 2008; Hirsi Ali 2008).

Even if the translation manages to survive the external pressures shaping it, it may still fail to convey the original work's *situation*, its saturation in local and national contexts; in indigenous genres, symbols, and styles; in the insider's perception of class, ethnic, and religious stratification; in the jargons and regional dialects through which power has been abused. The question is always, how much of this thick presence can travel beyond national borders? The most successful cases are when the human rights work's universality breathes *through* its particularity.

Immediate action versus structures of feeling

To craft a universal structure of feeling for a global audience, then, human rights culture must be supported by a dedicated infrastructure with the capacity to translate works into a common idiom. It must preserve their distinctiveness and at the same time promote their universality. When successful, human rights works reflect and help constitute an ethos, an atmosphere comprised of an intricate relationship between public opinion and the human rights practices or abuses carried out by (or in the name of) the state. Human rights works do not present rights as abstract ideas; instead, they embody ideas in concrete forms. Such productions represent a system of shared values, symbols, and sentiments. The reproduction of this system is long-term work that looks beyond any present crisis to the need to prepare citizens to defend against perpetual threats to the welfare of their community. These works may not result in immediate action on a given situation, but to the extent that they succeed in producing a sense of sympathetic identification for the victims of abuse, they fend off the numbness, voyeurism, and distance that are all too often the psychological effects of other mediated relations.

The modes of protest, testimony, lament, and laughter offer human rights artists basic tools they need to cry freedom, but the obstacles are great, and building a rights ethos is an endless process. Fortunately, these artists tend to be persistent. They know that, however many treaties there are, a rights-respecting world will not truly exist until people everywhere can imagine it. So they write it, sing it, act it, dance it, play it, paint it, film it, build it – dream it into being – and try to bring us closer.

References

Primary sources
PROTEST

Atwood, Margaret. 2006. *The Handmaid's Tale*. New York: Everyman's Library. Print.

Baldwin, James. 1991. *The Fire Next Time*. New York: Vintage. Print.

Blood Diamond. 2006. Directed by Edward Zwick. Warner Bros. Film.

Boal, Augusto. 2008. *Theater of the Oppressed*. London: Pluto. Print.

Coetzee, J. M. 2008. *Disgrace*. New York: Penguin. Print.

Cry Freedom. 1987. Directed by Richard Attenborough. Universal Pictures. Film.

'Darfur drawn: The conflict in Darfur through children's eyes.' 2005. Traveling exhibition sponsored by Human Rights Watch. www.hrw.org/legacy/photos/2005/darfur/drawings/.

Guess Who's Coming for Dinner. 1967. Directed by Stanley Kramer. Columbia Pictures. Film.

Kafka, Franz. 1998. *The Trial*. New York: Schocken. Print.

Okubo, Mine. 1983. *Citizen 13660*. Seattle: University of Washington Press. Print.

Orozco, José Clemente. 1931. *The Fraternity of All Men at the Table of Brotherhood and Ultimate Universality*. Mural at the New School for Social Research, New York. www.pbs.org/wnet/americanmasters/episodes/jose-clemente-orozco/gallery-paintings-by-orozco/84/. Web.

Orwell, George. 1961. *Nineteen Eighty-Four*. New York: Signet. Print.

Paine, Thomas. 1986. *Common Sense*. New York: Penguin. Print.

Paine, Thomas. 2009. *The Rights of*

Man. New York: Classic House. Print.

Sacco, Joe. 2002. *Safe Area: Goražde: The War in Eastern Bosnia, 1992–1995.* Seattle, WA: Fantagraphics. Print.

Solzhenitsyn, Aleksandr. 2000. *One Day in the Life of Ivan Denisovich.* New York: Penguin. Print.

Stowe, Harriet Beecher. 1998. *Uncle Tom's Cabin.* New York: Oxford University Press. Print.

Three Kings. 1999. Directed by David O. Russell. Warner Bros. Film.

Two Women. 2002. Directed by Tamineh Milani. Arman Film. Film.

Wollstonecraft, Mary. 2004. *A Vindication of the Rights of Woman.* Edited by Miriam Brody. New York: Penguin. Print.

Wright, Richard. 2005. *Native Son.* New York: Harper Perennial. Print.

Yevtushenko, Yevgeny. 1961. 'Babi Yar.' Translated by Ben Okopnik. Web. www.ess.uwe.ac.uk/genocide/yevtushenko.htm#Babi.

TESTIMONY

Achebe, Chinua. 1994. *Things Fall Apart.* New York: Anchor. Print.

Allende, Isabel. 2005. *The House of the Spirits.* New York: Dial. Print.

Beyond Rangoon. 1995. Directed by John Boorman. Castle Rock Entertainment. Film.

Drakulić, Slavenka. 1999. *As If I Am Not There* [aka *S: A Novel about the Balkans*]. New York: Penguin. Print.

Forche, Carolyn. 1993. *Against Forgetting: Twentieth Century Poetry of Witness.* New York: Norton. Print.

Frank, Anne. 2002. *The Diary of Anne Frank.* New York: Puffin. Print.

Goodman, Tanya. 2007. *Staging Solidarity: Truth and Reconciliation*

in a New South Africa. New York: Paradigm. Print.

Hirsi Ali, Ayaan. 2008. *Infidel.* New York: Free Press. Print.

Hotel Rwanda. 2004. Directed by Terry George. United Artists. Film.

Kundera, Milan. 1999. *The Unbearable Lightness of Being.* New York: Perennial. Print.

Menchu, Rigoberta. 1984. *I, Rigoberta Menchu: An Indian Woman in Guatemala.* New York: Verso. Print.

Partnoy, Alicia. 1998. *The Little School: Tales of Disappearance and Survival and Argentina.* San Francisco, CA: Cleis. Print.

Satrapi, Marjane. 2004. *Persepolis: The Story of a Childhood.* New York: Pantheon. Print.

Schindler's List. 1993. Directed by Steven Spielberg. Universal. Film.

Spiegelman, Art. 1986. *Maus: A Survivor's Tale: My Father Bleeds History.* New York: Pantheon. Print.

Spiegelman, Art. 1992. *Maus II: A Survivor's Tale: And Here My Troubles Began.* New York: Pantheon. Print.

The Great Debaters. 2007. Directed by Denzel Washington. Harpo Films. Film.

The Killing Fields. 1984. Directed by Roland Joffe. Enigma. Film.

Timerman, Jacobo. 2002. *Prisoner Without a Name, Cell Without a Number.* Madison: University of Wisconsin Press. Print.

Wiesel, Eli. 2006. *Night.* New York: Hill and Wang. Print.

LAMENT

Celan, Paul. 2001. *Selected Poems and Prose of Paul Celan*, edited by John Felstiner. New York: Norton. Print.

Darwish, Mahmoud. 2009. *Almond*

Blossoms and Beyond. Northampton, MA: Interlink. Print.

Galloway, Steven. 2008. *The Cellist of Sarajevo*. New York: Riverhead. Print.

Klepfisz, Irena. 1998. *Bashert. A Few Words in the Mother Tongue: Poems Selected and New (1971–1990)*. Portland, OR: Eighth Mountain. Print.

Morrison, Toni. 2006. *Beloved*. New York: Everyman's Library. Print.

Schroeder, Peter W., and Dagmar Schroeder-Hildebrand. 2004. *Six Million Paper Clips: The Making of a Children's Holocaust Memorial*. Minneapolis, MN: Kar-Ben. Print.

Stassen, Jean-Philippe. 2000. *Deogratias: A Tale of Rwanda*. Translated by Alexis Siegel. New York: First Second. Print.

LAUGHTER

Delisle, Guy. 2008. *Burma Chronicles*. Translated by Helga Dascher. Montreal: Drawn and Quarterly. Print.

Englander, Nathan. 2007. *The Ministry of Special Cases*. New York: Vintage. Print.

Kafka, Franz. 1998. *The Trial*. New York: Schocken. Print.

Kundera, Milan. 1996. *The Book of Laughter and Forgetting*. New York: HarperCollins. Print.

Rushdie, Salman. 2006. *Shalimar the Clown*. New York: Random House. Print.

Rushdie, Salman. 2008. *The Satanic Verses*. New York: Random House. Print.

Zoshchenko, Mikhail. 1975. *Nervous People and Other Satires*. Edited by Hugh Mclean. Bloomington: Indiana University Press. Print.

Secondary sources

Alexander, Jeffrey. 2007. *The Civil Sphere*. New York: Oxford University Press. Print.

Appiah, K. Anthony. 2000. 'Cosmopolitan reading.' In *Cosmopolitan Geographies: New Locations in Literature and Culture*, edited by Vinay Dharwadker. New York: Routledge. Print.

Bakhtin, Mikhail. 1984. *Rabelais and His World*. Translated by Helene Iswolsky. Bloomington: Indiana University Press. Print.

Crane, Diana (editor). 2002. *Global Culture: Media, Arts, Policy, and Globalization*. New York: Routledge. Print.

Donnelly, Jack. 2003. *Universal Human Rights in Theory and Practice*, 2nd edition. Ithaca, NY: Cornell University Press. Print.

Durkheim, Emile. 1972. 'Forms of social solidarity.' *Emile Durkheim: Selected Writings*. Edited by Anthony Giddens. New York: Cambridge University Press. Print.

Durkheim, Emile. 1992. *Professional Ethics and Civic Morals*. Edited by Bryan S. Turner. New York: Routledge. Print.

Durkheim, Emile. 1995. *The Elementary Forms of Religious Life*. Edited by Karen E. Fields. New York: The Free Press. Print.

Frye, Northrop. 2007. *The Anatomy of Criticism: Four Essays*. Edited by Robert D. Denham. Toronto: University of Toronto Press. Print.

Habermas, Jürgen. 1998. 'Kant's idea of perpetual peace: At two hundred years' historical remove.' In *The Inclusion of the Other: Studies in Political Theory*, edited by Ciaran P. Cronin and Pablo De Greiff, 165–201. Boston: Massachusetts Institute of Technology. Print.

Hunt, Lynn. 2007. *Inventing Human Rights*. New York: Norton. Print.

Jameson, Frederic, and Masao Miyoshi (editors). 1998. *The Cultures of Globalization*. Durham, NC: Duke University Press. Print.

McClennen, Sophia A., and Joseph Slaughter. 2009. 'Introducing human rights and literary forms; or, the vehicles and vocabularies of human rights.' *Comparative Literature Studies* 46(1): 1–19. Print.

McCloud, Scott. 1993. *Understanding Comics: The Invisible Art*. New York: Harper Books. Print.

Mill, John Stuart. 1989. *Autobiography*. New York: Penguin. Print.

Morretti, Franco. 2007. *Graphs, Maps, and Trees: Abstract Models for Literary History*. New York: Verso. Print.

Slaughter, Joseph. 2007. *Human Rights, Inc.: The World Novel, Narrative Form, and International Law*. New York: Fordham University Press. Print.

Sontag, Susan. 2003. *Regarding the Pain of Others*. New York: Picador. Print.

Swanson Goldberg, Elizabeth. 2007. *Beyond Terror: Gender, Narrative, Human Rights*. New Brunswick, NJ: Rutgers University Press. Print.

Tocqueville, Alexis de. 1969. *Democracy in America*. Edited by Jacob Peter Mayer. New York: Anchor. Print.

Tomlinson, John. 2007. 'Globalization and cultural analysis.' In *Globalization Theory: Approaches and Controversies*, edited by David Held and Anthony McGrew, 148–68. Malden, MA: Polity. Print.

White, Hayden. 1975. *Metahistory: The Historical Imagination in Nineteenth Century Europe*. Baltimore, ME: Johns Hopkins University Press. Print.

Williams, Raymond. 1977. *Marxism and Literature*. New York: Oxford University Press. Print.

3 | How editors choose which human rights news to cover: a case study of Mexican newspapers

ELLA MCPHERSON

Introduction

While much of this book is focused on the effects of human rights coverage on mobilization, we must remember that this coverage is not produced in a vacuum. During the day-to-day practice of journalism, members of the media are affected by a variety of influences that determine not only what information they choose to report and how they report it, but also what information they choose to ignore. These choices – or, as the case may be, commands – shape the human rights information transmitted by the media, and, if we presume that this information has an effect on its audiences, shape mobilization as well. It is therefore very important to understand the influences on human rights reporting.

Through a case study of human rights reporting at Mexican newspapers, I aim to provide an overview of what journalists are trying to do when they cover human rights stories and how these aims interact with overt influences on journalism, such as economic considerations and political pressures, to produce human rights news. To do this, I have developed a framework for thinking about how the headlines are plucked from the informational ether of every news day. Specifically, information is assessed against basic criteria of newsworthiness. Of that which is considered newsworthy, the more a particular piece of information is in line with a newspaper's journalistic, economic, and political aims relative to other bits of information, the more likely it is to be published. I explain these assessment categories in turn in this chapter, describing what kinds of human rights news survive this winnowing at Mexican newspapers.

Background

This chapter draws on a media ethnography conducted in Mexico in 2006 in the time preceding and following Mexico's first presidential election since what many consider to be its transition to democracy.[1] A watershed moment in this transition was the victory of the right-leaning opposition, the National Action Party (PAN), in the 2000 presidential election, ending the more than seven-decade reign of the Institutionalized Revolutionary Party (PRI). Mexico's media were instrumental in this political upheaval, not least because of reporting that challenged the government, a manifestation of particular news outlets' increasing economic and editorial independence from the state (Hughes 2006; Lawson 2002).

This independent sector of the media emerged as a core group of media leaders became disillusioned with the PRI, particularly following what is known as the 1976 Tlateloco Massacre, a violent clash between protesting students and the police that left hundreds of protestors dead. Until this point, the media largely sought a cozy, cash-for-coverage relationship with the government. In the days following this event, newspapers loyal to the PRI faithfully disseminated official government accounts of a few dozen killed, even though the word on the street was that the death toll ran into the hundreds. People took to the avenues in protest at the PRI's brutal repression, and one of their chants was '*Prensa vendida!*' ('Sell-out press') (Rodríguez Castañeda 1993, 120).

This novel, fierce public criticism of the press shook journalists (Lawson 2002). A core group, whom Hughes (2006) calls 'change agents,' all print journalists, decided that their journalism should break from Mexican tradition by focusing on democracy-enhancing journalistic aims and advocating a more watchdog stance. Some of these change agents were newspaper owners who implemented top-down change, some were groups of reporters who advocated change from below, and sometimes change spread laterally as staff left newspapers committed to the traditional journalistic model to join those more open to change. Democratic journalistic aims gradually diffused among these publications via training, the establishment of educational and reflexive forums, and the development of codes of ethics (Hughes 2003). As public demand burgeoned for the independent information published by these more autonomous newspapers and news magazines, change agents discovered that financial survival was possible without the help of the state. I call their newspapers 'market oriented' because of their financial dependence on audiences and advertisers rather than on financial-informational contracts with the state.

Despite Mexico's advances on the national level for democratization in general and democratic journalism in particular, the context in which regional newspapers operated in Mexico's poorest states was little different at the time of my research than during the heyday of the PRI. In 2006, the governments of Mexico's poorest states, Chiapas and Oaxaca, were all-powerful; they dominated the political and economic spheres, the latter through policies and favors, and because the private sectors of these states were relatively undeveloped – making the state the primary source of advertising revenue. Politics in Chiapas and Oaxaca were personalistic, with governors at the pinnacles of local political power, and constituents often forged allegiances directly with them rather than with their parties. Loyalty was rewarded, while dissidence was suppressed or punished. With respect to the media, these carrot-and-stick tactics included payment for commissioned articles, the criminalization of libel and slander, and the very real threat of physical intimidation. For example, a matter of days after I left Oaxaca, gunmen burst into one newspaper's newsroom and fired shots, injuring two reporters. As much as journalists might have liked to practice democratic journalism, events like this – in concert with the 'muzzle law,' as the defamation law is known in Chiapas, and with the fact that newspapers could find very few private-sector advertisers in these poor states – often silenced the watchdog at these 'state-oriented' newspapers – though not in all cases, as we will see later.

It is common, perhaps even compulsory, for both state-oriented and market-oriented newspapers in Mexico to have a human rights beat.[2] Although human rights reporters now cover human rights at large, including the activities of human rights non-governmental organizations (NGOs), journalists told me that their positions were originally created to cover Mexico's national and state human rights commissions. These semi-autonomous, government-funded commissions were established during the negotiations for the North American Free Trade Agreement, largely as a way to allay US concerns about the Mexican government's human rights record (Sikkink 1993). They monitor human rights situations in Mexico by investigating citizens' complaints about human rights infractions committed by state institutions. If a commission finds an institution to have violated a human right, it will issue that institution with non-binding recommendations for restitution. Correspondingly, human rights in Mexico are conceptualized as part of the relationship between the citizenry and the government. This means that human rights in Mexico is very much an issue of domestic importance; the critical lens is focused closely on the behavior of the Mexican state toward its citizenry, rather than aimed abroad, as is so often the case in Western nations. It also means that only state individuals and institutions can be categorized as violators of human rights. The same violation committed by a non-governmental civilian is classified as a crime, a category that has its own police beat at Mexican newspapers. Human rights reporting is therefore a relatively new but quite established part of Mexican journalism, categorized under political or society news (the latter in the sociologists' rather than the gossip columnists' sense of the word) and focused on state performance with respect to human rights. Some journalists measured this according to the Western idea of human rights, drawing on the UN's concept, while others preferred a more individualistic understanding of what they thought human rights should be in the particular context of Mexico.

A framework for understanding news selection

Figure 3.1 is a framework intended to illustrate how news selection occurs, though it necessarily simplifies this process drastically. This model clarifies the influences on the news arising from journalists' aims, tempered by contextual pressures. Of course, the practice of journalism may also be swayed by a whole host of more subtle influences, such as the social organization of the newsroom or cultural norms, which are insidious because they are largely structural (see McPherson 2010 for an analysis of these influences with respect to human rights reporting at Mexican newspapers). But this model plots the overt aspects of the determination of news – in other words, those attributable more to agency than to structure. This news selection

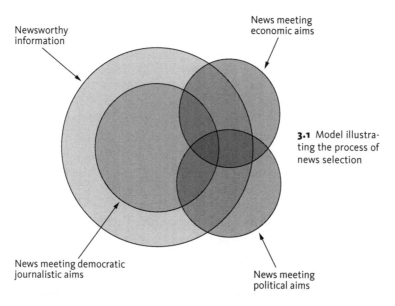

Newsworthy information

News meeting economic aims

News meeting democratic journalistic aims

News meeting political aims

3.1 Model illustrating the process of news selection

framework exists on a newsroom level, but each journalist also has his or her own version that may or may not align with that of the newsroom. In this section, I describe this model in broad strokes, whereas in the subsequent sections I describe more specifically the main criteria of news selection with particular reference to human rights reporting at Mexican newspapers – namely, what is considered newsworthy with respect to human rights and how human rights coverage relates to these newspapers' journalistic, economic, and political aims.

The model depicts various circumscriptions of information. The informational plane in which it is set is not *all* of the information in the world, but rather the information that reaches journalists. This is not a neutral process. This information depends on where journalists go, whom they know, and – crucially – which sources of information have the requisite resources to access and gain the attention of the newsroom. The resource in question might be social capital, held particularly, for example, by the communications officer of a human rights NGO who has, over time, become friends with the human rights reporter, or by the political movers and shakers who regularly lunch with editors to swap stories. It may be financial capital, reflected in the ability to attract journalists to press conferences with fax and email invitations requiring access to communication technologies – certainly not a given for Mexican human rights organizations. It may take the form of what Bourdieu (2007) calls symbolic capital, namely reputational characteristics such as credibility. For example, Mexican human rights NGOs struggle to build up their reserves of credibility, as they are not infrequently the targets of discrediting discourses levied by those they have accused of human rights violations. As a result, they can have trouble convincing journalists to consider their information (McPherson 2010).

For the print versions of Mexican dailies, the plane of available information has clear time delimitations, in that it consists of the information that crosses journalists' paths in a particular day. Even on the slowest of news days, this plane exceeds the space, in terms of column inches, and time, in terms of man-hours of reporting, that a newspaper can devote to news. Journalists therefore continuously rely on criteria to circumscribe this information so that their resources are deployed against the most valuable information – such as when editors assign or reporters choose stories, when reporters determine the direction of their daily beat, or when editors select headlines.

Figure 3.1 depicts the most relevant criteria considered for human rights news in Mexico: newsworthiness, journalistic aims, political aims, and economic aims. Of course, other criteria exist depending on the newspaper or the topic – goriness, for example, for Mexico's *nota roja* ('red news') crime tabloids, or safety, for reporting on the drug war. In the figure, the more important the criterion, the darker the shading of the sphere (in this version, each set of aims is depicted as equally important), and the darker the shading of the area in question, whether or not arising from sphere overlaps, the more likely it is that the information populating it will be published. The broader the criterion, the bigger its sphere. The broadest criterion – newsworthiness – is, as I describe in the next section, a hard-to-define concept – almost a sixth sense. It refers to, for example, the scale of the incident that the information describes or to the impact and/or exclusivity of the information. With some exceptions that I explain later in this section, information that appears in print is by definition newsworthy. Journalists do not, however, judge information on its newsworthiness alone. Much of the news they choose also serves ulterior aims – the conglomeration of which can be referred to as a newspaper's editorial line.

Journalistic aims refer to the role that journalists see their media as ideally playing in society. The dominant academic theory and the perspective of many practitioners mandate that journalism supports democracy and therefore journalists pursue democratic journalistic aims such as supporting pluralism and holding the state to account. Not all journalists are interested in democratic journalism, however – such as the owners of what are called 'ghost newspapers' in Mexico. These newspapers gather dust, unsold, on news stands, as they make money more on what they do *not* print than on what they do; these newspapers unearth scandalous gossip about the political and economic elite and then blackmail them, demanding payment to prevent publication. For ghost newspapers, as well as for some state-oriented newspapers, the journalistic aims criterion is non-existent. Not all reporters share their bosses' approach to classifying news, however – a clash that may lead to the subversive news dissemination tactics I describe later.

This leads us to economic aims. Most newspapers are also businesses, although in theory a Chinese wall exists between the business and information departments of media institutions. At many Mexican newspapers, however, information-gathering is very much influenced by the need to turn a profit in tough times – if not outright determined by owners' financial goals. The more important money is, the more influential the sphere of economic aims is in the choice of news. Another criterion is political aims, which again vary according to a newspaper's position on the political spectrum and its owner's personal and partisan allegiances. These economic and political aims are necessarily newspapers' responses to their economic and political contexts, as ignoring them could risk their very survival.

The diagram depicts these three criteria of aims as overlapping with each other and with the criterion of newsworthiness. The sphere of information that meets a newspaper's journalistic aims generally coincides in its entirety with the sphere of newsworthiness by dint of the fact that if the information is important for democracy, it is newsworthy.[3] The journalistic sphere overlaps with the political sphere when information that supports democracy also happens to support a newspaper's political proclivities. It overlaps with the economic sphere when it also meets reader or advertiser demands. On rarer occasions, information falls into all three categories. For example, Mexico's national left-leaning newspaper, *La Jornada*, conducted extensive and agenda-setting investigations into the human rights violations committed under conservative Mexican president Vicente Fox's administration during the May 2006 clash between street vendors and police in the town of San Salvador Atenco. These investigations met *La Jornada*'s journalistic aims of 'criticizing power,' in the words of one journalist. Although most of *La Jornada*'s journalists said they were unconcerned with economic aims, one editor told me that his newspaper always grows in times of national crisis such as the Atenco situation because of its critical, investigative coverage. With respect to political aims, it did not displease *La Jornada*'s journalists that the targets of their criticism were at the opposite end of the political spectrum ideologically.

Information in the political and economic spheres may still be newsworthy without contributing to democratic journalistic aims. For example, sensationalist crime coverage may sell newspapers without making the connection between crime and failures of the state, or an interview with a politician whose ideology aligns with the newspaper might be exclusive but not contribute information relevant for effective democratic governance. But some information that meets political or economic aims without technically being considered newsworthy may also end up in print. For example, celebrity gossip can be non-newsworthy but financially beneficial information. Coverage of newspaper owners and their cronies, such as the example one journalist gave me about her story on the launch party for a new hospital attended by her newspaper's owner, can be politically useful without being newsworthy. At this journalist's newspaper, the latter type of story is referred to as a *debe*, which literally means a debit, and they are non-negotiable assignments – as if reporters owe it to their bosses to cover them.

In sum, this model provides a way to think about how reporters go about choosing the information (whether news or not) with which to populate the headlines. Of course, the model for each actual newspaper differs from this generic representation depending on the newspaper's editorial lines, and the aims of these editorial lines reflect individual economic and political contexts. The conceptualization of newsworthiness, however, is remarkably stable across newspapers. In the next sections, I take a closer look in turn at the characteristics of news determination criteria at Mexican newspapers with particular reference to implications for the publication of human rights information.

Determining the newsworthiness of human rights information

When I asked journalists in interviews what news is, and in particular what human rights news is, they usually hemmed and hawed before tentatively embarking on an answer. That journalists cannot easily describe how it is that they determine newsworthiness, the activity that dominates their working days, is a phenomenon of much interest for media sociologists. In their research on crime reporting, for example, Hall et al. state that though news values are 'widely shared,' they are 'nowhere written down, formally transmitted, or codified' (1978, 54). Or, as Barnhurst (2005, 261) so cleverly puts it, 'journalists acquire a nose for news, but they cannot describe its smell.' My interviewees expressed similar attitudes toward news judgment, using vague words such as 'ethereal,' 'uncertain,' '[based on] intuition,' 'a sentiment,' 'improvised,' 'arbitrary,' and 'subjective.' In the midst of discussing newsworthiness, one editor at *La Jornada* introduced me to a colleague who walked into the room as '[she who is] trying to understand that which cannot be understood.'

This lack of 'formal rules' about 'how they [journalists] impose order on flux' can perhaps be unsettling for outside observers like Rock, who argues that 'such a lack of structure creates a great potential for anarchy' (1973, 74). The academic question that arises is thus how it is possible that the front pages of different newspapers, without any prescribed protocols, often closely resemble one another. Just because newsworthiness rules are not formalized, however, does not mean they do not exist or cannot be learned (in contradiction to Rock's [ibid.] statement that news is 'governed by an interpretative faculty called "news sense" which cannot be ... taught'). They represent what Bourdieu (Bourdieu and Wacquant 1992, 128) calls 'practical knowledge,' which 'explains that the agent does what he or she "has to do" without posing it explicitly as a goal, below the level of calculation and even consciousness, beneath discourse and representation.' Just because individuals cannot formulate their 'practical knowledge' does not mean it does not exist. Journalists were very clear that news judgment was a skill and one that they had to pick up on the job. As a relatively novice reporter explained it: 'You need to learn to look for it, you need to know what the article is, you need to have the journalistic touch to say, "This is the interesting thing here, this is what can be taken out, squeezed, and exploited to make the article."' I understood the importance of experience firsthand when one of the editors sat me down with a list of that day's articles and asked me to pick some to draw up a mock front page. I did, and my results were significantly different from what the editors had chosen. It was clear then to me that, as Tuchman (1972, 672) put it, 'news judgment is the sacred knowledge, the secret ability of the newsman which differentiates him from other people.'

News judgment's very lack of concreteness may be its greatest strength. As Jenkins (1992, 71) explains, paraphrasing Bourdieu, 'imagine the impossibility ... of having "on file" a rule or prescription for every conceivable situation which one might encounter in routine social life.' Human rights information can exist in infinite manifestations – different victims, perpetrators, violations, causes, consequences, etc. – and can coexist with an infinite variety of information on other topics, so to construct a fixed set of rules for relative news hierarchization would be impossible. The determination of newsworthiness must be improvisational, an attribute of this type of knowledge reflected in Thompson's (1990, 148) description of it as 'flexible schemata.'

In spite of newsmakers' insistent and persistent vagueness about their noses for news, their newsworthiness criteria eventually emerged during the course of our interviews, aided by discussions about particular human rights stories. First, human rights news is – as journalists ruefully acknowledged – usually about their violation. These newsmakers were rueful mostly about the state of human rights in their country rather than about the state of journalism's morbid preferences, although one editor did say, 'Unfortunately, we live off of bad news.' As the editor-in-chief of *La Jornada* explained when I asked him what a good human rights article was:

> The best story would be no story – when you don't have to write about the violation of human rights. I suspect that we are many years away from this good article, this marvelous article. All the rest depresses me. Every article that we do on the violation of human rights is a catastrophe for us because it speaks of the brutality of a system. There is

no good article about human rights – they are all horrible. Our obligation, like any media, is to publish it. The good article is the day when
you don't have to do an article on this because the violation of human
rights has ended. The day that the human rights defenders disappear,
that will be the article of *ocho columnas* [eight columns]![4] Then we will
be speaking of a society – a world – that is more in accordance with
what it should be.

A journalist echoed this sentiment when he speculated that the
reason that human rights reporting in Mexico focuses on the violation
rather than the respect of human rights is because their violation is
more prevalent than the respect for them. It also is more compelling,
as one human rights reporter explained it, stating that a story about
the military destroying houses in a community is just more interesting
and 'tells us more' than the story of an NGO and the government
signing an agreement. Besides their prevalence and intrigue, human
rights violations are newsworthy because, as an editor at *El Universal*
explained it, 'human rights are there to be taken care of ... Therefore
it is news when they are violated.' His colleague at *La Jornada* echoed
these sentiments, saying that 'speaking of breaking a human right is
speaking of breaking society and of the social contract being broken.'
These human rights journalists are not alone in their rationales for
focusing on the 'bad' of human rights news; Hall et al. (1978, 68) explain
the prevalence of crime news, and particularly of violent crime news,
as attributable in part to the fact that 'violence represents a basic
violation of the person ... Violence is also the ultimate crime against
property, and against the state. It thus represents a fundamental rup-
ture in the social order.'

In tandem with the fundamental characteristic of human rights
newsworthiness as being about violations, journalists search for information that is characterized by as many of the following features
as possible: novelty, exclusivity, impact, representativeness, and timeliness. Novelty, as an editor at *La Jornada* described it, refers to 'information on something you don't know about.' Exclusivity is valued not
only for the 'scoop' factor but also for its shelf life, which lasts as long
as the information can be kept from other media. This relatively long
shelf life means that the exclusive article is valuable for the flexibility
it gives editors in planning their pages.

Journalists think about impact in several ways. Several mentioned
the importance of political impact, especially in the context of an
avowedly political paper such as *La Jornada*. Given that human rights

news almost always involves a governmental authority accused of a violation, it inherently has a political impact, though the scale of that impact can vary depending on the accused or on the type of accusation. Newsmakers also measure impact according to the scale and/or severity of the violation. Usually, a human rights situation is deemed newsworthy if it involves multiple victims (the most-cited examples of this were Mexico's Dirty War and the 2006 Atenco conflict), though exceptions are made in cases with a single victim when the violation was considered severe. For example, one journalist mentioned Paulina Ramírez's case, which went to the Inter-American Commission on Human Rights. At the age of 13, Paulina became pregnant as the result of a rape. State officials illegally denied her right to an abortion. This journalist considered Paulina's case newsworthy because of the age of the victim, the 'adding insult to injury' aspect of the violation, and the nature of the human rights violation itself.

Single-victim violations can also be valuable in terms of newsworthiness if they are representative of a wider phenomenon. In one journalist's words, a newsworthy story has 'sufficient elements to represent or crystallize an activity or a way of being that is repetitive and continuous on the part of the authorities, that is not restricted to the individual complaint but that is representative of a real problem that is repeated.' Human rights stories about particular victims provide a way to vividly illustrate these problems. An editor at *El Universal* gave me the example of how his 'Society and Justice' section thus treated a report about gender inequality across Mexico:

> There are two ways of publishing this information. The day that the report is presented, you can say, 'Chiapas is the least equal and the Federal District is the most,' and that's it – and include a graph. But what we did was look for a story of two women and to talk about it through people, so that tomorrow, when people read it, women will identify with one or the other woman ... If you present the numbers, they will rapidly see that there is a great inequality. But these figures won't stay in their heads over time. The idea is this – that when we talk of inequality or poverty, people have a point of reference ... The image of the woman comes to their head.

The more timely a human rights story is, the more newsworthy journalists see it as being. They refer to such a story as having 'conjuncture' (*coyuntura*) because of its relatedness to current events – what journalists in the US often call a 'news peg.' This requirement of conjuncture can be frustrating for journalists at times, as it can keep information that is unrelated from current events but nonetheless considered important out of the news.

Journalists see newsworthiness as a relative rather than an absolute concept, which means, as one editor put it, that the same news could be front page today but in the interior pages tomorrow, based simply on what else happens that day. Schlesinger (1987, 57) explains this well with reference to the ranking of information at the BBC: 'When the editors have found a story which they think is sufficiently newsworthy to head the bulletin, they have a yardstick against which to judge the newsworthiness of others.' Layered over this newsworthiness assessment is the assessment of how well information fits particular newspaper aims, which I turn to next, beginning with an exploration of Mexican newspapers' journalistic aims.

Journalistic aims of human rights reporting: supporting democracy and stopping violations

As mentioned above, journalistic aims refer to the ideal role that journalists see their media institution as playing in society; for many journalists, such as the change agents in the Mexican media sphere, the media should aspire to practicing democratic journalism focusing on, among other goals, generating accountability and supporting pluralism. Democratic journalism was the original mission of Mexico's fledgling market-oriented newspapers, so it is no surprise that democratic journalistic aims were 'top of mind' for journalists when I asked them to describe their editorial lines. At *La Jornada*, for example, journalists explained their aims as including 'giving voice to those who don't have it' and 'criticizing power.' *El Universal* has a Code of Ethics encapsulating these ideals with phrases such as: 'All activities of the media and of journalists should be inspired by the public interest, keeping in mind that pursuing any private interest in the transmission of information is contrary to the principles guaranteed by the Universal Declaration of Human Rights.' Like talismans for democratic journalism, dog-eared copies of this Code of Ethics nestled in journalists' pockets and adorned their desks.

Complementary to its Code of Ethics, *El Universal* has a special agenda of topics that one editor described as addressing 'the basic principles of democracy.' He explained further: 'The country we live in has poverty and discrimination, has millions of migrants, drugs, corruption. Faced with this, what the paper has to do is tackle these problems. We are convinced this is what we should do.' The topics on this agenda, which editors must ensure receive particular attention in their sections, include the problem of human rights in Mexico. In fact, at several newspapers, resources are devoted to human rights reporting in part because it is a surefire route to pursuing democratic journalistic aims.

Beyond the wide-ranging notion of these democratic journalistic aims, journalists have specific journalistic aims with respect to their human rights coverage. They outlined several concrete means by which they wished their human rights news to have an impact on their society. Human rights coverage can serve as a check against violations, journalists said, both through its publication and through its practice, namely both through *bearing* witness and through *being* witness.

In terms of bearing witness, journalists described a process where their human rights reporting makes them what one reporter called a 'counterpart' and 'counter-power' to the state. Human rights coverage can awaken a moral outrage in the public, journalists said, by, as one explained it, causing readers to think: 'How great that I am not in that situation. What can I do so that those people no longer live like that?' Clearly, one possible action for constituents is to put pressure on their elected officials, resulting in governmental action and thus achieving what Protess et al. (1992) would describe as the classic policy agenda-building aim of this type of journalism. If politicians themselves are readers, journalists hope that human rights coverage could also appeal to their humanity directly and stir them to act. As one journalist described it: 'It has to be a daily battle – opening spaces in the media and the national debate, putting it [human rights] on the candidates' agendas.' In so doing, as one editor explained it: 'I think that here we fulfill one of the roles of journalism – ... ensuring that institutional machinery functions.'

Journalists recognized that they have a vital partner in this function, and one that equally depends on them: the human rights community (though this relationship is often fraught; see McPherson 2010). Journalists spoke in particular of their duty to work with Mexico's human rights commissions by publishing their recommendations for redressing human rights violations issued to infringing institutions. As one journalist described it:

The force of all the human rights commissions in Mexico is the public denouncement because they don't have the possibility to sanction. For them, it is the moral power. So when they generate a recommendation, what we do is publish it, because we understand the work of the human rights [commissions]; they do their part, and we do our part when we publish their recommendations.

Another journalist described this partnership in a similar manner, emphasizing the singular importance of the media in holding the state accountable through the generation of public moral pressure:

The blacklist of authorities who don't comply with the commission recommendations is an important article because that is the name of the game. The human rights commission morally pressures the [governmental] institution, but if the media doesn't pick up this moral pressure, the institution says, 'Well, nothing happened, the Commission said that I didn't fulfill [the recommendation] ... but nothing has happened [to me] ...' But if [the commission] says it and ten newspapers publish it, Amnesty International might find out, [and the institution] feels pressure to fulfill. This is how it works. If the people don't find out because we don't publish – if no one finds out, the authority just says, 'Whatever.' Moral pressure is how this system functions because the commissions cannot legally oblige authorities to obey.

The media's ability to stop human rights violations does not only rely on pressure generated by publication; it can also occur via face-to-face monitoring as well. The physical practice of covering human rights – being witness – is a powerful tool for stopping human rights violations, journalists said. In essence, the threat of the media's coverage is enough to prevent violations from occurring if that coverage is guaranteed. One editor described this phenomenon with respect to one of 2006's biggest human rights stories in Mexico. He refers to this story in shorthand as Atenco, the name of the town where a clash took place between police and a crowd supporting the street vendors the police were trying to relocate, resulting in serious casualties on both sides:

For example, everyone is aware of the issue of Atenco. It was televised. Lots of human rights were violated. But if there had not been live television coverage or live photographers, I think there would have been more deaths – because they would have acted without anyone watching.

The media's presence is not always an antagonistic act toward the government, positioning a defender of democracy and the people against a violator of human rights. It can be a symbiotic event, where the media get their story, the people are protected from violations, and Mexico's post-transitional state can burnish its democratic image as a respecter of human rights. As this editor went on to explain:

So now in many police operations ... like relocations, they invite the National Human Rights Commission. They say, 'Accompany us so that you see how we are going to use force, because the state has the privilege or the obligation to use force when it is necessary, but we are going to use it adhering to the respect of human rights. We are going to remove them, but we are not going to hit them or kill them or wound them.' So they invite the Human Rights Commission and often they invite the media, so the media are witnesses. And they do this precisely to avoid being accused of human rights violations.

It seems that the media's presence has had this sort of effect only since it has put an end to its relationship of cronyism with the state. As one reporter described it: 'Before, it was very common that the police hit people in front of us journalists. With the advancement of the media, the government has been obliged to train its police ... They don't do it in front of witnesses, but it still happens.' An editor concurred: 'Unfortunately, when they have planned on violating human rights, they don't invite the Commissions or the media.' As such, this effect is limited to potential violation triggers that the media know about. Furthermore, as a journalist pointed out, it is also limited to particular categories of rights. As one journalist said, the government may have 'its hands more tied with respect to these rights, but it is harder to go and document the rights to health and housing.'

Journalists did not just hope to be able to protect rights on their own or in collaboration with human rights organizations, but also by empowering the citizenry. They felt that their coverage has an important educational aspect. When I asked them about their aims for their coverage, several mentioned that they wrote about human rights with the aim that their readers 'learn that they have rights.' Beyond informing for information's sake, journalists hoped that the public would deploy human rights knowledge to their advantage in their relationship with the state. As one said, 'If people know their rights, they can organize to defend them or even just to demand that they be respected,' and, as another said, so armed, the public 'themselves can defend their integrity, their citizenship, their lives.' By implication, the idea is that the citizenry does not have to wait for a human rights organization or the media to come to their rescue.

Journalists like the fact that their human rights reporting can reverberate beyond the page in these ways particular to this type of coverage – that, as one reporter said, it can change a situation, no matter how small. A few journalists called this 'transcendence,' a concept that, self-consciously or not, seemed to be a loose interpretation of the Horkheimer and Adorno (1979) idea based around the same word – the notion that a cultural form can create a moment in which the observer of that form transcends reality and can achieve a critical stance that can fuel change. As one human rights reporter explained it:

> This beat ... allows you to make contributions that you couldn't as much in the political section. When you denounce that someone's rights were violated, they may get help or rise above the situation. This is why I like the beat so much – that it does not just stay a denouncement. People can benefit from you, whereas not so much from the political section, which is only what the politicians declare. It doesn't go beyond the declaration.

Some journalists called their human rights reporting an act of consciousness-raising, while others considered it a form of activism or almost-activism. As one reporter described it: 'What happens to a lot of us working on this beat is that we feel that ... we have to do more than just inform; rather we must participate in the defense and the promotion of human rights.' No doubt the fact that some reporters' career paths move back and forth between employment by media companies and employment by human rights organizations normalizes the blurring of boundaries between journalism and activism. Not all journalists were comfortable with this tendency, however. One reporter said: 'I know people who are obsessed with the topic and sometimes lose the distinction between their work as reporters and their militancy for human rights. You lose objectivity and you give priority to things that may not be certain or people who aren't right.' But most reporters seemed to feel that they were productively operating somewhere between the two practices; as one reporter described it, 'it is not exactly that we are doing militant journalism, but generally it is about making denouncements.' As another put it, 'rather than being a protagonist, the journalist is a mediator between the public and political and social actors.'

Overall, then, journalists involved in human rights reporting at Mexican newspapers see their coverage as both fulfilling their general democratic journalistic aims and meeting particular journalistic aims related to acting as watchdogs against power abuses and serving the public. As one journalist aptly summed it up: 'This is news that serves two things: informing and preventing. Inform the competent authorities so that they work in favor of justice. Prevent the next generations from the same errors.' Given this multilayered emphasis on the journalistic aims of human rights reporting, we can imagine that the journalistic aims sphere is deeply shaded in the news determination framework for human rights reporters. It may even, at times, extend beyond the boundaries of newsworthiness. As one editor put it, 'what we are looking for – more than newsworthiness – is that it [the violation of human rights] doesn't happen anymore.' At the newspapers where human rights coverage is a priority – namely, market-oriented newspapers – the newsrooms' overall news determination framework matches that of these journalists. Furthermore, as we will see below, the human rights news that falls within the journalistic aims category is often reinforced by newspapers' economic aims. However, at state-oriented newspapers, the newsroom's news selection framework often clashes with that of the human rights reporter because of the importance of newspaper owners' economic and political aims, which often contraindicate human rights coverage.

Economic aims of human rights reporting: meeting reader demand and filling column inches

Most Mexican newspapers were quite concerned with their economic aims, which varied according to whether they were financially market-oriented or whether they depended on sponsors from the political classes. Market-oriented newspapers faced growing competition from electronic media for a private advertising market constrained by Mexico's status as an emerging economy as well as by a limited audience size. Despite adult literacy rates above 90 per cent (United Nations Development Programme 2007), Mexico is characterized by what one editor called a 'culture of not reading.' Furthermore, newspaper prices can be prohibitive; a newspaper can cost about one-quarter of the minimum daily wage. As a result, newspaper circulation in 2000 was 93 per 1,000 inhabitants – less than half that of the United States (UNESCO Institute for Statistics 2011). State-oriented newspapers had to continually curry the favor of their sponsors or risk perishing, as market alternatives are even more constrained for regional newspapers than for their national counterparts. The context-influenced variety of economic aims of a newspaper largely determines how much its economic aims overlap with journalistic aims, and therefore how influential economic aims are in determining human rights news.

For market-oriented newspapers, overlap between economic and journalistic aims with respect to human rights news corresponds with the extent to which journalists see their readership as interested in human rights stories. Although some newspapers did track readership demand through surveys and hit rates on the web versions of their newspapers, journalists' understanding of their readers was not always grounded so much in data as in feeling. Readers were perceived as interested in human rights news for several reasons. First and foremost, journalists at market-oriented newspapers conceive of their audiences as, like them, interested in information relating to democratic governance. As one editor said, 'the violation of human rights is frequently among our articles, and the paper gives it space, because it sells. People want to know. If someone was beaten, if their rights were violated, people want to know about it – yes, it is news.' His colleague at another newspaper echoed this sentiment, saying that the middle- and upper-class readers his newspaper targets are very interested in human rights coverage, as 'they are interested in the law being respected, that the authorities don't abuse [it].' This perceived interest is a very strong driver of human rights coverage at some newspapers – as long as the demand is seen to last. Journalists who had previously worked at *Reforma*, a right-leaning national newspaper targeted at Mexico's economic elite, told me that readership research there revealed a relative lack of interest in human rights among readers, perhaps because *Reforma*'s relatively privileged readers are so infrequently the victims of violations. Coverage was decreased accordingly. It is not that human rights do not matter to *Reforma*, one ex-employee said, but rather that they became seen as the relatively dispensable pieces of news in the information hierarchy, given lackluster reader demand; in other words, this shift in reader demand meant that human rights news was no longer so heavily populating the overlap between journalistic aims and economic aims for *Reforma*.

Beyond its content, market-oriented journalists see their readers as interested in human rights news for what it conveys and conjures. Particular types of human rights news, they believe, can generate emotional reactions in readers that draw readers to the newspaper in question. This includes a feeling of affiliation important for gaining and retaining audiences. One national Mexican newspaper wished to shore up its numbers of female readers and young readers, whom the directorship viewed as being especially concerned with situations of injustice and with human rights violations in particular, since they are the sectors of Mexican society vulnerable to violations. The directorship saw human rights reporting as capable of generating stories to which women and youths could relate because similar things had happened to them, to people they knew, or to people like them. This tactic, while encouraging certain types of human rights coverage, may also limit other sorts, such as coverage of violations committed against other vulnerable populations less likely to buy newspapers, including the elderly or indigenous.

Another emotional reaction among readers that journalists attribute to human rights coverage is that of titillation, the province of tabloid-style journalism. In Mexico, one of the most popular forms of tabloid is *nota roja*, practiced predominantly by its regional and popular newspapers. *Nota roja* is disturbingly graphic, featuring photographs of decapitated bodies, terrible accidents, and abused victims; these photographs are so horrific that, for example, *nota roja* newspaper *La Prensa*'s website, featured, for a period, a disclaimer that popped up when one navigated to its homepage, warning: 'The content of this site could be considered not appropriate for minors and for sensitive people. Do you want to enter?' Particular categories of human rights stories – 'the most bloody, those that have to do with rapes of women, sexual violations, deaths, murders,' in the words of one reporter – are prime candidates for *nota roja* coverage and are therefore pursued avidly by newspapers that practice this type of journalism. Of course, the particular economic aim of attracting readers via *nota roja* journalism has the effect of circumscribing the human rights information that meets both journalistic and economic aims, potentially excluding non-violent violations such as the denial of rights to education and health care.

A third economic aim of human rights coverage is related to what it conveys about its newspaper: credibility. Given the tradition of the cozy state–media relationship in Mexico, which persists in many pockets, market-oriented newspapers are continually interested in proving their credibility with respect to independence from the state. Their journalists see this credibility as key to attracting readers, as illustrated by a story told by an editor at a newspaper in Oaxaca transitioning from state- to market-orientation. A local tae kwon do champion had been beaten by the police 'like Rodney King' and then taken to the jungle, where he died from his injuries. Members of the police set up the scene of his death to look like suicide, but, following a long court case, they were eventually convicted. This editor said his newspaper covered the story in part because:

> We are a new paper that aspires to credibility, a higher circulation – that wants to gain the confidence of the people. This article brings credibility because it converts us into a trustworthy media. *Tiempo* tells the truth. *Tiempo* doesn't hide things. They say, 'Well, *Tiempo* defends

the interests of society. It is playing the role it was given as a paper: denouncing abuses so that they are solved, so that the authorities create order.' So, this gives us credibility.

Conceivably, even readers uninterested in human rights may become loyal readers of a newspaper that covers human rights, not for the information this type of story contains but for what it connotes about the credibility of the rest of the information in the newspaper. Like reader interest related to democratic information, affinity generation, and tabloid titillation, this perceived demand maintains an overlap between journalistic and economic aims related to human rights coverage at market-oriented newspapers as long as the demand continues – or at least continues to be perceived. The framework is very different, however, at state-oriented newspapers, where financial concerns often make the spheres of economic and journalistic aims look less like a Venn diagram than like a game of marbles.

Much of state-oriented newspapers' incomes derive from financial-informational contracts with individual politicians who want to, in the words of one journalist, 'buy protection.' Protection comes in several forms. For example, politicians can buy 'ad articles,' where a reporter is commissioned to cover a particular political story in a particular way; they can purchase a guarantee that all their press releases will be published; and they can rent a prominent news space to publish whatever they please, including discrediting information about their opponents. The newspaper's end of the bargain boils down to excluding the bad news and including the good news about paying politicians and their cronies, and vice versa for their political opponents. Traditionally, journalism in Mexico operating in this fashion was a lucrative endeavor, and economic goals remain paramount for many journalists and owners at contemporary state-oriented newspapers. One reporter in Chiapas explained his boss's perspective on news selection in the following way:

> For example, if I was the owner of a newspaper ... and a denouncement arrived concerning someone whose rights were violated, for me it's not news because it is not useful to me. I don't obtain anything from it ... for my economic interests. So it is better that I omit it and use the space for something that really will benefit me. I think this is the logic of the newspaper; for this reason there is no diffusion of human rights violations.

In the upper echelons of news decision-making, therefore, economic aims may entirely eclipse democratic journalistic aims.

Despite this, human rights coverage can slip into the pages of state-oriented newspapers, largely under the aegis of individual reporters for whom these journalistic aims are a priority. Of course, this coverage must adhere to these newspapers' financial-informational contracts, so stories accusing paying politicians and their pals of human rights violations are taboo. Outside this restriction, however, concerned reporters can publish human rights stories because they can serve an important function for the state-oriented newspaper: filler. With reference to market-oriented media outlets in the United States, McManus (1994, 124) describes a type of information as 'hamburger helper,' in that it serves as filler, rounding out the newspaper once the meat of information meeting journalistic and economic aims has been selected. In contrast, informational filler at state-oriented newspapers in Mexico – where it is known as 'chorizo' because it is assessed not so much by its content as by its length – is any information not directly related to financial sponsors, including information that one might consider emblematic of democratic journalism.

Whether human rights information makes it into the news depends, therefore, on which politician or agency is the target of the accusation. For example, a reporter in Chiapas told me that his newspaper 'has an unwritten pact that you have to look after the governor,' but that he could write about the human rights violations committed by 'the rest [who] don't matter,' namely, state employees and entities that, unlike the state executive's office, do not have enough funds in their budgets for advertising contracts. These stories included the abuse of street children, discrimination in the classroom, rape allegations levied against teachers, and the situation of women in Chiapas. Another reporter told me that her articles criticizing the legislature are often published, even on the front page, because that governmental body cannot afford to pay newspapers, even to get the legislative agenda published.

The content of state-oriented newspapers, therefore, is often determined by multiple news selection frameworks, with economic aims more important among those at the top of the newsroom hierarchy and journalistic aims more important among those at the bottom, the reporters. These reporters are very careful to respect the limits of tolerance for democratic journalism, though, as they may face dismissal for crossing the line, not to mention legal and physical recriminations from disgruntled targets of their coverage. As one reporter said: 'There are many newspapers that prefer to sacrifice their reporters than to lose advertisements.' Differences between individual news selection frameworks within one newsroom – where hierarchy trumps – are not, however, confined to state-oriented newsrooms. I witnessed the same at market-oriented newspapers, though to a lesser extent. There, journalists would gift unpublished stories they thought newsworthy and journalistically important to colleagues at other media outlets as a way to circumnavigate the restrictive aims of their superiors: 'You have to make information flow, and even more when it concerns things that need to be denounced,' said one reporter in describing this practice. Besides economics, another area in which editors and reporters clash at times is the type and prominence of newsroom political aims.

Political aims of human rights reporting: limited partisan and personal motives

A lot of what seems political in traditional Mexican journalism – the pandering to one party accompanied with ferocity toward another – is actually economic in nature. Purely political aims are therefore relatively minor compared with economic aims in terms of their importance in determining news selection. Political aims that do exist at Mexican newspapers fall into two camps: partisan political aims and personal political aims.

Some of Mexico's biggest market-oriented newspapers are openly – even avowedly – partisan to a particular political perspective. *La Jornada*, for example, is aligned with the political left. Under a conservative government, it is not difficult for its newsroom to line up its political aims with its journalistic aims of speaking truth to power. Although many journalists there stated that their political aims were ideological rather than party-based and that their critical stance would persist should the left rule in Mexico, others were not so convinced. 'This is the challenge the paper faces,' one reporter there told me: 'Not to forget that this human rights denunciation has to continue no matter which party the government is.'

Personal politics can also play a role during both state- and market-oriented newspapers' news deliberations. These are instances where an editor's or owner's personal ambitions or relationships may affect the information covered by their newspaper – a situation magnified by the close social and professional circles of journalists and politicians in Mexico. For example, a journalist in Chiapas told me that one of his state-oriented newspaper's owners already holds a political position but hopes to move upwards in the local governmental bureaucracy. He therefore allegedly struck a deal with one of the candidates for state governor, promising his campaign favorable coverage in return for a coveted job should the candidate be elected. At a market-oriented newspaper, a journalist explained to me that coverage of ex-president Luis Echeverría's 2006 indictment for his involvement in a 1971 fatal suppression of student protestors – front page at many other newspapers – was limited to a photograph in the back, 'practically with the cinema listings,' because the owner of her paper is good friends with Echeverría. Although striking, overall this practice seemed to be quite limited, at least in comparison with the effects on coverage of trying to successfully operate a newspaper in a harsh economic environment.

Conclusion

In this chapter, I have shown that human rights news is the outcome of a news determination process where newsworthiness is assessed in concert with a number of newsroom aims that coexist under the umbrella of the editorial line. Human rights information must usually be about violation rather than protection to be considered newsworthy. Beyond that, the more novel, exclusive, impactful, representative, and timely it is, and the more it meets newspapers' journalistic, economic, and political aims, the more likely it is to be published.

For journalists who strongly subscribe to democratic journalistic aims and practice human rights reporting accordingly, a clear link exists between human rights news and activism. Journalists can be activists both by being witness, whereby their physical presence impedes violations, and by bearing witness, whereby their publishing of human rights information helps puts a stop to it. In the latter scenario, this information is intended to raise public awareness, leading to pressure on politicians, or to influence politicians as readers directly. In so doing, journalists often work hand in hand with human rights organizations, providing the access to audiences so necessary for generating public moral outrage. Human rights news can also be aimed at educating the public, so that citizens can act in defense of their rights on their own behalf. While some human rights journalists are comfortable calling their work 'activism,' others are wary of the blurring of boundaries between journalism and activism, fearing that it might compromise journalistic objectivity.

The journalistic aims that impel human rights reporting coexist alongside other aims – some countervailing, some reinforcing, and varying between and within newsrooms. Human rights coverage correspondingly differs. At market-oriented newspapers, human rights coverage receives a boost from its ability to dovetail with journalistic aims, which are relatively prominent in these newsrooms. It is also seen as helping to generate audiences through demonstrating news-papers' critical independence from the state and providing in-demand, democracy-enhancing information. Furthermore, particular types of human rights news are prioritized for their ability to attract particular audiences, including *nota roja*-style stories and information about vio-lations targeting certain segments of society. Human rights coverage benefits from the pursuit of market-oriented economic aims, therefore, but only for as long as the readers are perceived as being interested in it. At state-oriented newspapers, human rights news may be prized by reporters for its content but by the directorship for its usefulness as filler. As long as it causes no trouble for financial sponsors of these newspapers, it may occupy column inches. Furthermore, at both types of newspapers, human rights news must be in line with partisan and personal politics when these political aims are salient.

The mechanics of the framework of news determination I have outlined in this chapter are as important for the news they include as for that they leave out. In addition to considering the effects of the media on human rights mobilization, we must remember the fact that a significant proportion of human rights information never reaches a public because it is not witnessed, it is not considered newsworthy, or it contraindicates the media's editorial line aims. The particular examples outlined in this chapter include human rights information concerning sectors that do not make up significant proportions of the readership, and, at *nota roja* newspapers, human rights information that does not involve bloodshed, for example coverage of health and education rights. These 'news silences' (Cottle 2007, 5) can have just as much of an effect on public opinion and policymaking with respect to human rights as can human rights news.

Notes

1 As part of my media ethnogra-phy, I interviewed 26 reporters and 26 editors at 16 of Mexico's market-oriented newspapers, headquartered in Mexico City, and state-oriented newspapers, located in Oaxaca and Chiapas, who held positions along the production chain of human rights reporting. Interviews were tape-recorded, transcribed, and translated by me. These interviews, supplemented by participant ob-servation in the newsrooms of two

of Mexico's largest market-oriented newspapers, *La Jornada* and *El Universal*, allowed me to parse the influences on human rights report-ing at Mexican newspapers.

2 Accordingly, rather than impos-ing my own definition of human rights reporting or of human rights on this research, I was guided by how my informants defined these categories – interesting data in and of itself.

3 Though not depicted in this

diagram, exceptions to this do occur. For example, one might be a Mexican newspaper's publication of the outcome of a children's drawing competition at the Federal District's Human Rights Commission – not a newsworthy piece of information, but one that, by maintaining human rights on the news agenda and educating the public about human rights, supports democracy. An editor told me that they publish every bit of information sent out by that Commission because he sees their work as intertwined – namely, the Commission relies on the media to generate the public pressure to prevent or stop human rights violations.

4 This is the Mexican equivalent of saying that the article will be placed 'above the fold' on the front page. Traditionally, Mexican newspapers had front pages with eight columns of text, so to say that the article gets eight columns means that it is considered important enough to be assigned all eight of the front-page columns.

References

Barnhurst, Kevin G. 2005. 'News ideology in the twentieth century.' In *Diffusion of the News Paradigm, 1850–2000*, edited by Svennik Høyer and Horst Pöttker, 239–62. Gothenburg, Sweden: Nordicom.

Bourdieu, Pierre. 2007. *Distinction: A Social Critique of the Judgment of Taste*. Cambridge, MA: Harvard University Press.

Bourdieu, Pierre, and L. Wacquant. 1992. *An Invitation to Reflexive Sociology*, 1st edition. Chicago, IL: University of Chicago Press.

Cottle, Simon. 2007. 'Ethnography and news production: New(s) developments in the field.' *Sociology Compass* 1(1): 1–16.

Hall, Stuart et al. 1978. *Policing the Crisis: Mugging, the State, and Law and Order*. London: Macmillan.

Horkheimer, Max, and Theodor Adorno. 1979. *Dialectic of Enlightenment*. London: Verso.

Hughes, Sallie. 2003. 'From the inside out: How institutional entrepreneurs transformed Mexican journalism.' *Harvard International Journal of Press/Politics* 8(3): 87–117.

Hughes, Sallie. 2006. *Newsrooms in Conflict: Journalism and the Democratization of Mexico*. Pittsburgh, PA: University of Pittsburgh Press.

Jenkins, Richard. 1992. *Pierre Bourdieu*. London: Routledge.

Lawson, Chappell. 2002. *Building the Fourth Estate: Democratization and the Rise of a Free Press in Mexico*. Berkeley: University of California Press.

McManus, John H. 1994. *Market-Driven Journalism: Let the Citizen Beware?* Thousand Oaks, CA: Sage Publications, Inc.

McPherson, Ella. 2010. *Human Rights Reporting in Mexico*. Cambridge: Cambridge University Press.

Protess, David L. et al. 1992. *The Journalism of Outrage: Investigative Reporting and Agenda Building in America*. New York: Guilford Press.

Rock, Paul. 1973. 'News as eternal recurrence.' In *The Manufacture of News: Social Problems, Deviance and the Mass Media*, edited by Stanley Cohen and Jock Young, 73–80. London: Constable.

Rodríguez Castañeda, Rafael. 1993. *Prensa Vendida: Los Periodistas y los Presidentes, 40 Años de Relaciones*. Mexico City: Grijalbo.

Schlesinger, Philip. 1987. *Putting

'Reality' Together: BBC News. London: Methuen.

Sikkink, Kathryn. 1993. 'Human rights, principled issue-networks, and sovereignty in Latin America.' *International Organization* 47(3): 411–41.

Thompson, John B. 1990. *Ideology and Modern Culture*. Stanford, CA: Stanford University Press.

Tuchman, Gaye. 1972. 'Objectivity as strategic ritual: An examination of newsmen's notions of objectivity.' *American Journal of Sociology* 77(4): 660–79.

UNESCO Institute for Statistics. 2011. 'Daily newspapers: Total average circulation per 1,000 inhabitants.' Montreal: UNESCO Institute for Statistics. http://data.un.org.

United Nations Development Programme. 2007. '2007/2008 human development report: Adult literacy rate.' New York: United Nations Development Programme.

4 | Framing strategies for economic and social rights in the United States

DAN CHONG

Introduction

In early 2009, proponents of economic and social rights[1] in the United States had substantial reason for optimism. After a half-century of neglecting rights to food, housing, and health care during the Cold War, human rights activists in the United States were finally beginning to realize the importance of these rights. Over the past decade, an increasing number of organizations such as Amnesty International expanded their mandates to focus their considerable moral power and legal authority on the realization of economic and social rights. New organizations and coalitions dedicated to these rights emerged in the United States, such as the Center for Economic and Social Rights (CESR), the National Economic and Social Rights Initiative (NESRI), the US Human Rights Network (USHRN), and the International Network for Economic, Social and Cultural Rights (ESCR-Net). For the first time since the signing of the Universal Declaration of Human Rights in 1948, the majority of human rights organizations in the United States were now actively fighting for the rights that most directly affect impoverished people's lives.[2]

In early 2009, the overall political atmosphere in the United States also appeared to soften to economic and social rights. In the country where official policy for decades was to consider these rights un-American, collectivist, and 'alien in spirit and philosophy to the principles of a free economy' (Alston 1990, 383), the American public had just elected a presidential candidate who campaigned on a platform to restore human rights to the center of foreign policy, double foreign aid to $50 billion by 2012, and provide universal access to health care in the United States (*Guardian* 2008). Public opinion polls showed that a majority of Americans supported a health-care reform proposal that included regulations on private insurers, subsidies for low-income families, a mandate for employers to provide insurance, and tax increases on the wealthy. As many as 76 per cent of Americans supported a public option to ensure universal access to health insurance (Stein 2009). Thus, US human rights activists had cause to be hopeful that their increased advocacy was beginning to pay dividends and that the protection of economic and social rights would expand. In the years since, the optimism of economic and social rights activists has been dampened. While President Obama's initial budget did increase anti-poverty aid, once the effects of the economic recession became clear, his administration was forced to pull back from his pledge (LaFranchi 2009). Legislation to protect immigrants' rights to education and work (the DREAM Act as well as attempts at comprehensive immigration reform) or to ensure the right to a healthy environment by mitigating climate change had stalled in Congress. More visibly, as the debate over comprehensive health-care reform (HCR) drew on in 2009, public support for the legislation decreased, even as support for most of its individual elements remained strong (Rasmussen Reports 2010). While HCR did narrowly pass Congress with virtually no Republican support,[3] it simultaneously became a major rallying point in the burgeoning Tea Party protests across the country which targeted HCR as 'socialist' and linked it to Nazi Germany (Gardner 2009). The Tea Party movement drew as many as 1,000,000 people to Washington DC in September 2009, and opposition to HCR helped lead to Republican victories in the 2010 midterm elections.

Why does the expansion of economic and social rights in the United States appear to be more distant today, several years after 2009? Analysts could reasonably point to a number of different causes for this change in atmosphere: the policy constraints caused by the 'Great Recession' of 2008 and the federal budget deficit; the inability of Democrats in Congress to maintain party discipline in the face of a united opposition; the lack of commitment by the President to realizing his campaign promises; conservative backlash against a center-left party in power in Washington; or perhaps the procedural rule of the Senate that requires only forty-one votes to block legislation. All of these factors in some combination have played a role in the fate of HCR, as well as current American attitudes toward economic and social rights.

The role of framing

In this chapter, however, I focus on the role of framing strategies used by proponents and opponents of economic and social rights. Framing analysts argue that human rights activists have not yet been successful in framing rights such as food, housing, and health care in a way that appeals to a broad section of the American public. While it is impossible to measure precisely the impact of framing strategies on political outcomes, researchers in the fields of political communication, social psychology, and constructivist theory have demonstrated that framing strategies have an important role to play in setting political agendas and guiding public opinion (see Cress and Snow 2000; Gamson and Meyer 1996). Although effective framing strategies do not guarantee immediate success, they are often able to tilt the competitive political arena toward one side of an issue or another. As such, framing strategies are designed to help win short-term legislative battles as well as to incite long-term shifts in political culture. For human rights activists, framing strategies attempt to 'mediate atrocity' by making us aware of, sympathetic to, and actively engaged in the daily, and often unseen, suffering of others.

A frame is defined as a fundamental cognitive structure, or schema, through which we interpret the world around us (Goffman 1974). Frames are both verbal and visual, conscious and subconscious, intellectual and visceral. By serving as basic cognitive lenses through which we see reality, frames help us select which aspects of reality are important and lead us to define those issues in a certain way.

Because frames serve as important mental gateways to reality, political actors deliberately attempt to frame issues in the media and other public forums so that the perception of an issue develops in a way that is advantageous for the actor. Because political actors exist at all levels, and because these actors are often in competition, framing contests become one of the central battlegrounds in political struggles. The prizes for victory are legitimacy and public support, which in democracies tend to drive elite thinking and behavior (Jackson 2006, 139). When an actor is able to frame an idea in such a way that it resonates with existing social practices and cultural assumptions, his or her idea is more likely to be perceived as legitimate and subsequently adopted and followed (Franck 1990). As Mary Ann Glendon (1991, 11) argues: 'The way we name things and discuss them shapes our feelings, judgments, choices, and actions, including political actions. History has repeatedly driven home the lesson that it is unwise to dismiss political language as "mere rhetoric."'

Researchers of social movements have examined these contests over issue-framing in some detail and have concluded that certain kinds of framing strategies tend to be more effective than others (McAdam, McCarthy, and Zald 1996). Frames are successful when they *resonate* with people (i.e. when they have an immediate visceral appeal or match up with existing personal or cultural beliefs) rather than when they try to *persuade* people of the logic of a position. Visual images, sensationalism, and personal stories tend to resonate more deeply than merely citing facts and statistics. Indeed, a frame can be effective even when it is being argued against, because even as it is being refuted, the frame still serves as the primary point of cognitive reference (Lakoff 2004). Frames that represent a consistent message, repeated over and over again, are more likely to become embedded in public discourse and ingrained in the public imagination.

Issues also tend to gain political support when they are framed as universal moral claims rather than as the narrow desires of a particular interest group. For example, framing strategies that emphasize bodily harm, innocent or vulnerable victims, and basic ideas of human dignity are likely to be widely accepted across populations and situations (Keck and Sikkink 1998). For example, in the 1980s human rights activists were successful at persuading transnational corporations such as Nestlé to adopt a code of conduct for marketing infant formula in the Third World (despite the corporations' perceived better interests) because activists used universalistic language to call attention to the bodily harm directly inflicted upon vulnerable children (Sikkink 1986).

Framing strategies must also be tailored for a specific audience to fit within a specific context. Even as political actors try to frame their issues in terms of universal principles, these efforts take place within an existing cultural context that determines the 'standards of appropriateness' of these principles (Finnemore and Sikkink 1998, 897). In other words, framing strategies that appeal to existing cultural assumptions, and yet simultaneously challenge and reform them, have a greater likelihood of effectiveness than frames perceived as entirely new or foreign. The success of frames depends more upon how stories and images resonate culturally – how general ideas are activated for certain constituencies – than upon the detailed substantive content of the issue (Klandermans and Goslinga 1996, 336). The cultural resonance of a frame is therefore even more important than its veracity, as is demonstrated by the ongoing effectiveness of political messages that are refuted by fact-checking organizations.

In the cultural context of the United States, then, economic and social rights must be promoted in a manner that appeals to dominant cultural norms such as individual liberty, limited government, patriotism, and respect for private property – even as activists seek to co-opt or modify these cultural norms to achieve universal access to basic economic goods. In the context of the Cold War, this task proved enormously difficult, as economic and social rights could easily be branded as a 'Soviet, Third World creation' and linked to an actual

Communist threat to America (Alston 1990, 383). Since the end of the Cold War, much greater political space has opened up for US human rights organizations to advocate for economic and social rights (Chong 2010, 8), but as the public debate over health care has made clear, the specters of 'socialism' and 'expanding government' remain at the forefront of the public mindset. While economic and social rights have achieved mainstream legitimacy throughout Europe and much of the developing world, the political culture of the United States presents some unique challenges to human rights advocates.

Indeed, there is actually no single political culture in the United States, but many. For example, not only has public opinion been divided in its support for HCR, but the public is also split on the reasons why. Both supporters and opponents were internally divided over whether the HCR legislation went too far or not far enough in expanding access to health care, controlling costs, and regulating insurance companies (CBS News 2010). Thus, the need to tailor framing strategies for specific audiences would suggest that a different message should be crafted for each of these audiences, depending on their particular political beliefs. Perhaps arguments for food, housing, and health care should be framed in radical ways for activists but in centrist ways for moderates and skeptics. Indeed, studies of the 'radical flank effect' in the social movement literature have shown that more extreme elements within a social movement can have a beneficial effect on political outcomes by making moderates' positions appear more attractive and safe (Tarrow 1998). However, other studies have shown that the diversity of messages can have a negative effect on political outcomes, when moderates' positions are disregarded or demonized by becoming associated with more radical positions (Haines 1997). Perhaps this can be called the 'guilt-by-association' effect. These negative effects are especially pronounced when the distinctions between the messages of moderates and radicals are not clearly framed or understood (Gupta 2002). As such, the need to tailor framing strategies for specific audiences across the ideological spectrum comes into conflict with the need to have a coherent frame repeated consistently in public discourse.

Given these challenges, what framing strategies are currently being pursued by proponents of economic and social rights? How well do these strategies appeal to different audiences, and how well do they address the competing frames of political opponents? Are the various framing strategies easily tied together into a single coherent narrative,[4] or is an inconsistent set of messages fighting against itself?

Framing strategies for economic and social rights

In this chapter, I examine a selection of framing strategies used by human rights activists in the United States in recent years: legality, radical social justice, bipartisanship, patriotism, and narrative. These strategies are not mutually exclusive, but each approach has unique strengths and appeals to a different kind of audience. Although this selection is not comprehensive, it does represent a range of different approaches, allowing us to analyze their strengths and weaknesses when used alone or in combination. These strategies are widely employed to advocate for all economic and social rights, but because of the prominence of the health-care debate in the United States since 2009, many of the examples will be drawn from this issue.

Legality The first framing strategy used by economic and social rights advocates is an appeal to legality, specifically international human rights law. An appeal to legality is common among traditional human rights organizations because many of them are staffed with lawyers and activists who identify human rights primarily as legal instruments (Chong 2010, 41). In other words, economic and social rights are defined as the principles embodied in the Universal Declaration of Human Rights and other international instruments, which states are legally bound to follow upon ratification.

Claiming that housing (or health care) is a human right, the primary message within this strategy is that the United States has failed to live up to its obligations under international law. For example, in October 2009 the Secretary-General of Amnesty International, Irene Khan, urged the United States to ratify the International Covenant on Economic, Social and Cultural Rights (ICESCR). In her speech, Khan criticized the United States for its perception of health care as 'needs to be met by markets as opposed to legal entitlements possessed by all' (Corsi 2009). NESRI is also confronting the US government on its record of protecting the rights to health, housing, work, and education. Among the many tactics that NESRI employs, its legal strategies have included working with the UN Special Rapporteur on Adequate Housing in 2008 to conduct an official visit to the United States; analyzing legal entitlements to health care in US state constitutions; and critiquing HCR proposals through the lens of international human rights law (NESRI 2010). Similarly, the Poor People's Economic Human Rights Campaign (PPEHRC 2010), a coalition of dozens of grassroots organizations across the country, brought hearings before the Inter-American Commission on Human Rights in 2005 to investigate the US record on adequate housing.

TABLE 4.1 Common framing strategies for economic and social rights

Framing strategy	Typical message	Sources	Audiences	Strengths	Weaknesses
Legality	'Housing is a human right'	Amnesty International, National Economic and Social Rights Initiative, International Network for Economic, Social and Cultural Rights	Human rights activists, international supporters	Universality; legal authority; specificity in analysis	Public view of international law as elitist and 'foreign'
Radical social justice	'Take back the land'	Poor People's Economic Human Rights Campaign, US Human Rights Initiative	Grassroots activists	Mobilizes base activists; visceral appeal	Alienates moderates; reinforces 'socialism' counter-frame
Bipartisanship	'Divided we fail'	American Association of Retired Persons, ONE	Political independents and moderates	Political legitimacy	Alienates base activists; increasing partisanship means dwindling center
Patriotism	'Christianized medicine' and 'Americans can do better'	Bono, Michael Moore	All Americans	Appeals to patriotism while trying to redefine what it means	May lack specific policy implications; may lead to nationalist response
Narrative	'It can happen to you'	International Network for Economic, Social and Cultural Rights, *Sicko*	Everyone, especially women	Inspires sympathy; visceral resonance	May lack specific policy implications; limited media formats

The main strength of the legality frame is the universality of its appeal to a higher legal authority. Basing claims to economic and social rights on a set of objective legal standards accomplishes two broad goals. For human rights activists at home and abroad, who comprise the main audience for this message, it contains the promise of holding the United States government accountable to the obligations it has formally agreed to (or, in the case of the ICESCR, pressing for a formal agreement). As a former Amnesty International official stated, 'the crucial thing is legal accountability and the legal framework. That's absolutely essential, and that's why human rights organizations are full of lawyers' (interview with the author, June 2003). For grassroots activists, the legal approach legitimizes their struggle for housing, work, and health care by framing their claims in terms of universal principles. As one practitioner explained, people 'get excited about human rights because it gives them a legitimacy they didn't feel they had. That the whole world recognizes that their claim is valid means a lot to them' (interview with the author, September 2005).

Another important strength of this approach is that it allows for considerable specificity in policy analysis and recommendations. Although legal norms for economic and social rights are still somewhat vague, human rights organizations are translating those norms into increasingly specific policy proposals. Thus, for example, ESCR-Net (2009) provided detailed analyses of government responses to the 2008 economic recession, focusing on principles of non-discrimination, adequate livelihood for the most vulnerable, and transparent and accountable processes under international law. ESCR-Net (2010) is currently collecting information from hundreds of member organizations worldwide about whether governments are adhering to these principles as they enact financial bailouts, stimulus packages, and new tax and welfare policies.

Conversely, the legality frame also contains some inherent weaknesses. Historically, international law has served as a barrier to the empowerment of grassroots activism because legal discourse can be inaccessible to laypersons. Making legal claims that the United States should uphold its human rights obligations can easily get bogged down by arguments over which treaties apply, or what precise obligations are implied by the requirement to 'take steps ... through international assistance and cooperation ... to the maximum of its available resources, with a view to achieving progressively the full realization of the rights' in Article 2(1) of the ICESCR. Indeed, as the legality frame tries to remove economic and social rights advocacy from the mud-slinging of political discourse by appealing to the technical expertise of lawyers, it can also make that discourse dry and uninspiring.

This weakness is being mitigated by the fact that human rights organizations are increasingly translating legal instruments into more accessible language that can serve as the basis for an effective grassroots social movement. However, another challenge for the legality frame is the American public's low level of awareness (and perhaps opinion) of international law. Although strong majorities of Americans hold international law in high regard in the abstract (Global Envision 2007), Americans tend not to be very knowledgeable about specific international legal instruments and do not broadly support having international law restrict US policymaking.[5] As such, the legality frame, especially when it appeals to international legal instruments that the United States has not signed or ratified, is vulnerable to attack from opponents who claim that economic and social rights are 'foreign' instruments that do not fit within the US political culture or serve the national interest.

Radical social justice One alternative approach to framing economic and social rights in the United States could be called the radical social justice frame, which is more common among grassroots activists and the poor themselves. Although there are many definitions of social justice, this framing strategy is distinguished by its direct attack on US economic policies and structures as the root causes of violations of economic and social rights. For example, a 2005 brochure from the PPEHRC claims that US economic policies 'impoverish and kill people' and are the 'real weapons of mass destruction.' Likewise, at the 2005 inaugural conference of the USHRN, a coalition of grassroots organizations dedicated to addressing US human rights violations, one speaker received a standing ovation when she labeled herself a 'communist' (which she defined as equalizing resources), and another called for a 'revolution.' The title of the conference itself was 'No Retreat, No Compromise,' which highlights the more confrontational approach of this framing strategy. The USHRN (2010) has also supported the 'Take Back the Land' campaign, which uses non-violent direct action to protect access to housing for people who have been threatened by eviction, foreclosures, natural disasters, or the removal of public housing. Protestors in the Occupy Wall Street movement in 2011 also used this strategy by placing blame directly on corporations for violating rights to housing, food, fair labor, and education.[6]

The main strength of this framing strategy is that it is extremely energizing for activists involved in the struggle. The rhetoric and imagery used are direct, unambiguous, and easy to understand. It precludes hiding behind legal technicalities and non-ratified treaties, and asks its audience a basic question: Whose side are you on? Will you take action to reinforce your moral and political beliefs? As such, this strategy follows one of the most important rules of framing: to represent your issue in a manner that will have an immediate, visceral appeal. Indeed, even as the economic recession has reduced public support for universal access to health care, it has probably increased public sympathy for those whose right to housing has been threatened. As unemployment and foreclosures mounted, a handful of local jurisdictions enacted a moratorium on evictions, and a judge in New York cancelled an entire mortgage for one struggling couple (Woods 2009). 'Taking back the land' has some potential appeal in this context.

Even as the radical social justice frame mobilizes people to action, it can also alienate political moderates and invite a backlash. It plays to the popular fear that economic and social rights are a step toward socialism and totalitarian government. As one health-care advocate notes: 'Why talk to us about equality in health care, they'll ask you, when all you really want to do is redistribute wealth? [There's a] suspicion that a sweeping agenda underlies the call for redistribution' (Mandler 1995). As the Tea Party movement has shown, that suspicion is more widely shared and more deeply felt than many social justice activists would like to admit. Thus, as much as this framing strategy activates its adherents, it also activates strident opposition that is linked to enduring assumptions about American identity (for example, the 'freedom versus tyranny' frame of the Tea Party).

Bipartisanship The bipartisanship frame tries to mute such conservative opposition to economic and social rights by explicitly appealing to the political center in the United States. It argues that the basic principles underlying economic and social rights (not legal entitlements, but principles of universal access and equitable treatment) are shared by Republicans and Democrats, conservatives and liberals, CEOs and labor unions. Instead of trying to protect economic and social rights from political discourse, as the legality frame attempts to do, this strategy explicitly relies on political bipartisanship and ideological centrism to provide legitimacy for these rights.

A typical example of this framing strategy is illustrated by the 'Divided We Fail' campaign – a coalition led by the American Association of Retired Persons (AARP), Business Roundtable, Service

Employees International Union, and the National Federation of Independent Business – that supported HCR efforts. These powerful lobbying groups joined forces to argue for universal health care under the notion that 'the biggest divide in America is not between its people, but between the public and our leaders in Washington.'[7] The mascot for this campaign, with its obvious symbolic intent, is a purple creature that is half-donkey and half-elephant. Another example is the ONE campaign, which uses a bipartisan strategy to frame its advocacy for a greater US commitment to eliminate AIDS and extreme global poverty. This approach is evident in the fact that ONE refuses to endorse political candidates, but tries to get every candidate to sign a pledge to support ONE's principles. In the 2008 election campaign, Republican Bill Frist and Democrat Tom Daschle worked closely together as ONE's senior advisors in this effort. A final example comes from the 'We Can Solve It' campaign, an organization founded by Al Gore to combat climate change. In one commercial for this campaign, televangelist Pat Robertson sits on a couch with Reverend Al Sharpton, saying that they are 'polar opposites … who strongly disagree except on one issue, taking care of the planet.' Another commercial has Democrat Nancy Pelosi sharing a couch with Republican Newt Gingrich, saying that 'our country must take action on climate change.'[8]

The major strength of this appeal to bipartisanship is the political legitimacy it confers. The American public, particularly moderates and independents, want to see Democrats and Republicans work together to enact policy. In a recent poll, an overwhelming 93 per cent of Americans believed that there is 'too much partisan infighting' in Washington (Murray 2010). Because most populations are ideologically distributed in roughly the shape of a bell curve, more public support is typically found in the center of the distribution than in the two tails. In other words, as energizing as the radical social justice frame can be, it can at best appeal to only a limited population in the United States. And since the political culture in the United States is further to the ideological right on economic and social rights than in most other developed countries, it may be even more necessary to appeal to the center.[9] In justifying his organization's centrist approach, one progressive anti-hunger activist stated: 'We live in a conservative country, let's face it' (interview with the author, June 2004). Legislation typically does not survive for long in the US Congress without at least some bipartisan support, particularly given the filibuster rule in the Senate.

On the other hand, many analysts have argued that the problem of partisanship is not unique to Washington, but is strong and increasing among the US population as well. Although roughly a quarter of Americans self-identify as 'independent' when asked in surveys, many of those lean strongly toward Democrats or Republicans, so some analysts argue that only one-tenth of the population are truly centrist independents (Jones 2009). Similarly, in a survey in early 2009, 58 per cent of Americans wanted President Obama to stick to his own policies rather than work in a bipartisan way (Sargent 2009).[10] Under this polarized interpretation of the political climate, the population distribution resembles the two humps of a camel rather than a bell curve. If the political center is so small, and perhaps disappearing, the effectiveness of a bipartisan approach would be severely limited. Indeed, pursuing bipartisanship is analogous to the Prisoner's Dilemma game, where both parties gain more by working together, but each party can gain individually by defecting.

Even if the political center remains strong, there are significant costs to adopting a bipartisan framing strategy. In order to get Nancy Pelosi and Newt Gingrich to agree on any issue, it must either be framed vaguely enough to omit controversial policy details or it must represent a significant policy compromise. The 'Divided We Fail' campaign appears to be an example of the former, where signatories to the pledge did not commit themselves to any specific reform proposal. This is not necessarily a weakness, as long as vague commitments build momentum toward actual legislation. But as the health-care debate demonstrated, when it came down to specific bills, these initial commitments did not lead to bipartisan support in Congress. Lastly, if the bipartisan frame represents a real policy compromise (such as the removal of the public option and universal coverage from HCR), then it can easily alienate activists who tend toward ideological purity. This point is illustrated in polls showing that a plurality of Americans believe that HCR *did not go far enough* in expanding coverage, controlling costs, or regulating the insurance industry (Condon 2010). This suggests that the political compromises necessitated by an appeal to bipartisanship have not produced the kind of centrist support they were designed to attain.

Patriotism Another way of framing economic and social rights in the United States that is very compatible with a bipartisan frame is to tie them into traditional American ideals and values. By claiming that access to food, housing, and health care is an inherent part of the American identity, this framing strategy attempts to resonate with Americans' patriotism even as it tries to emphasize its more socially responsible aspects.

American identity is a contested discursive ground, but most popular notions of American identity would likely include some mention of freedom, progress, a strong work ethic, individualism, and Christianity. The patriotic frame draws upon those American myths, but also emphasizes other common aspects of our identity, such as Emma Lazarus' poem at the Statue of Liberty: 'Give me your tired, your poor, your huddled masses yearning to breathe free.'

This framing strategy was illustrated by Irish rock band U2's lead singer, Bono, as he led the Heart of America tour in 2002 to launch what would become the ONE campaign against global poverty and disease. In arguing why Americans should increase their commitment to eliminate AIDS and extreme poverty, Bono stated: 'My prayer is that this country, which has unparalleled economic, technological, military, and cultural power, will rethink its humble origins, the purpose that made it great' (Falsani 2003). Bono regularly referred to the United States as the 'city on a hill,' and appealed to Americans' optimistic sense of progress rather than criticizing their past foreign policy failures. Stating that 'America is not just a country, it's an idea,' Bono (2004) told a University of Pennsylvania graduating class that 'we're the first generation that can look at poverty and disease, look across the ocean to Africa and say with a straight face, we can be the first to end this sort of stupid extreme poverty.'

Oprah Winfrey and her guests also appealed to patriotism when they discussed filmmaker Michael Moore's documentary *Sicko* on the *Oprah* television show in 2007.[11] Arguing for universal access to health care, Winfrey asked rhetorically: 'What do we really believe? Do we all have the same right to health care in this country?' Moore replied:

> If you're a member of any of the great faiths, Christian, Jewish, Muslim, Buddhist, whatever, all the great faiths have already answered that question many years ago. Jesus said that the way to get into heaven is: When I was hungry, did you feed me? When I was homeless, did you give me shelter? When I was sick, did you take care of me? And I – when you're called socialist or what they call socialized medicine, I think we need to change the terms. I'd like to call it Christianized medicine, because this is what Jesus would do, right?

Moore later continued:

> We have socialized medicine in the Army. Thank God, right? I mean, what if we forced the soldiers to pay for their own health insurance? We would never do that. We believe in socialized medicine so much, we make sure the Army has it first.

The obvious strength of this kind of framing strategy is that it appeals to an extremely strong, visceral sentiment held by the vast majority of the target audience in the United States. It links economic and social rights to core beliefs about our national identity and basic moral values. It is able to directly confront the counter-frame, 'socialism,' without making claims that can easily be dismissed as foreign or radical. As such, the patriotism approach seems to adhere to the principles of effective framing strategies quite closely.

There are two possible weaknesses in this strategy, at least insofar as it has been adopted in the United States to date. First, with some exceptions, this strategy has not been widely used by advocates of economic and social rights. As such, the intended audience may not distinguish the message from the messenger; the image and source of a frame are as important as its actual content. Irish rock stars and left-wing documentarians are probably not the best messengers for a patriotic framing strategy. Second, an appeal to patriotism can lack the specificity in policy implications that framing strategies based in legality or bipartisanship may have. Because patriotism is such a contested term, there is no guarantee that framing economic and social rights through the lens of patriotism will lead to policies that ensure non-discrimination, universal access, and the protection of the most vulnerable. At worst, an appeal to patriotism may even bias policy solutions toward domestic needs rather than much more urgent international needs.

Narrative A final framing strategy that is evident among advocates of economic and social rights is what might be called the anecdotal or narrative approach. This approach frames rights to food, housing, and health care by telling the personal accounts of people who have suffered through or overcome certain deprivations. Everyone loves a good story, and the persuasive power of narrative has been well documented (Green, Strange, and Brock 2002). Although a collection of personal anecdotes does not add up to logical evidence for a particular position, the narrative approach is an extremely powerful persuasive strategy precisely because the visceral appeal of a frame is as important as its content. The narrative approach is therefore ubiquitous in political discourse.

One example of this strategy being employed for economic and social rights is an anthology of stories about personal experiences with the American health-care system (Mullan, Ficklen, and Rubin 2006). Another example is Michael Moore's film *Sicko*, which follows the trials and tribulations of citizens who suffer from the invisible hand of the American health-care system. Human rights organizations such as ESCR-Net and the PPEHRC have also used this strategy quite consistently, running projects that document people's stories of abuses of economic and social rights in the context of the economic recession.[12]

The importance of this framing strategy revolves around its ability to inspire sympathy in its audience. Stories persuade in a way that facts and evidence can never do, by psychologically linking the audience to actual people who are the victims of an abusive system. The title of the *Oprah* episode that discussed Moore's film was 'Sick in America: It Can Happen to You.' Anecdotes make us realize that abuses can indeed happen to us, and as cognitive studies have shown, when we internalize sympathy we are much more likely to be persuaded intellectually. This is true of virtually everyone, but is arguably an even more effective strategy when women comprise the audience. As Carol Gilligan (1982) noted in her groundbreaking work, women tend to engage in a different process of moral reasoning than men typically do, a process that is contextual and interpersonal rather than rooted in abstract rationality.[13] As such, when asked the question 'Does everyone deserve the same minimum quality of health care?' women tend to make a judgment by empathizing with an actual person in a social context, rather than derive a principle based on some kind of Kantian moral code.

Although the strengths of storytelling are clear, there are a couple of potential weaknesses. First, like some other framing strategies, a set of anecdotes does not necessarily lead to a specific legislative or policy recommendation. As such, anecdotes, patriotism, and bipartisanship are useful for setting the agenda and shaping the context of debate, but ultimately implementation of economic and social rights will depend on further kinds of discourse. Second, anecdotes typically require some time to tell, so they do not easily fit into a news media format composed of ten-second sound bites and two-word labels. This is why the narrative strategy is more commonly used in full-length books, films, articles, and speeches.

Conclusions

Having surveyed five common framing strategies for economic and social rights in the United States, we return to the original question: Which strategies are effective, alone and in combination? As the above discussion demonstrates, each of these strategies is useful in different contexts for different audiences. However, it is apparent that some frames do not fit together as well as others, particularly the 'radical social justice' and 'bipartisanship' frames. With that exception, the remaining frames are mutually inclusive, and it is conceivable that advocates could successfully combine several frames simultaneously. They would be wise to remember, however, that effective framing strategies are consistent, coherent, and oft-repeated. Thus, for example, 'Health care for all Americans' could be a master frame that would combine several different framing strategies. If activists, human rights organizations, Democratic members of Congress, and the President had consistently repeated a slogan like this in every health-care debate, it is possible (though certainly not guaranteed) that public support for HCR today would be different.

So what went wrong? In the second presidential debate with Republican candidate John McCain in October 2008, Barack Obama stated:

I think [health care] should be a right for every American. In a country as wealthy as ours, for us to have people who are going bankrupt because they can't pay their medical bills; for my mother to die of cancer at the age of 53, and have to spend the last months of her life in the hospital room arguing with insurance companies because they're saying that this may be a pre-existing condition and they don't have to pay her treatment; there's something fundamentally wrong about that.[14]

This was a powerful and unambiguous statement that used at least two of the framing strategies mentioned above: patriotism and the use of narrative. However, instead of continuing to proactively frame the health-care debate over the ensuing year, Democrats largely ceded discursive ground to the conservative and Republican opposition. The debate over HCR eventually revolved around terms such as 'socialism,' 'government spending,' 'cost-cutting,' and the rather astounding 'death panels.' Instead of fighting to have their own framing strategies control the playing field, supporters of HCR tended to respond to their critics with detailed evidence from 1,000-page bills, trying to disprove their opponents' claims. However inaccurate the criticisms might have been, debunking them by pointing out that page 425 of the House bill does not in fact authorize death panels (FactCheck.org 2009), or that independent economists believe that the bill will 'bend the cost curve' over the long term (Cutler, Davis, and Stremikis 2009), is simply not as effective as *any* of the framing strategies discussed above.

In sum, proponents of economic and social rights should recognize that framing these rights in the United States entails some unique challenges. However, these challenges can be met by effective framing strategies that are grounded in existing research and tailored to specific audiences and contexts. Ensuring universal access to a set of basic needs – nutrition, adequate housing, health care, education, and a safe environment – is a message that can potentially resonate deeply with people. More proactive framing strategies could even persuade the public that, in a country as great and wealthy as America, it is an *atrocity* that millions of its citizens continue to go to bed each night hungry, sick, and homeless.

Notes

1 Economic and social rights are the subset of human rights that deal with material livelihood and social welfare. These rights include rights to education, marriage, fair working conditions, property, and so forth. However, the core of these rights are 'subsistence rights,' or demands that a person's material survival be socially guaranteed – survival that depends on the ability to achieve a minimum standard of living and acquire goods such as nutrition, housing, and health care (see Shue 1996, 13).

2 For a detailed description of this trend, see Nelson and Dorsey (2008), and Chong (2010).

3 The Patient Protection and Affordable Care Act was passed by the US Congress and signed into law by President Obama in March 2010. It seeks to make health coverage nearly universal by, *inter alia*, mandating that individuals purchase insurance coverage, increasing regulations on private insurance companies, and providing subsidies for low-income individuals.

4 A single concept that ties together different framing strategies has been called a 'master narrative' or 'master frame' (Snow and Benford 1992). For example, a master frame for economic and social

rights might be 'equal dignity for all,' while specific framing strategies might refer to legality or patriotism. Each framing strategy would then lead to tactical decisions such as the specific audience to target, the images to display, the wording of particular slogans, and the timing of campaigns.

5 For example, in 2006, only a slight majority of Americans (57 per cent) explicitly favored having the CIA abide by the Geneva Conventions in interrogating terror suspects (see Global Envision 2006). Three years later, a majority of Americans favored the use of waterboarding and other 'aggressive interrogation techniques' against Umar Farouk Abdulmutallab, the Nigerian man who attempted to destroy an airplane in December 2009 (see Rasmussen Reports 2009).

6 The first official statement from the Occupy Wall Street movement referred repeatedly to these rights. See the full text at www.dailykos.com/story/2011/10/01/1021956/-First-official-statement-from-Occupy-Wall-Street.

7 Additional information on the 'Divided We Fail' campaign can be found on the AARP's research and policy website at www.aarp.org/research/.

8 The commercials can be viewed by searching at www.youtube.com.

9 Results of polls that ask respondents to identify their political philosophy have been fairly consistent over the past three decades. Twice as many people self-identify as 'conservative' than as 'liberal' (roughly 36 per cent and 18 per cent, respectively), while a plurality self-identify as 'moderate' (see Harris Interactive 2005).

10 Ironically, in the same survey, an overwhelming 79 per cent wanted Republicans to be more bipartisan – in other words, to support Obama's agenda. And yet over the ensuing year, as Republicans remained united in opposition to Obama's agenda, they made clear political gains in the 2010 elections.

11 'Sick in America: It Can Happen to You,' 27 September 2007.

12 See, for example, ESCR-Net's Business and Human Rights documentation project at www.escr-net.org/actions/actions_show.htm?doc_id=1117505. For PPEHRC, see http://weap.org/ca-ppehrc.htm.

13 Note that neither Gilligan nor I argue that these gender differences are universal, invariant, or essential; but rather that they are socially conditioned tendencies.

14 For a video of this statement, see www.youtube.com/watch?v=zAR8K2KCiGc.

References

Alston, Philip. 1990. 'US ratification of the Covenant on Economic, Social and Cultural Rights: The need for an entirely new strategy.' *American Journal of International Law* 84(2): 365–93.

Bono. 2004. 'Because we can, we must.' Commencement address at the University of Pennsylvania, 19 May. www.upenn.edu/almanac/between/2004/commence-b.html.

CBS News. 2010. 'The President, health care and terrorism,' *CBS News*, 11 January. www.cbsnews.com/htdocs/pdf/poll_obama_011110.pdf?tag=contentMain;contentBody.

Chong, Dan. 2010. *Freedom from Poverty: NGOs and Human Rights Praxis*. Philadelphia: University of Pennsylvania Press.

Condon, Stephanie. 2010. 'Poll: Obama health care marks hit new low.' *CBS News*, 11 January. www.cbsnews.com/blogs/2010/01/11/politics/politicalhotsheet/entry6084856.shtml.

Corsi, Jessica. 2009. 'Amnesty head urges US ratification of economic and social rights treaty.' *Harvard Law Record*, 22 October.

Cress, Daniel M., and David A. Snow. 2000. 'The outcomes of homeless mobilization: The influence of organization, disruption, political mediation and framing.' *American Journal of Sociology* 105(4): 1063–104.

Cutler, David M., Karen Davis, and Kristof Stremikis. 2009. 'Why health reform will bend the cost curve.' Center for American Progress and The Commonwealth Fund, 7 December. www.commonwealthfund.org/Content/Publications/Issue-Briefs/2009/Dec/Why-Health-Reform-Will-Bend-the-Cost-Curve.aspx.

ESCR-Net. 2009. 'ESCR-Net statement on the financial crisis and global economic recession: Towards a human rights response.' June. www.escr-net.org/usr_doc/EconomicCrisisHRStatement_ESCR-Net_final_eng_withendorsements.pdf.

ESCR-Net. 2010. 'Is your government respecting its human rights obligations in confronting the economic crisis?' Questionnaire circulated in 2010. www.escr-net.org/actions/actions_show.htm?doc_id=1129717&attribLang_id=13441.

FactCheck.org. 2009. 'False euthanasia claims,' 29 July. www.factcheck.org/2009/07/false-euthanasia-claims/.

Falsani, Cathleen. 2003. 'Bono's American prayer.' *Christianity Today*, 1 March. www.christianitytoday.com/ct/2003/march/2.38.html.

Finnemore, Martha, and Kathryn Sikkink. 1998. 'International norm dynamics and political change.' *International Organization* 52(4): 887–917.

Franck, Thomas. 1990. *The Power of Legitimacy Among Nations*. Oxford: Oxford University Press.

Gamson, William A., and David S. Meyer. 1996. 'Framing political opportunity.' In *Comparative Perspectives on Social Movements,* edited by Doug McAdam, John D. McCarthy, and Mayer N. Zald, 275–90. Cambridge: Cambridge University Press.

Gardner, David. 2009. 'A million march to US Capitol to protest against "Obama the socialist."' *Mail Online*, 14 September. www.dailymail.co.uk/news/worldnews/article-1213056/Up-million-march-US-Capitol-protest-Obamas-spending-tea-party-demonstration.html.

Gilligan, Carol. 1982. *In a Different Voice: Psychological Theory and Women's Development*. Boston, MA: Harvard University Press.

Glendon, Mary Ann. 1991. *Rights Talk: The Impoverishment of Political Discourse*. New York: Free Press.

Global Envision. 2006. 'Americans want CIA to respect Geneva Convention.' GlobalEnvision.org, 20 September.

Global Envision. 2007. 'Polls reveal Americans' attitudes about U.S. role in the world.' Global Envision.org, 14 August. www.globalenvision.org/library/8/1728.

Goffman, Erving. 1974. *Frame Analysis: An Essay on the Organization of Experience*. New York: Harper.

Green, Melanie C., Jeffrey J. Strange, and Timothy C. Brock. 2002. *Narrative Impact: Social and Cognitive Foundations*. Hove, UK: Psychology Press.

Guardian. 2008. 'Full text: Obama's foreign policy speech.' *Guardian*, 16 July. www.guardian.co.uk/world/2008/jul/16/uselections2008.barackobama.

Gupta, Devashree. 2002. 'Radical flank effects: The effect of radical-moderate splits in regional nationalist movements.' Paper presented at the Thirteenth International Conference of Europeanists, Chicago, Illinois, March 14–16. http://falcon.arts.cornell.edu/sgt2/pscp/documents/RFEgupta.pdf.

Haines, Herbert. 1997. 'Black radicalization and the funding of civil rights: 1957–1970.' In *Social Movements: Readings on their Emergence, Mobilization and Dynamics*, edited by Doug McAdam and David Snow, 440–9. Los Angeles, CA: Roxbury.

Harris Interactive. 2005. 'Party affiliation and political philosophy show little change, according to national Harris Poll.' Harris Interactive, Inc., 9 March.

Jackson, Patrick T. 2006. 'Relational constructivism: A war of words.' In *Making Sense of International Relations Theory*, edited by Jennifer Sterling-Folker, 139–55. Boulder, CO: Lynne Rienner Publishers.

Jones, Jeffrey M. 2009. 'More independents lean GOP; party gap smallest since 2005.' *Gallup*, 30 September. www.gallup.com/poll/123362/independents-lean-gop-party-gap-smallest-since-05.aspx.

Keck, Margaret E., and Kathryn Sikkink. 1998. *Activists Beyond Borders: Advocacy Networks in International Politics*. Ithaca, NY: Cornell University Press.

Klandermans, Bert, and Sjoerd Goslinga. 1996. 'Media discourse, movement publicity, and the generation of collective action frames: Theoretical and empirical exercises in meaning construction.' In *Comparative Perspectives on Social Movements: Political Opportunities, Mobilizing Structures, and Cultural Framings*, edited by Doug McAdam, John D. McCarthy, and Mayer N. Zald, 312–37. Cambridge: Cambridge University Press.

LaFranchi, Howard. 2009. 'Economy forces Obama to rein in foreign-aid goals.' *Christian Science Monitor*, 23 March. www.csmonitor.com/USA/Foreign-Policy/2009/0323/p03s07-usfp.html.

Lakoff, George. 2004. *Don't Think of an Elephant! Know Your Values and Frame the Debate*. White River Junction, VT: Chelsea Green Publishing.

Mandler, M. 1995. 'Economic and social rights and the right to health.' Report from a discussion held at Harvard Law School in September 1993. Cambridge, MA:

Harvard Law School Human Rights Program.

McAdam, Doug, John D. McCarthy, and Mayer N. Zald (editors). 1996. *Comparative Perspectives on Social Movements: Political Opportunities, Mobilizing Structures, and Cultural Framings*. Cambridge: Cambridge University Press.

Mullan, Fitzhugh, Ellen Ficklen, and Kyna Rubin. 2006. *Narrative Matters: The Power of the Personal Essay in Health Policy*. Baltimore, MD: Johns Hopkins University Press.

Murray, Mark. 2010. 'NBC/WSJ poll: Public fed up with DC.' *MSNBC Online*, 26 January. http://firstread.msnbc.msn.com/archive/2010/01/26/2185944.aspx.

Nelson, Paul, and Ellen Dorsey. 2008. *New Rights Advocacy: Changing Strategies of Development and Human Rights NGOs*. Washington, DC: Georgetown University Press.

NESRI (National Economic and Social Rights Initiative). 2010. www.nesri.org/programs.

PPEHRC (Poor People's Economic Human Rights Campaign). 2010. http://old.economichumanrights.org/actions.html.

Rasmussen Reports. 2009. '58% favor waterboarding of plane terrorist to get information.' Rasmussen Reports.com, 31 December. www.rasmussenreports.com/public_content/politics/general_politics/december_2009/58_favor_waterboarding_of_plane_terrorist_to_get_information.

Rasmussen Reports. 2010. 'Health care reform.' RasmussenReports.com, 22 January. www.rasmussenreports.com/public_content/politics/current_events/healthcare/september_2009/health_care_reform.

Sargent, Greg. 2009. 'Poll: Majority doesn't want Obama to be bipartisan.' *Who Runs GOV* (blog), 24 February.

Shue, Henry. 1996. *Basic Rights: Subsistence, Affluence and US Foreign Policy*. Princeton, NJ: Princeton University Press.

Sikkink, Kathryn. 1986. 'Codes of conduct for transnational corporations: The case of the WHO/UNICEF Code.' *International Organization* 40(4): 815–40.

Snow, David A., and Robert D. Benford. 1992. 'Master frames and cycles of protest.' In *Frontiers in Social Movement Theory*, edited by Aldo D. Morris and Carol M. Mueller, 133–55. New Haven, CT: Yale University Press.

Stein, Sam. 2009. 'Obama boost: New poll shows 76% support for choice of public plan.' *Huffington Post*, 18 July. www.huffingtonpost.com/2009/06/17/obama-boost-new-poll-show_n_217175.html.

Tarrow, Sidney. 1998. *Power in Movement: Social Movements and Contentious Politics*. Cambridge: Cambridge University Press.

USHRN (US Human Rights Network. 2010). 'Take Back the Land campaign.'

Woods, Kathy. 2009. 'New York judge nullifies mortgage.' *Legal Newsline*, 30 November. www.legalnewsline.com/news/224281-new-york-judge-nullifies-mortgage.

5 | 'Fresh, wet tears': shock media and human rights awareness campaigns

TRISTAN ANNE BORER

Introduction

In February 2005, after a year of increasingly frustrated writing about the growing conflict in the Darfur region of Sudan, Nicholas Kristof, a regular *New York Times* op-ed columnist, resorted to filling part of his weekly column space with pictures of dead and mutilated bodies, along with text describing the atrocities in detail (Kristof 2005). His frustration obvious, Kristof explained that the pictures were meant to spur his readers to action. After chastising his readers – 'It's time for all of us to look squarely at the victims of our indifference' – he exhorted them to take action, arguing that the only way to end the genocide was for individuals to respond personally with direct political action. Likening the situation to the Rwandan genocide a decade earlier, Kristof cited former Senator Paul Simon's statement that 'if every member of the House and Senate had received 100 letters from people back home saying we have to do something about Rwanda, when the crisis was first developing, then I think the response would have been different.' Finally, Kristof asserted a causal link between viewing pictures of atrocities and acting to oppose them. 'Americans will be stirred,' he claimed, 'if they can see the consequences of their complacency' (ibid.).

Kristof had arguably done more to bring attention to the plight of Darfuris than any other journalist, using his column to spread awareness of the emerging humanitarian crisis there. Exasperated that his writing was apparently not translating into either policy changes or individual action, he decided to try to shock his readers into action by publishing pictures of, and describing in detail, the tortured and mutilated bodies of four civilian victims of the conflict, one of whom was a small child. In turning to shock to elicit reader response, Kristof was borrowing a tactic well known in the field of advertising. Shock advertising, or 'shockvertising,' is advertising that deliberately, rather than inadvertently, attempts to startle, offend, or shock an audience (Manchandra et al. 2003, 268). Ann Cooper defines shockvertising as 'the desire to shock the audience into taking notice by whatever means possible' (quoted in ibid., 268). The shock is elicited using a variety of methods, such as the display of images or the use of words that are repulsive, gruesome, and graphic. They are intended to provoke feelings of disgust, revulsion, fear, and anger. A subset of shock advertisements are those that go beyond just getting the audience to take notice by also attempting to provoke personal behavioral changes by shocking the audience into action. It is in this spirit of public service advertisements, designed to heighten public awareness of social issues and force a reaction to them, that Kristof offered his viewers graphic images accompanied by explicit descriptions of victims of a vicious conflict far removed from the reality of the vast majority of his readers. In deciding to take the shock route, Kristof appears to have been working under the assumption, as described by Laurent Berlant, that the use of such images 'has to be a good thing, because it produces *feeling* and with it something at least akin to *consciousness* that can lead to *action*' (quoted in Szörényi 2006, 30; italics in original).

While the use of shock is a well-known marketing tool, little has been written about shock media from a human rights perspective. What can the findings in the first field tell us about the second, i.e. the use of shock to elicit action to end atrocities? Does it work? Do people remember these ads more than others? If so, does remembering necessarily translate into action to change behavior? Are there any downsides to using shock ads? While research in the advertising field suggests that Kristof and others are correct in thinking that shock media can motivate readers to act, other perspectives, including feminist analysis, point to negative consequences of trying to shock people into action through graphic depictions (both in images and prose) of atrocities, especially those occurring far away. Ultimately, this chapter argues, while Kristof and other human rights activists mean well, they may well undermine their own goals through their tactics. These arguments are explored through an analysis of three types of shock media aimed at raising awareness about human rights abuses: op-eds, 'objective' news reporting, and petitions.

Shock public safety advertisements (PSAs)

Most commonly, shock ads are used to sell products. Examples of these profit-motivated ads might include those from French Connection's 'FCUK' campaign (see Owens 2001), which were banned in New York City taxis, or Volkswagen's depiction of a deadly car crash to advertise the Jetta (see Stevenson 2006). There is, however, another type of shock ad – one that is used to raise awareness of a pressing public policy issue. This category of shock advertisement is the focus of this chapter. Referred to here as shock public safety advertisements, or 'shock PSAs,' the goal of these ads is to shock the viewing or reading audience into changing personal behavior, very often in relation to a public-health crisis.[1] As Manchandra et al. note, 'particularly in public service announcements, it is hoped that shock appeals will gain attention, encourage cognitive processing, and have an immediate impact on behavior, e.g. drinking and driving, or condom usage' (2003, 268). Some examples should suffice to demonstrate how shock has been employed in the hopes of prompting behavioral changes.

In 2000, an organization called the Breast Cancer Fund ran a breast cancer awareness campaign using several posters that mimicked contemporary women's magazine ads and catalogs. Each ad, however, featured a supermodel clad in a sexy bra and panties revealing mastectomy scars where breasts once were. Using the slogan 'It's no secret,' one ad, for example, looked nearly identical to a Victoria's Secret lingerie catalog.[2] Other posters mimicked ads for Obsession perfume and *Cosmopolitan* magazine. The pictures of missing breasts and vivid mastectomy scars juxtaposed with sexualized female bodies were indeed shocking (and controversial – some billboard companies and mass transit systems refused to run them). They were meant to be. The Breast Cancer Fund stated that 'the goals of the provocative ad campaign are to increase public awareness and involvement in breast cancer issues' (Imaginis.com). A second health-related shock PSA is the US Food and Drug Administration's (FDA) anti-smoking campaign. In keeping with the terms of the Family Smoking Prevention and Tobacco Control Act passed by Congress in June 2009, the FDA developed new regulations requiring the top half, both front and back, of all cigarette packs sold in the United States to be covered with warning labels with one of nine graphic color images of, for example, diseased lungs, a man exhaling smoke through a tracheotomy, and a mouth with lip cancer (see *Los Angeles Times* 2011 for the images). Health advocacy groups lauded the campaign, hoping that the 'images [will] shock and deter new smokers and motivate existing smokers to quit' (Wilson 2011). Although slated to take effect by September 2012, at the time of writing the FDA and tobacco companies are engaged in a legal battle after the latter successfully challenged the new labeling rules in federal court. A third, better-known shock PSA is the 2011 'From Drugs to Mugs' campaign, which pairs shocking 'before' and 'after' pictures of drug addicts to show the toll that drug use takes on users' faces. The pictures show mugshots of drug users at the time of their first arrests paired with a subsequent mugshot showing often-severe facial deterioration; examples include addicts who have lost teeth or who have scratched their skin down to the bone. This campaign is a sequel to another anti-drug initiative – both were created by the Multnomah County Sheriff's Office in Oregon in the United States – the 2004 'Faces of Meth' project. Explicitly acknowledging their intention to scare drug users straight, one campaign organizer stated, 'we want everyone, not just high school kids, to look at these pictures and to be shocked' (Daily Mail Reporter 2011).

Other public-health shock appeals have been directed at alcohol abuse, seat belt safety, AIDS awareness, and domestic violence (Manchandra et al. 2003, 269). Health advocates have not cornered the shock market tactic, however; activists in other movements, spanning the political spectrum, have also adopted its use. Perhaps most controversial has been the use of graphic images by anti-abortion activists. Indeed, one anti-abortion organization, Priests for Life, offers perhaps the clearest rationale for the use of shocking images to promote behavior change – the very definition of a shock PSA: 'When you want people to act to reform deeply embedded trends in society, it is not enough simply to know that the trends are wrong. One must be profoundly disturbed so as to be stirred to action' (Priests for Life, n.d.). In line with this argument, the organization encourages the anti-abortion movement to use pictures of aborted fetuses in its campaigns:

> The experience of those who use horrifying pictures teaches that those who haven't seen abortion only think they know how evil it actually is. Some say aborting mothers believe God will punish but ultimately forgive abortion; but there are different levels of 'believing' and a mother with a functioning conscience will find it easier to trivialize the spiritual consequences of abortion if she has never seen one ... Many women have told us that they aborted because no one showed them a picture ... (ibid.).

Human rights shock PSAs

All the ad campaigns described above are specifically intended to shock an audience into taking notice of an issue and, more importantly, to spur the audience into taking action by changing their personal behaviors around the issue. This chapter argues that a similar approach can be seen in some human rights-related activism. That is, human rights activists often use the tactic of shock to heighten awareness of atrocities in the hope that the audience will respond in a sequence akin to that noted by Berlant above: the shock will raise their consciousness; this will produce a feeling of compassion; the feeling will lead to action to stop abuses. This was clearly the hoped-for process in Kristof's 2005 Darfur column noted in the introduction (evident in his causal claim that 'Americans will be stirred if they can see the consequences of their complacency'). Exhortations that use shock to spur human rights action will be referred to here as human rights shock public safety announcements (hereafter, HR shock PSAs). This chapter will examine three types of these human rights shock ads. The first category is op-eds. Because editorials are explicitly subjective, they are a natural place for writers to offer their opinions on political events and to try to persuade readers to do something about them. A second category includes news stories that are ostensibly objective reporting of facts but nevertheless are presented in such an overtly shocking way that they appear to contain an underlying message about human rights atrocities and an implicit call to action. Petitions are the final type of HR shock PSA examined here. Since the whole point of these appeals is to urge signers to support – or take action on – a cause, they are another obvious vehicle for conveying a human rights PSA. While shock can obviously be effectively conveyed through the use of images, they are not the only means available; shock prose is also sometimes used. Some of the HR shock PSAs examined here combine both images and prose, while others use only one or the other. The various types of HR shock PSAs are described in the next section, with examples provided of each. This section is then followed by more in-depth analysis of the merits, drawbacks, and ethical implications of using shock to prod action on behalf of those suffering from human rights abuses. The focus is largely, although not exclusively, on gender-based HR shock PSAs.

Op-eds Because the *New York Times* is a national paper of record, perhaps no journalist has done more to raise awareness about the reality of human rights abuses, especially in Asia and Africa, and the plight of their victims than Nicholas Kristof, who, since 2001, has devoted many of his *New York Times* op-eds to these issues. While not the exclusive focus of his work, much of his writing has been devoted specifically to gender-based violations, including the book *Half the Sky: Turning Oppression into Opportunity for Women Worldwide*, co-authored with his wife (Kristof and WuDunn 2009). A two-time Pulitzer Prize winner, Kristof frequently explicitly employs the tactic of shock.

Indeed, he was rewarded specifically for this choice of tactic when the Pulitzer committee cited his *'graphic*, deeply reported columns' in 2006 (Pulitzer Prizes 2006; italics added). Kristof sometimes tries to shock through the use of images, such as in the Darfur column described in this chapter's introduction; at other times, he uses only words. In addition to the Darfur column, numerous other examples of Kristof's writing illustrate his use of shock. Many of these highlight gender-based violations resulting from cultural norms relating to the treatment of women in various countries, as in the following three examples.

On 30 November 2008, Kristof, reporting from Pakistan, wrote in his *Times* column about the issue of acid burning, which he likened to a form of terrorism as cruel as exploding bombs. These attacks are 'commonly used to terrorize and subjugate women and girls' and involve 'flinging acid on a woman's face to leave her hideously deformed' (Kristof 2008). Kristof introduces Naeema Azar, telling his readers that:

> acid had burned away her left ear and most of her right ear. It had blinded her and burned away her eyelid and most of her face, leaving just bone. Six skin grafts with flesh from her leg have helped, but she still cannot close her eyes or her mouth; she will not eat in front of others because it is too humiliating to have food slip out as she chews.

A picture of Azar, her face burned away, accompanies the text (ibid.). He ties acid attacks to the status of women in countries where these attacks are prevalent:

> I've been investigating such acid attacks, which are commonly used to terrorize and subjugate women and girls in a swatch of Asia from Afghanistan through Cambodia (men are almost never attacked with acid). Because women usually don't matter in this part of the world, their attackers are rarely prosecuted and acid sales are usually not controlled ... Acid attacks and wife burnings are common in parts of Asia because the victims are the most voiceless in these societies: they are poor and female.

On 30 March 2011, Kristof turned his attention to punishment meted out for honor crimes[3] in Bangladesh. His article focuses on Hena, a fourteen-year-old girl who, after being abducted and raped, was found guilty of adultery by a local imam and sentenced to 100 lashes by public whipping. According to Kristof, Hena's last words were 'protestations of innocence,' and he quotes a CNN blog post that reported that her parents 'watched as the whip broke the skin of their youngest child and she fell unconscious to the ground.' Hena reportedly collapsed after 70 lashes and died a week later. Invoking the cultural norms sur-rounding women's and girls' behavior, Kristof concludes, 'all accounts that I've seen suggest that this was a brutal attack on a helpless girl in the name of sharia and justice' (Kristof 2011a).

Six weeks later, on 11 May, Kristof tackled the issue of female genital cutting (FGC) in Africa generally (with a focus on Somalia), which he referred to as female genital mutilation, a term that itself carries a certain amount of shock value. The op-ed is devoted primarily to the most extreme form of cutting, infibulation. Going for maximum shock value, Kristof (2011c) writes:

> Let's not be dainty or euphemistic. This is a grotesque human rights abuse that doesn't get much attention because it involves private parts and is awkward to talk about. So pardon the bluntness about what in-fibulation entails. The girl's genitals are carved out, including the clit-oris and labia, often with no anesthetic. What's left of the flesh is sewn together with three to six stitches – wild thorns in rural areas, or needle and thread in the cities. The cutter leaves a tiny opening to permit uri-nation and menstruation. Then the girl's legs are tied together, and she is kept immobile for ten days until the flesh fuses together. When the girl is married and ready for sex, she must be cut open by her husband or by a respected woman in the community.[4]

Likening the process to torture, Kristof again attributes FGC to cultural traditions that exist to control the behavior, in this case sexual, of women but not men in certain societies.

News stories While op-eds are purposely subjective, HR shock PSAs sometimes appear in more objective news reporting. The use of sen-sationalism in journalism is certainly not new, and much scholarship has analyzed whether shock sells more newspapers and has discussed the ethics of showing graphic pictures of dead and dying people – whether victims of state-sponsored violence or soldiers in war. While this literature is important and interesting, the focus of this chapter remains HR shock PSAs – the uses of shocking images and words to highlight human rights abuses with the specific goal of eliciting behavioral changes in the audience; these changes might include bring-ing pressure to bear on governments or providing financial support for non-governmental organizations (NGOs). Key aspects of an HR PSA, then, include intentionality and advocacy. Since news reporting is ostensibly meant to be objective, it would appear that hard news (i.e. objective reporting) and HR PSAs (i.e. advocacy of a particular position to elicit readers' action) are mutually exclusive. On occasion, however, the line between the two becomes blurred, and a story is presented in such a way that, despite claims of neutrality, it appears to have a clear underlying call to action. When such a call is related to human rights abuses and when shock is used to prompt readers to act, what is billed as objective news becomes an HR shock PSA. An example that could be read as such, and which garnered a tremendous amount of attention – much of it negative – was *TIME Magazine*'s 9 August 2010 cover photograph of an eighteen-year-old Afghan woman, Aisha, whose nose and ears had been cut off for fleeing her abusive in-laws. The picture is accompanied by the declarative headline: 'What happens if we leave Afghanistan' (*TIME Magazine* 2010). As if the picture is not shocking enough, the accompanying article makes heavy use of shock prose. Aisha's attack is described thus:

> The commander gave his verdict, and men moved in to deliver the punishment. Aisha's brother-in-law held her down while her husband pulled out a knife. First he sliced off her ears. Then he started on her nose. Aisha passed out from the pain but awoke soon after, choking on her own blood. The men had left her on the mountainside to die.

A more general discussion of the status of women under the Taliban is also offered:

> Under the Taliban, who ruled Afghanistan from 1996 to 2001, women accused of adultery were stoned to death; those who flashed a bare ankle from under the shroud of a burqa were whipped. Koofi remembers being beaten on the street for forgetting to remove the polish from her nails after her wedding (Baker 2010).

While *TIME Magazine*'s managing editor Richard Stengel denied any underlying political motive for running the picture and article (for example, to generate support for continuing the US military mission in Afghanistan), or that the story contained an implicit call to activism, many readers vehemently disagreed. As one writer for a blog dedicated to counter-insurgency and post-conflict environments argued: 'Stengel's assertion that the decision to run the image was judgment-neutral strains credulity; will anyone view that photo and say "this helps confirm my view that we must withdraw?"' (Gulliver 2010). Undoubtedly the editors believed that the tactic of shock would be most useful in bringing Taliban-ordered, gender-based human rights abuses to the attention of the magazine's readers. What is less clear is whether the goal of this HR shock PSA was to elicit individual action to ensure that no other women suffer similar fates (à la the Kristof op-eds) or to influence public policy (i.e. by justifying an extended occupation). In some cases a fine line may exist between shock in the service of prompting individual activism and shock in the service of promoting particular governmental policies, which some would consider propaganda. Either goal would arguably fit our definition of the use of shock to highlight human rights abuses for the purpose of influencing outcomes. The line between the Aisha story as HR shock PSA versus HR shock propaganda will be explored in detail below.

Petitions Petitions have long been used to bring awareness of an issue to the general public and to elicit individual action ('please sign this petition') in the service of political change. Petitions are a popular medium for human rights activism in the age of the Internet, especially through social networking sites, as signatures are gathered electronically or through the click of a mouse rather than through the old-fashioned method of physically signing. Websites such as GoPetition.com and thepetitionsite.com allow individuals to create and disseminate petitions on any topic, but by far the most popular and arguably most professional and respected petition site with an explicit human rights and social justice focus is Change.org, which describes itself as an 'online activism platform for social change that raises awareness about important causes and connects people to opportunities for powerful action' (Change.org 2011). The website provides suggestions for creating effective petitions, one of which is to include powerful (read: shocking?) pictures. The suggestion page notes: 'The old cliché is right: a picture is worth a thousand words. Catch your readers' attention with a great graphic that pulls them in and leaves them wanting to learn more' (ibid.). This suggestion is followed by various 'powerful' examples, including a jarring picture of a pelican covered in crude oil. The website further suggests the use of 'attention-grabbing email subject lines.' Petitions, then, seem ripe for use as HR shock PSAs. Two gender-related examples are examined here. Although both pre-date social media websites such as Facebook, which is arguably now the most common method for distributing petitions, the petition organizers did try to harness the power of the Internet by using email lists.

The first, from 1998, was entitled 'The Taliban's War on Women,' and is reported to have been started by a Brandeis University student. The petition aimed to highlight the treatment of Afghan women under the Taliban and to protest this treatment by asking the US government to take action to end it (although no specific action is mentioned). The petition relies on shock prose to make its point, including the following:

> Since the Taliban took power in 1996, women have had to wear burqua [sic] and have been beaten and stoned in public for not having the proper attire, even if this means simply not having the mesh covering in front of their eyes. One woman was beaten to DEATH by an angry mob of fundamentalists for accidentally exposing her arm while she was driving [capitalization in original] ... At one of the rare hospitals for women, a reporter found still, nearly lifeless bodies lying motionless on top of beds, wrapped in their burqua, unwilling to speak, eat or do anything, but are slowly wasting away. Others have gone mad and were seen crouched in corners, perpetually rocking or crying, most of them in fear ... Husbands have the power of life and death over their women relatives, especially their wives, but an angry mob has just as much right to stone or beat a woman, often to death, for exposing an inch of flesh or offending them in the slightest way (Emery 1999).

Recipients of the petition were asked to add their names to the bottom of the petition, copy and paste the text into a new email, and resend it, preferably to fifty people. When the number of names reached fifty, recipients were asked to email a copy of it to a specific Brandeis University email address. Brandeis University deemed the petition an unauthorized chain letter under its email policies and deleted the email address, but not before its email system was swamped with hundreds of thousands of messages (ibid.). However, the petition took on a life of its own, and for several years variations on the original one were still circulating on the Internet, all of which employed similar shock prose.

A second, also very popular, email petition spread like fire across the globe in 2003. Reputed to have originated with a Spanish branch of Amnesty International (although that was never confirmed), the petition – which will be analyzed in more detail below – concerned the apparent imminent execution by stoning of a young Nigerian woman, Amina Lawal Kurami, who had been found guilty of adultery in an Islamic court in Katsina, her home state in northern Nigeria, for having a child out of wedlock (Sengupta 2003). The petition, which is the length of a short paragraph, is addressed to Nigeria's President Olusegun Obasanjo. The petition refers to the 'barbarian judgment imposed upon the unwed mother.' It also implores Obasanjo to 'ensure that this cruel and inhuman sentence is not carried out' (PetitionOnline.com, n.d.).[5]

Why use shock? Does it work?

The use of shock in advertising Why is shock so often employed in HR PSAs? Some scholars argue that the media are self-interested and the use of shock is simply a business practice designed to sell newspapers (Boyle and Hoeschen 2001). It seems unlikely, however, that Nicholas Kristof uses shock primarily to sell copies of the *New York Times*. Moreover, human rights-focused petition creators are not in the business of making money. Even the decision to publish the picture of Aisha on the cover of *TIME Magazine*, which probably *did* increase sales of that particular issue, was likely driven as much by a desire to heighten awareness of human rights abuses against women in Afghanistan as by a desire to make money. If profit is thus not the only, or even primary, motivating factor for the use of shock media, why then is it used? The field of advertising, where shock has long been used both generally and more specifically for public service announcements, might reveal insights that can help make sense of HR shock PSAs. As Manchandra et al. note, advertisers typically justify the use of shock for its 'ability to "[break] through the clutter," "get noticed," and "get people's attention."' The clutter that must be broken through is the increasing number of ads with which consumers are confronted. Advertisers must ask, 'in an age when consumers are exposed to an estimated 3,000 advertisements per day, what does it take to get an advertisement noticed?' For many advertisers, 'the answer is shock' (Manchandra et al. 2003, 268 and 269). The expectation, of course, is that consumers will be more likely to remember ads with shocking content. This process 'attempts to surprise an audience by *deliberately violating norms* for societal values and personal ideals. It is the norm violation aspect of the shock appeal that is assumed to underlie its ability to break through advertising clutter and capture the attention of a target audience who then listens and acts on the related message' (ibid., 269; italics in original).

Narrowing the advertising field down to PSAs, another reason for using shock is that most consumers are generally aware of the negative consequences of such behaviors as smoking, taking drugs, or eating junk food; thus, purely informational advertisements are not terribly effective. Moreover, consumers are often focused on the short-term pleasure of behaviors, while the long-term effects seem less real. Shock is thus used to highlight these long-term consequences (Marketplace 2009). This combination of striving to be memorable while educating consumers about long-term consequences of negative health behaviors is evident in the US government's anti-smoking shock campaign described above. The chief executive of the American Heart Association commented, for example, that the graphic photographs 'strongly depict the adverse consequences of smoking. They will get people's attention. And they will certainly be much more memorable than the current warning labels' (Wilson 2011).

Turning from the advertising field to the human rights field, a third reason for using shock in HR PSAs comes from Paul Slovic's psychology-based theories of 'genocide neglect.' Slovic, drawing on studies in psychology, offers an affect-based argument that states that human beings experience psychological numbing with regard to large-scale loss. Slovic quotes Mother Teresa, who is reported to have said: 'If I look at the mass I will never act. If I look at the one, I will' (Slovic 2007, 80). He argues that it is difficult for mass atrocities to 'feel real' to people. In a sense, he says (ibid., 84), apathy for large-scale suffering that takes place at a distance is simply hardwired in humans:

> Affect is a remarkable mechanism that enabled humans to survive the long course of evolution ... [It] evolved to protect individuals and their small family and community groups from present, visible, immediate dangers. This affective system did not evolve to help us respond to distant, mass murder ... The circuitry in our brain is not up to this task.

He sums up his argument with the simple statement, 'our capacity to feel is limited' (ibid., 90). Slovic then asks: 'How can we impart the feelings that are needed for rational action?' In answering his own question, Slovic (ibid., 86) makes an argument that is tantamount to a psychology-based justification for human rights shock media:

> For whatever reasons, images often strike us more powerfully, more deeply than numbers. We seem unable to hold the emotions aroused by numbers for nearly as long as those of images. We quickly grow numb to the facts and the math. Images seem to be the key to conveying affect and meaning, though some imagery is more powerful than others.[6]

HR shock PSAs employ shock for the various reasons noted above. In justifying publishing the picture of Aisha on the cover of *TIME Magazine*, for example, editor Richard Stengel offered something of a 'cutting through the clutter' argument. Referring to information about the war in Afghanistan that had recently surfaced through the release of classified documents by WikiLeaks, Stengel said, 'what you see in this picture and our story is something that you cannot find in those 91,000 documents: a combination of emotional truth and insight into the way life is lived in that difficult land and the consequences of the important decisions that lie ahead' (*TIME Magazine* 2010). Perhaps no one is more honest about the use of shock in the service of raising awareness of human rights atrocities than Nicholas Kristof. Indeed, Kristof explicitly advocates borrowing tactics from the advertising world. 'What would happen if aid organizations and other philanthropists embraced the dark arts of marketing spin and psychological persuasion used on Madison Avenue?' Kristof asks. 'We'd save millions more lives,' he answers. After feeling enraged by what he deemed a 'collective shrug' in response to his many op-eds about Darfur, Kristof came to the conclusion that 'those of us who care about human rights and global poverty can do a far better job in our messaging. Like Pepsi, humanitarian causes need savvy marketing' (Kristof 2009b). Explaining why he so frequently uses it, Kristof articulates all three reasons for using shock media – (1) cutting through the clutter ('Isn't that what Africa is always like? People slaughtering each other?'); (2) the fact that readers are already aware of negative consequences ('yet these columns on AIDS sank with barely a ripple. Readers already knew AIDS was catastrophic'); and (3) psychic numbing to mass atrocities ('the more who die, the less we care') (ibid.). In crafting his message, Kristof cites Slovic's work, and, like Slovic, Kristof believes that the use of shocking images and prose is not only helpful but is a necessary ingredient in eliciting compassion. Both Kristof and Slovic seek to discover how to convey adequately the reality of mass atrocities in a way that will prompt people to act. Both agree that simply reporting the scale of suffering does little to overcome apathy and may well make it worse. Slovic argues against simply reporting death tolls, arguing that dry statistics are 'human beings with tears dried off that fail to spark emotion or feeling and thus fail to motivate action' (Slovic 2007, 79). Kristof concurs: 'When we want to get help, we make logical arguments about the scale of the suffering: *Five million people have died in Congo!* ... All the psychological research shows that we are moved not by statistics but by fresh, wet tears, with a bit of hope glistening below' (Kristof 2009b; italics in original).

Does shock work? Although shock has long been used in advertising, its effectiveness has been relatively understudied. In terms of PSAs, Manchandra et al. examined the effectiveness of shock advertising in the context of HIV/AIDS prevention in comparison with two other advertising tactics: fear and information. They found that 'shocking advertising content is superior to non-shocking content in its ability to attract attention and facilitate memory for the advertisement' (Manchandra et al. 2003, 276). However, does remembering a shocking ad necessarily translate into acting on its message – the behavioral change sought by those who develop and produce PSAs? The findings of Manchandra et al. suggest that shock appeal may have some impact on message-relevant behavior.[7] Other scholars have argued that, while public-health shock PSAs maybe be memorable, they are most likely to translate into action when they are part of a larger campaign (Marketplace 2009).[8]

These studies suggest that those interested in arousing interest and activism around human rights violations are on the right track in employing shock in their appeals to readers. Indeed, Manchandra et al.'s conclusions (2003, 277) must be quite heartening to Kristof and others who engage in HR shock PSAs:

> In a public policy context we have shown that, although a shock advertisement generates an acknowledgment of norm violations among viewers, it also ensures that subjects remember the message and engage in message-relevant behavior. In a cluttered advertising environment, shocking advertising content ensures that the message will be heard.

Indeed, Manchandra et al. (ibid.) practically urge human rights activists including Kristof, Stengel, the writers of the human rights petitions, and others to carry on their shock-based work: 'Our findings suggest that advertising practitioners as well as public policymakers should consider the use of shocking content in their advertising campaigns' (ibid., 278).

Other factors, however, suggest that some curbing of enthusiasm might be in order. First, there is a difference between a public-health PSA and an HR PSA. The point of a public-health PSA is to raise awareness of an issue in order to change personal behavior ('here's shocking information about HIV/AIDS; you'd better use a condom'). The goal is to prompt behavior change in order to make the viewer's/reader's life better. In an HR PSA, an audience is prompted to take action to make someone *else's* life better – probably someone who lives far away ('here's shocking information about the HIV/AIDS pandemic in Africa – please be shocked enough to take action to stop it'). In other words, there is a much more direct connection between the message of a public-health PSA and its audience ('take action to save your own life') than between an HR PSA and its audience ('take action to save someone else's life'). For example, one person recalls being scared away from taking drugs after being shown a film in school of an autopsy on a drug addict: 'It did not pull any punches, it was a straight film showing everything from the pulling of the girl out of the freezer to cutting open [*sic*] right through to the pictures showing what drugs do to the body ... It scared me ****less' (Daily Mail Reporter 2011). It seems less likely that this sense of fear would be as present for the audience of an HR PSA because the message is much further removed ('don't change your behavior and you may die' versus 'don't change your behavior and someone else may die'). One can only conjecture that this added distance between a policy issue and the intended audience impacts how effective HR shock PSAs are. Much more research needs to be done before we can be confident that Manchandra et al.'s conclusions translate from public-health PSAs to HR PSAs.

A second factor that might undermine the idea that shock should be used in the service of HR PSAs is the question of whether there is such a thing as too much shock – that is, whether pictures of starving children or mutilated bodies can actually turn people off, or be deemed too upsetting, disturbing, or disgusting. There is a fine line between turning the page because of insufficient shock (either because of 'bad news' clutter or psychic numbing – 'same old stories coming out of Africa') and turning the page because of too much shock ('I can't bear to look at these pictures, so I must look away'). Either way, the message is tuned out and the page is turned, defeating the behavior-inducing purpose of an HR PSA. Again, more research needs to be done on what makes an HR PSA too mild versus too graphic before we can fully understand how well they work and when they may best be used.

There is also a third reason why, despite Manchandra et al.'s conclusions that shock works and should be considered, those wishing to elicit action around human rights abuses might think twice about using an HR shock PSA to do so: they may, in fact, have unintended consequences. First, they may make the audience less likely, rather than more likely, to act by undermining the sense of cosmopolitanism needed to elicit action on behalf of distant suffering. More serious is the possibility that HR shock PSAs can backfire and actually do the victims of human rights violations more harm than good. Finally, HR shock PSAs, precisely because they are so shocking, run the risk of being co-opted for political purposes. For reasons explained below, all three unintended consequences are especially likely to occur around HR shock PSAs that focus on gender-based violations.

Most of the HR shock PSAs described above – the petitions on the treatment of Afghan women and the possible stoning of Amina Lawal, acid burning of women in Pakistan, female genital cutting, and Aisha's and Hena's punishment under sharia law – relate to private-sphere violations suffered by women living in non-Western societies. Obviously shock can be used to raise awareness about all types of human rights violations (for example, Kristof's graphic op-ed on the Darfuri genocide, as described above); it does, however, seem to be a particularly favored tactic to highlight gender-based violations. Some feminists have pointed out that non-Western cultural traditions surrounding the sexual behavior of women (and control thereof) are particularly prone to being sensationalized by Westerners, academics and media alike. If this is true, then HR shock PSAs may be getting caught up in the universalist/cultural relativist debate,[9] with Western human rights activists such as Nicholas Kristof and the writers of the 'Save Amina' petition taking the universalist position, decrying the 'barbaric' cultural practices 'endured' by women in non-Western settings. Exoticized violence against women – especially to control their sexuality – is perhaps unsurprisingly then carried over into HR PSAs to end these cultural practices. What do feminists make of this sensationalizing of violent cultural practices for the sake of condemning them, and how might this affect the efficacy of HR PSAs that use shocking prose and images for the same purpose? Three possible effects are examined in the next section.

Exoticizing the 'other' Some feminists, mainly postcolonial feminists, view the universalist approach as tantamount to imperialism: 'Postcolonial feminism charges that global feminist [i.e. universalist] criticisms of cultural practices outside the West frequently are forms of "imperial feminism" or "feminist Orientalism," often exoticizing and sensationalizing non-Western cultural practices by focusing on their sexual aspects' (Jagger 2005, 56). Alison M. Jagger, for example, argues that the use of sensational language to denounce some non-Western cultural practices is a favorite means by which Western feminists have endeavored to 'save' women subject to these practices. She notes that 'the popular press regularly runs stories about non-Western practices it finds disturbing, especially when these practices concern women's sexuality,' mentioning several practices that could almost serve as an index of Kristof op-eds: 'arranged marriage, "sexual slavery," dowry murder ("bride burning"), "honor" killings, genital cutting ("circumcision," "mutilation"), sex-selective abortion and female infanticide' (ibid.). Feminist legal theorist Leti Volpp concurs: 'Only certain problems receive coverage or generate concern, namely those used to illustrate the alien and bizarre oppression of women of color; for example, sati [widows' self-immolation], dowry death, veiling, female genital surgeries, female infanticide, marriage by capture, purdah [concealment of women from men], polygamy, foot-binding, and arranged marriages' (Volpp 2001, 1208). In what could be a direct response to Jagger or Volpp, not only is Kristof aware of the charge of cultural imperialism, he almost appears to embrace it: 'is it cultural imperialism for Westerners to oppose genital mutilation?' he asks; 'yes, perhaps, but it's also justified. Some cultural practices such as genital mutilation – or foot-binding or bride-burning – are too brutish to defer to,' he replies (Kristof 2011c). Jagger finds this sensationalized/shocking approach to gendered injustices problematic because it creates a dichotomy of 'their' (traditional/illiberal) treatment of women versus 'our' (advanced/liberal) treatment of women.

This dichotomy is problematic for various reasons, Jagger argues. First, it is premised on what she calls the 'injustice by culture' argument, which asserts that a major cause of suffering among women in poor countries is unjust treatment in accordance with local cultural traditions (Jagger 2005, 61). While it is true, she argues, that women in these societies tend to suffer disproportionately from religious and cultural laws that apply only to members of specific religions or cultures, this thesis ignores that many of the abuses women suffer in non-Western cultures are compounded by extreme poverty – a poverty that cannot be understood exclusively in terms of unjust local traditions. Jagger points instead to contemporary processes of economic globalization 'regulated by the Western-inspired and Western-imposed principles and policies of neoliberalism' (ibid., 62). In other words, the West is highly complicit in the suffering of non-Western women, but the witting or unwitting endorsement of the 'injustice by culture' thesis obscures this reality. Cultural practices, this argument states, are constrained by structural forces, and well-meaning pleas to eradicate violent cultural practices will come to naught if human rights activists fail to acknowledge this fact. Relating this to HR shock PSAs, Jagger would argue that their relentless and graphic focus on exotic sexual violence ignores deeper root causes of violence against women. This, of course, has important consequences for the type of activism that might result from any call to action. Should one fight to end female genital cutting (as Kristof would have his readers do[10]), or should one instead fight to improve women's economic independence so that they have economic survivability outside marriage and can thus forgo the practice if they so choose (an action more in line with Jagger's argument). In a provocative statement, Jagger adds, 'rather than simply blaming Amina Lawal's culture, we should begin by taking our own feet off her neck' (ibid., 75).

A second, and related, problem with Western press treatments of non-Western women's human rights violations, according to Jagger, is that they tend to overlook just how much Western interventionism has accompanied these violations. Again, Western complicity is evident, as Jagger notes: 'It must be acknowledged that some of the same Western powers that trumpet democracy and liberalism at home support undemocratic and gender-conservative regimes abroad, fomenting coups, dictatorships, and civil wars.' Indeed, 'Western powers may reinforce or even impose gender-conservative cultures on non-Western societies by supporting conservative factions of their populations' (ibid., 69 and 66). In terms of our HR PSA analysis, it can appear contradictory or even hypocritical to try to motivate an audience to care about the treatment of women overseas by using shock, without also acknowledging how the audience members' own governments may have played a role in the violations that are so shockingly portrayed. While the Aisha cover photo was criticized for many reasons, discussed in more detail below, one criticism was precisely related to what was perceived to be the US government's (and *TIME Magazine*'s) hypocrisy. As one blogger wrote, using the mutilated face of Aisha to make an implicit argument for a continued US presence in Afghanistan is 'one of the most rank propaganda plays of the Afghanistan war' (Crowe 2010). Derrick Crowe – writing in the blog *SpeakEasy* that is linked to the online news magazine *AlterNet* – and many others are perhaps most upset by the headline featured alongside Aisha's picture: 'What happens if we leave Afghanistan' (no question mark; a simple, declarative statement). As Crowe points out, Aisha's punishment at the hands of the Taliban 'isn't the picture of some as-yet-unrealized nightmarish future for Afghan women. It's the picture of the present.' He draws on a *Human Rights Watch* report on violence against women in Afghanistan to argue that current and former Taliban warlords operate with impunity, 'often with the tacit approval of key foreign governments and inter-governmental bodies' (*Human Rights Watch* 2010, 10, quoted in Crowe). Thus, despite *TIME Magazine*'s dire warning, through the shocking image of a woman with no nose, of what will happen to women's rights should the United States leave, Crowe and others respond with scorn: 'the fox is already in the henhouse. There is a very powerful set of anti-women's-equality caucuses already nested within the Afghan government that the US supports' (Crowe 2010). As a result, Crowe concludes that while *TIME Magazine* argues that women's rights will vanish should the US withdraw, the opposite will in fact occur: 'The US's massive troop presence and the escalating instability is strengthening the hand of the political forces that want to roll back women's political equality, so the longer we stay, the worse off women will be as they attempt to navigate the eventual political settlement of the conflict' (ibid.).

A third negative consequence of the essentializing and dichotomizing approach to non-Western 'illiberal' cultures versus Western 'liberal' ones, according to Jagger, is that it leads to a '"West is Best" mentality that takes for granted that Western culture is more advanced than non-Western culture' (Jagger 2005, 67). Western cultures are portrayed in Western media (which would include some HR shock PSAs) as 'dynamic, progressive, and egalitarian,' while non-Western cultures are portrayed as 'backward, barbaric, and patriarchal' (ibid.). Volpp concurs, arguing that the discourse surrounding sharia law by US academics and the media tends to 'reinscribe certain popular assumptions – that there exist communities of people who think it may be perfectly appropriate to engage in domestic violence, namely, those who are too ignorant, too primitive, too backward to know any better' (Volpp 2001, 1183–4). This is problematic for a host of reasons, not least of which is that it obscures gender-based human rights violations in the West; or, when such violence *is* acknowledged, it is seen as anomalous and individual in the West but intrinsic to non-Western cultures. Jagger sums up the problem by quoting Uma Narayan: 'When cultural explanations are offered only for violence against poor women in poor countries, the effect is to suggest that these women suffer "death by culture," a fate from which Western women seem curiously exempt' (Narayan 1997, 15, cited in Jagger 2005). Volpp adds that 'incidents of sexual violence in the West are frequently thought to reflect the behavior of a few deviants – rather than as part of our culture.'[11] Moreover, she argues, while culture is invoked to explain violence against foreign women, it is not similarly invoked to explain forms of violence that affect Western women. She offers the example of dowry murders in India versus death by domestic violence in the United States and argues that 'only one is used as a signifier of cultural backwardness' (Volpp 2001, 1186–7).

Returning to our analysis of shock media, feminists such as Jagger, Narayan, and Volpp would likely not be surprised that the number of HR PSAs that Nicholas Kristof devotes to violence against women in non-Western countries outnumbers those devoted to gender-based violence in the West by an order of magnitude. Domestic violence is, of course, endemic in the United States; one would be hard pressed, however, to find a single op-ed about US domestic violence in the *New York Times* with the kind of shock prose about acid burning and the accompanying graphic image of a faceless woman that Kristof used to highlight domestic violence in Pakistan.[12]

Moreover, the 'West is Best' mentality means that because HR shock PSAs are (overly) focused on civil and political rights violations in the form of bodily integrity violence (torture in the form of infibulation or cutting off noses or burning away faces, or cruel and unusual punishment in the form of lashings, for example), violations of other rights, such as social and economic rights, especially in the United States, are ignored. Jagger (2005, 69) writes that:

> ... the feminization of poverty is especially conspicuous in the United States, where women continue to suffer extensive violence. Thus, it must be recognized that the human rights especially of poor women are routinely violated even in liberal Western societies, and on some accounts women fared better in the erstwhile Second World than in the First World, for much of the twentieth century.

HR shock PSAs regularly highlight poverty-based violence suffered by women around the world. Kristof, for example, has written numerous shocking op-eds about maternal mortality in Africa, or the consequences of insufficient prenatal medical care, such as obstetric fistulas (describing one woman sufferer thus: she 'endures internal injuries that leave her incontinent – steadily trickling urine and sometimes feces through her vagina. She stinks. She becomes a pariah' [Kristof 2009a]). In contrast, shocking descriptions of the real consequences of poverty borne by US women are conspicuous by their absence.

While all of the aforementioned effects of using shocking language and images to raise awareness of gender-based human rights violations suffered by women in non-Western cultures are obviously problematic in and of themselves, taken together they produce what is arguably the most serious negative side effect of gender-based HR shock PSAs: that rather than prompting action to end violations, they instead reinforce apathy. In other words, HR shock PSAs may produce the wholly unintended consequence that they make the audience less, rather than more, likely to act. The reason for this relates to the theory of cosmopolitanism offered by Lilie Chouliaraki. Focusing on television reporting of human rights atrocities, Chouliaraki's interest lies in determining when the media are able to create a global public with a sense of social responsibility toward the distant sufferer; she calls such an ethically engaged public the cosmopolitan citizenry. Referring to the need to cut through the disaster clutter, she asks whether, in an era of 'constant bombardment with humanitarian emergencies,' the media can shape 'an ethical sensibility that extends beyond our own "neighborhood"?' (Chouliaraki 2006, 1). The questions she poses are clearly applicable to this study of shock media: 'How are certain scenes of suffering construed as being of no concern to Western spectators or capable of arousing the spectators' emotions? How can we differentiate between representations of suffering that may simply bring a tear to a spectator's eye and those that may actually make a difference in the sufferers' lives?' (ibid., 7). In sum, Chouliaraki investigates the conditions under which media reports, in our case HR PSAs, 'induce displays of global care for people we know nothing about and will never meet' or promote 'the conditions under which it is possible for the media to cultivate an ideal identity for the spectator as a citizen of the world – literally a cosmopolitan' (ibid., 2). She is skeptical that media can serve as a motivator for activism – arguing that 'despite the instantaneous and global reach of visibility that [media] technologies have achieved, the optimistic celebration of our planet as a global village or the [audience] as a new cosmopolitan should be held in check' (ibid., 4) – and the reason for her pessimism relates precisely to the various feminist critiques of shock media noted above. The crux of her argument is that some 'news texts construe the misfortune of distant sufferers as a case of action,' while others 'construe the scene of suffering as being of no concern to the specta-tors' (ibid., 6). Like Jagger, Volpp, and others, Chouliaraki is concerned with news constructions that create the dichotomous 'we' versus an 'other.' The 'we' is construed as inhabiting an imagined community and residing in a zone of safety called the West, while the 'other' is construed as living in a zone of suffering (ibid., 10). The task for media is to 'cultivate a "beyond the nation" cultural resonance among Western audiences' (ibid., 12). Her analysis of why this is so difficult to accomplish (she decries the 'relatively weak potential for public identifications in Western media' [ibid.]) points again in the direction of questioning the tactic of trying to shock the audience into action. Cosmopolitanism is so rare, she says, because the current 'politics of pity' in the media produces 'narcissistic emotions about the suffering "other" that cannot move the spectator beyond the reflex of caring only for those like "us."' Rather, she argues, a 'culture of intimacy' is created that 'reserves the potential for us to pity "our" own suffering and leaves the far away "other" outside our horizon of care and responsibility' (ibid., 13–14). When media portrayals of suffering fail to reduce the proximity between the audience and the sufferer, any proposed action to alleviate their misfortunes is less likely to follow. Combining Chouliaraki's argument with the feminist critique of Western media treatments of non-Western cultural practices surrounding women's sexuality, one can argue that HR shock PSAs are the form of activism *least* likely to connect the spectator with the sufferer. HR shock PSAs, in other words, despite their goals to the contrary, do not – in this theory – serve as a 'space of cosmopolitan agency,' capable of moving the public beyond its own community – that of the West. As a result, members of the viewing or reading public are rarely more than communitarian spectators, who respond one-sidedly to Western suffering alone (ibid., 187–90). Referring to Western media constructions of the Amina Lawal case, Chouliaraki argues that 'the humanness of the Nigerian woman, for example, remains suspended between a condition thoroughly "universal" – her motherhood – and thoroughly "alien" to Western experience – her life under the sharia rule' (ibid., 191).

Anna Szörényi, in a study on visual representations of refugees, makes an argument very similar to Chouliaraki's. Her work has focused on collections of refugee images that were created specifically as part of a 'worldwide project of arousing sympathy for refugees,' a project with which Kristof would undoubtedly identify.[13] Szörényi's argument, like Chouliaraki's, links the feminist critique of shock media and the likelihood of action on behalf of refugees, arguing that the images of and texts about refugees 'work to produce spectacle rather than empathy in that they implicitly propagate a world view divided along imperialist lines, in which the audience is expected to occupy the position of privileged viewing agent while refugees are positioned as viewed objects' (Szörényi 2006, 24). The result of this dichotomy, she argues, is that refugees are 'constructed both visually and verbally so as to make it clear that one of the most persistent and telling of these lines of demarcation is that between "us" and "them." The end result is that in spite of their professed humanitarian concern, such books seem designed to reiterate, rather than challenge, the uneven distribution of suffering across the globe' (ibid.). Like Chouliaraki, Szörényi is pessimistic about the ability of images of refugees, who are presented as both homogeneous and exotic, to produce action to help them. When their conditions are presented as inevitable (just another African humanitarian crisis), refugee images tend to 'emphasise the *distance* between the viewer and (any responsibility for) the geo-political realities that have created this particular scene' (ibid., 30; italics in original). Even worse, they may well have the opposite effect, because 'much can go astray with this projected progression from feeling to action. Not least ... is the tendency for such images, which always seem to depict something occurring "elsewhere" and at a distance, to induce *mourning* – a distinctly non-active response ... One does not try to help the already dead. And so there is a risk that [refugee images], unparalleled in provoking *feeling*, also tend to provoke resignation and passivity' (ibid.; italics in original).

Backlash If the first unintended consequence of HR shock PSAs, especially those focused on gender-based violence, is that their portrayal of an exoticized 'other' makes action on their behalf less likely, a second consequence is that they may backfire, producing a backlash that actually does these women more harm than good. The argument here is that the use of shocking language – language that depicts non-Western cultures as 'barbaric' – can serve to further entrench those cultural practices, as a defense against a Western neocolonial onslaught. Such was the case with the 'Save Amina' shock petition. Soon after the petition made the global rounds, lawyers for two Nigerian human rights NGOs representing Lawal sent their own email appeal – urging people to ignore the petition, arguing that the intense international pressure was resulting in a real threat of vigilantism, with proponents of sharia law threatening to take matters into their own hands if the death sentence were overturned. 'In trying to save the woman's life, they said, the signers may be putting her – and her Nigerian supporters – at risk' (Sengupta 2003). As evidence, the lawyers pointed to a 1999 case, in which an unmarried teenage girl was sentenced to 100 lashes by cane in an Islamic court for fornication. To pre-empt a reversal of the decision as a result of international protest, the pro-sharia governor of the state had the sentence carried out before an appeal could be filed (ibid.). There was a real threat, Lawal's lawyers argued, of this happening to her, especially because of the use of shock media to 'save' her:

> Dominant colonialist discourses and the mainstream international
> media have presented Islam (and Africa) as the barbaric and savage
> Other. Please do not buy into this. Accepting stereotypes that present

Islam as incompatible with human rights not only perpetuates racism but also confirms the claims of right-wing politico-religious extremists in all of our contexts (quoted in Jagger 2005, 73).

Volpp perhaps best sums up how HR shock PSAs have the potential to backfire, resulting in the exact opposite of what they intended: 'a missionary feminist effort assuming West is Best incurs a defensive reaction from members of criticized communities, and thus plays into the hands of those who choose to defend sex-subordinating behavior in the name of cultural nationalism' (Volpp 2001, 1216).

The political uses of shock media A third unintended consequence of HR shock PSAs is that they can be co-opted for reasons for which they were never intended; in other words, they can be manipulated for political purposes. One major cause of the outcry against the Aisha cover photograph in *TIME Magazine* is the belief that human rights abuses against women were invoked for propagandistic purposes. The most vociferous criticism of the cover picture and its accompanying article could be found on political blogs and online news websites, where numerous bloggers and online journalists, along with hundreds of readers, asserted that the picture and article had little to do with US concern for Afghan women; rather, women's rights were conveniently exploited to score political points.[14] Derrick Crowe, for example, argued that 'using the rights of women as a justification for extending our massive US troop presence in Afghanistan is a recipe for failure on this issue and for the betrayal and heartbreak of those who care about the fate of Afghan women' (Crowe 2010). In another example, Michael Shaw, writing for *Bag News Notes*, a web news site dedicated to the analysis of news images and the politics of imagery, posed a series of questions about the Aisha pictures for his readers to contemplate, all of which related to the political manipulation of Afghan women. A few of these questions include: 'Any surprise that this "tug at your heart" cover comes out just days after WikiLeaks brings the failure of the Afghan campaign into the light?' and 'Isn't this title ... applying emotional blackmail and exploiting gender politics to pitch for the status quo – a continued US military involvement?' Readers of this post agreed overwhelmingly with these sentiments, with one writing that 'it's emotional manipulation designed to provoke knee-jerk revulsion and pity (which it does) in order to get those home (war) fires burning again regarding this "war" (read occupation).' Another reader posed the question more succinctly: 'Since when was the US military a feminist organization?' (Shaw 2010). In another example, Allison Kilkenny, in a blog called *Unreported* that is dedicated to independent journalism, accuses *TIME Magazine* of 'slap[ping] this poor girl on the cover as a way to pimp their nation-building bias' (Kilkenny 2010). In fact, peace scholar David Cortright claims on the *24 Peace Scholars* blog that the US government and NATO were not only aware that Afghan women could be, if not exploited, then at least used to shore up public support for the war effort, they encouraged it. Cortright reveals that among the almost 10,000 documents leaked by WikiLeaks was a March 2010 Central Intelligence Agency (CIA) memorandum that offered recommendations on how to bolster public opinion in Europe in the face of growing skepticism. One recommendation read:

> Afghan women could serve as ideal messengers in humanizing the ISAF [International Security Assistance Force] role in combating the Taliban because of women's ability to speak personally and credibly about their experiences under the Taliban, their aspirations for the future, and their fears of a Taliban victory. Outreach initiatives that create media opportunities for Afghan women to share their stories with French, German, and other European women could help to overcome pervasive skepticism among women in Western Europe toward the ISAF mission (Cortright 2010).

Thus, when *TIME Magazine* published its 'Aisha' issue, it did not take long for critics of the war to see it as the CIA's recommended media strategy at work. One blog reader summed up the strategy of using Aisha to boost public support: 'the counter-sanctuary, anti-safe-haven, going-after-AQ [al Qaeda] rationale is so obviously bankrupt as to leave the human rights argument as the single reed in the wind, the one thing that supporters of the war can point to as an unvarnished evil of US departure: innocent people will be killed' (Gulliver 2010).

This was not the first time that the treatment of women by the Taliban was invoked as a reason for US military intervention in Afghanistan. It was also not the first time that shock was used to make the argument. In November 2001, Laura Bush, wife of then-President George Bush, took over the presidential weekly radio address (the first time a first lady had done so since the inception of these addresses in 1982) to condemn the treatment of women in Afghanistan. The use of shock prose for political ends was obvious. Noting, for example, that 'only the terrorists and the Taliban threaten to pull out women's fingernails for wearing nail polish,' Bush asserted that 'civilized people throughout the world are speaking out in horror – not only because our hearts break for the women and children in Afghanistan, but also because in Afghanistan, we see the world the terrorists would like to impose on the rest of us' (White House 2001).

Is there something about HR shock PSAs that leads people to use them opportunistically? One could argue that there is indeed a correlation between the type of sensationalized language used to denounce gender-based cultural practices that Jagger, Volpp and others warn against, and exploiting the condition of women for political purposes. In other words, the more that non-Western societies are 'othered' and the more their cultures are portrayed as 'barbaric,' the easier it is to manipulate gender-based human rights violations for propagandistic purposes. In short, Laura Bush and *TIME Magazine* were able to use Aisha and other Afghan women for their own political purposes precisely *because* people like Nicholas Kristof had long made the treatment of women under sharia law a focus of their HR shock PSAs. HR shock PSAs, in other words, may have inadvertently created a ready-made trope – women who live in Afghanistan are forced to endure cruel and unusual (i.e. exotic) violent cultural practices and are punished unjustly for refusing to do so – that could easily be tapped into for political purposes.

To conclude and summarize this long analysis of how HR shock PSAs may undermine their own goals, we can compare Nicholas Kristof's op-eds with the work of feminist critics of gender-based PSAs – two bodies of work with the shared goal of reducing worldwide violence against women – to see just how divided feminists can be when it comes to identifying the best tactics to promote women's rights. The crux of the feminist critique of Western media portrayals of gender-based violence is that they promote the idea that women in non-Western cultures are in need of 'saving' and that the saving will be done by Westerners through, as Jagger says, 'proselytizing supposedly Western values or raising consciousness about the injustice of non-Western practices' (Jagger 2005, 70). Nowhere was the act of 'saving' more explicit than when Kristof himself bought two Cambodian teenage sex workers from their traffickers and returned them to their families. Not surprisingly, the act was met with some criticism, such as that of the reader who wrote that 'the same Western paternalist theme emerged. The women were victims, and Nick was there to rescue them' (Kristof 2010). Kristof is aware of his critics, noting that some readers have asked 'why many of my columns about Africa seem to portray "black Africans as victims," and '"white foreigners as their saviors."' Rather than denying the charge, Kristof responded that 'very often I do go to developing countries where local people are doing extraordinary work, and instead I tend to focus on some foreigner, often some American, who's doing something there.' In explaining why he does this, Kristof reiterated the view of Paul Slovic, noting that 'it's very difficult to engage readers and viewers in distant crises' and repeating his claim that humanitarians need to become better marketers of their causes (ibid.). What exactly are Kristof's self-described marketing tools? First, he uses bridge characters – people with whom readers can immediately identify. Given that we tend to identify most with people who are like us (a sentiment with which both Slovic and Chouliaraki would agree), Kristof concludes that 'often the best way to draw readers in is to use an American or European as a vehicle to introduce the subject and build a connection' (ibid.). In an article un-ironically titled 'Nicholas Kristof's advice for saving the world' (Kristof 2009b), he provides further details of his methodology. The second method he suggests is to focus on the individual and not the crisis, arguing that 'donors [didn't] want to help ease a crisis personified by a child; they just wanted to help one person – and to hell with the crisis.'[15] Third, he says, 'I learned that readers cared above all about girls, so when I came across a young man with a compelling story, I would apologize and ask him if he knew any girls with similar problems' (ibid.). Finally, he advises his readers interested in becoming humanitarians, 'come back with photos of her – or, better, video that you put on a blog or web site.'

This analysis highlights an apparent disconnect. On the one hand, what are the main concerns of feminist critics of HR shock PSAs? That their focus on shocking images and descriptions of women that are not contextualized (Jagger's 'root cause' complaint) leads to the idea that these women can only be 'saved' by Westerners. On the other hand, what is prescribed in the 'how to' guide of the best-known author of these PSAs in Western mainstream media, Nicholas Kristof? Focus on Westerners doing good in foreign lands, use images, focus on women, and leave out the context. Both sides are concerned with alleviating suffering. Both, however, seem miles apart in their analysis of how to get there. The first side argues that the type of 'advertising' in which Kristof engages will not only be ineffective (i.e. it will fail to elicit a cosmopolitan response), it will backfire and do these women more harm than good. Kristof, on the other hand, after years of writing about humanitarian crises in the global South, insists that the type of HR shock PSA he uses is the only way to get anyone to notice, much less care about, human rights atrocities that occur a great distance away from his audience.

Conclusion

This chapter has applied what is known about the effectiveness of shock advertising, especially in relation to public safety advertisements or PSAs, to the field of human rights. Human rights shock advertisements, in the form of op-eds, petitions, or 'objective' news reporting, use graphic and disturbing images and prose to try to shock readers into taking action on a particular human rights issue, from genocide in Darfur, to female genital cutting, to the treatment of women under sharia law, to famine in Somalia. The analysis here of the pros and cons of using HR shock PSAs has focused largely on the feminist critique of gender-based 'shockvertising.' While they certainly garner much attention and generate debate – Nicholas Kristof's op-ed on female genital cutting generated 224 online reader responses and a Google search for '*TIME Magazine* Aisha cover' generates 300,000 hits – there are also some unintended consequences that should temper any unbridled enthusiasm for their use.

Lingering ethical issues There are many other issues regarding HR shock PSAs that this chapter has not delved into, but that are important and should be studied. For example, there are a number of ethical issues surrounding the use of shocking images of mutilated women – their noses cut off, their faces burned away – or dead bodies – beaten so badly they are unrecognizable. Two such issues are noted very briefly here, both of which deserve a chapter unto themselves. First, some people have pointed to an apparent double standard in which images of dying or dead Africans or other people of color are regularly published by Western news media that would never, out of a sense of respect, show similar pictures of Western white people. Criticizing a *TIME Magazine* photo essay on AIDS in Africa that contains ten images of a woman slowly bleeding to death as she struggles to give birth to a second twin, twenty-four hours after the first (see Addario 2010 for images), Kenyan journalist Rasna Warah, referring to the images as 'death pornography,' asks:

> Why is it that death is considered a private, sacred affair when the person dying is not an African, but a public event when the dying is an African? ... Here, the author and photographer strip [the woman] of all dignity, parading her in her very desperate moments for the world to see. Would these pictures have been published if she was white?

Warah acknowledges that the photo essay was meant to be an HR shock PSA, intended to raise awareness about the high rates of maternal mortality in Africa. Nevertheless, she says: 'Westerners give their own dead the respect they deserve, but strip others – Africans in particular – of this respect at every opportunity' (Warah 2010). Allison Kilkenny (2010) makes a similar point from another angle. Writing about the Aisha cover, she notes the hypocrisy of being unwilling to show dead American soldiers while at the same time willing to show pictures of mutilated Afghans:

> ... the media hesitates to show the true consequences of war. For a long time, the Bush administration placed a ban on photographing military coffins, and though the Obama White House has since lifted that ban, the media appears to be complacent in shielding the US population from the ugliness of occupation – unless, of course, it's for the purpose of nation-building propaganda. In that event, *TIME* is willing to put a copy of a horrifically mutilated young girl in every household.

A second ethical issue with HR shock PSAs, not unrelated to the first, is the commodification of suffering. As Warah notes: 'the Dying African's last moments are often captured on film and shown at fundraisers.' Indeed, 'the more graphic [the images] are, the more money they help to raise' (Warah 2010). What's more, Nicholas Kristof quite publicly urges aid NGOs and humanitarians to 'embrace the dark arts of marketing spin' (Kristof 2009b).[16] What is the fine line between exploitation and raising awareness, and how does that line shift when requests for money are added to the equation? As much as most NGOs would be loath to admit that they use graphic images in part to raise funds, as one writer points out, 'the truth is that the development sector, just like any other business, needs revenue to survive. Too frequently, this quest for funding uses these kinds of dehumanizing images to draw pity, charity, and eventually donations' (McNicholl 2010). Arthur and Joan Kleinman, writing about cultural appropriations of suffering, sum up the issue by asking, 'to what uses are experiences of suffering put?' They conclude that 'ultimately, we will have to engage the more ominous aspects of globalization, such as the commercialization of suffering, the commodification of experiences of atrocity and abuse, and the pornographic uses of degradation' (Kleinman and Kleinman 1996, 3 and 19).

Future research directions This chapter is certainly not the final word on the use of shock to motivate activism to end human rights abuses.

Even on the core question of the chapter – whether HR shock PSAs actually accomplish their goals – much is still unknown and in need of further study. As Chouliaraki states: 'it is, in my view, a key question on the agenda of media research today to investigate further, rather than celebrate, whether transnational news flows reproduce the spectators' communitarian concerns in the zone of safety or cultivate new connectivities between spectators and distant sufferers' (Chouliaraki 2006, 196). Beyond this, research could move into new directions, tackling related – but equally important – questions. For example, does shock work in the same way for economic rights violations as it does for violations of civil and political rights? As this chapter is being written, the world is witnessing an almost unprecedented famine in Somalia. The humanitarian crisis is front-page news on an almost daily basis, frequently accompanied by images that are in every way as shocking as arguably the most shocking depiction of suffering of all, Kevin Carter's 1994 *New York Times* photograph of a vulture perching near a little girl in Sudan who had collapsed from hunger (Lorch 1993).[17] Do these pictures have the same impact on viewers as pictures of tortured bodies? If not, how are they different? Is an audience more or less likely to respond to pictures of starving Africans as it is to pictures of Africans whose limbs have been hacked off in a civil war?

Further research is also warranted on the role of new media in shocking an audience. All sorts of videos of shocking human rights abuses are available for viewing on YouTube, for example, including the flogging of a teenage girl by militants in Pakistan's Swat Valley. Most theorizing about media, such as Chouliaraki's argument about how difficult it is to create a cosmopolitan citizenry, or Jagger's claims about the exoticizing of violence against women, have focused on either television or newspaper coverage of atrocities. Whether and how these claims translate to new media forms such as YouTube needs further investigation.

Finally, a third area ripe for further exploration is whether there exists some sort of 'shock fatigue,' similar to the better-known concept of compassion fatigue in which overexposure to suffering results in public apathy and a weakened sense of compassion and charity toward distant sufferers (Moeller 1999). If, as noted above, shock is used to cut through the clutter of bad news (just another African crisis or just another example of sharia law's treatment of women), what is to stop HR shock PSAs from contributing to this clutter? In other words, what if people become as desensitized to these 'shockvertisements' as they were to all the bad news that they were meant to break through? And what are the implications of an increasingly desensitized audience? Will those human rights activists and NGOs, in trying to get the attention of the audience, resort to more and more shock? Is there a way to stop the shock/fatigue spiral? Nicholas Kristof, frustrated and outraged by what he perceived to be insufficient response to his writing about the violence in Darfur, ratcheted up the shock by putting pictures of dead Darfuri children in his column. Kleinman and Kleinman question whether this type of ratcheting up actually achieves the goal of shocking an audience into action. What if, they ask, it backfires and leads to a sense of helplessness rather than empowerment? They write: 'another effect of the postmodern world's political and economic appropriation of images of such serious forms of suffering at a distance is that it has desensitized the viewer. Viewers are overwhelmed by the sheer number of atrocities. There is too much to see, and there appears to be too much to do anything about' (Kleinman and Kleinman 1996, 9). This, for them, is one of the lasting legacies of this particular moment in history: 'Thus, our epoch's dominating sense that complex problems can be neither understood nor fixed works with the massive globalization of images of suffering to produce moral fatigue, exhaustion of empathy, and political despair' (ibid.).

In the end, this Kristof/Kleinman debate sums up one of the major moral, ethical, and political dilemmas of our time. Nicholas Kristof believes, in effect, that 'if I show you these pictures of dead people, you will be moved to action,' to which Kleinman and Kleinman respond, 'if I look at more pictures of dead people, I will feel overwhelmed and feel as if there is nothing I can do.' In a world that is ever more rife with suffering, sorting out the answer to this debate is more important than ever and deserves serious and sustained analysis.

Notes

1 It is almost impossible to read about shockvertising without coming across the ads from the Italian clothing company Benetton, especially those created by Oliviero Toscani, the company's creative director between 1982 and 2000. Toscani was responsible for some of the most controversial and memorable advertisements in history, which included, among others, a photograph of a war cemetery during the Gulf War, an image of a boat overcrowded with Albanian refugees rejected by Italy, a picture of a Liberian soldier holding a human thigh bone, a series of photographs of real death-row inmates, a slain Croatian soldier's bloody uniform, a duck covered in oil, and – perhaps most famously – the final moments of a man dying of AIDS. More than any others, these ads appear to be a combination of both profit-seeking and PSA: each ad had a clear consciousness-raising message about pressing social issues

such as human rights infringements, war, racism, environmental degradation, slavery, and HIV/AIDS, among others, and yet no Benetton garment ever appeared in any of the ads (although a small Benetton logo did appear in the corner of each ad). In equal measure, the ads both evoked praise (and garnered awards) and produced outrage and boycotts. If nothing else, they elicited – as intended – pure shock. Many of these shocking Benetton images can be seen at www.fashionist.ca/2010/07/ benettons-most-controversial-advertising-campaigns.html.

2 The rest of the ad read: 'It's no secret society is obsessed with breasts, but what are we doing about breast cancer?'

3 According to Sally Engle Merry, an honor killing 'is the murder of a woman by her father or brother for engaging in sex outside marriage or for being suspected of doing so.' The function of these crimes, she argues, is to regulate women's sexuality, maintain a family's reputation, and to reinforce communities by preventing transgressions of their norms (Merry 2009, 129).

4 The use of shocking language to describe human rights violations is not the sole province of op-ed or petition writers. On occasion academic scholars also use language almost certainly chosen for its shock value. See Alison T. Slack (1988) for a description of infibulation that is almost exactly the same as Kristof's.

5 While Lawal did indeed face the threat of death by stoning at the time of the petition's distribution, her conviction was eventually overturned, after the Nigerian NGO BAOBAB for Women's Human Rights took up her case.

6 The use of shock media to change behavior spans the political spectrum, as seen in a pro-life/anti-choice argument for the use of shocking images of aborted fetuses that is nearly identical to Slovic's: 'Shocking pictures are indispensable for influencing that process precisely because they evoke emotion which crashes through psychic defenses impenetrable to "facts and logic"' (Priests for Life, n.d.).

7 This was measured in their study by the number of subjects who picked up HIV/AIDS-related material after exposure to fear appeals, information appeals, or shock appeals. Approximately one-half of the subjects exposed to shock and fear appeals picked up an AIDS-related item, compared with approximately 20 per cent in the information and control conditions (Manchandra et al. 2003, 276).

8 For example, one public-health shock campaign adopted by New York City was the use of graphic images to highlight the negative consequences of drinking sugar-laden drinks. One image, for example, showed a soda being poured into a glass, with the drink turning into globs of fat. While the image was shocking, it was embedded in a larger campaign designed to educate consumers about making healthier food choices, calorie counting, and physical exercise; the 'abominable abdominal' shock ads alone would do little but grab attention, some scholars argue, if they were not embedded in educational outreach about the root causes of obesity (Marketplace 2009).

9 According to Ann Elizabeth Mayer, the universalist position holds that all humans possess the same inalienable rights, and that the international community has

the right to judge, by reference to international standards, how states treat their own citizens. States, under this approach, are required to reform their constitutions and laws to bring them into conformity with international norms. In a conflict between traditional practices and international norms, in other words, the former must give way to the latter: international human rights trump local practices. Cultural relativists, on the other hand, argue that no cross-cultural or universal standards for evaluating state treatment of citizens exist; therefore, no society can legitimately judge or condemn another for its traditional practices. Often, cultural relativists object to the universalist approach as an attempt to foist Western values on non-Western cultures. The charge of cultural imperialism is frequently levied (Mayer 1995, 176). However, some feminists, such as Martha Nussbaum, argue that cultural relativism often serves as a pretext for excusing culturally based violations of universal human rights. Jagger quotes Nussbaum, for example, as referring to cultural relativism as '"politically correct" anti-essentialism that rationalizes "ancient religious taboos, the luxury of the pampered husband, ill health, ignorance, and death"' (Jagger 2005, 58). Leti Volpp argues the opposing position, noting that in the universalism/cultural relativism discourse, 'the values of Western liberalism are reified, defined as the opposite of culture ... What becomes codified are two falsely divided packages, one with the "stamp of human rights," and one without, each of which depends upon the other for its meaning and identity' (Volpp 2001, 1203).

10 In fact, it is difficult to know exactly what actions Kristof would have his readers take because he rarely recommends specific actions in his op-eds. Although his Darfur op-ed does urge his readers to contact their congressional representatives, none of the three gender-based op-eds described above contains any specific recommendations; this despite the fact that the op-ed on acid burning mentions the International Violence Against Women Act co-sponsored by Senators Joe Biden and Richard Lugar. While Kristof (2008) states his 'hope that with Mr. Biden's new influence the bill will pass in the next Congress,' he never urges his readers to take action to help ensure this.

11 Volpp cites a 1998 survey conducted by the Family Violence Prevention Fund to support her contention that domestic violence can be described as a cultural practice in the US: 31 per cent of American women report being physically or sexually abused by a husband or boyfriend at some point in their lives, and almost one-fifth of women reported experiencing a completed or attempted rape at some time in their lives (Volpp 2001, 1212).

12 To be fair to Kristof, he has not been completely silent on the issue of violence against women in the United States. In April 2011, for example – a month after writing about Hena's lashing in Bangladesh and a month before his column on infibulation in Africa – Kristof wrote an op-ed about sex trafficking in the United States entitled 'What about American girls sold on the streets?' (Kristof 2011b). It contains little shock prose and is not accompanied by any images, however. Most importantly, it is a rare exception

to his focus on violence against women in other countries. Even his 2002 op-ed, whose title 'Bush vs. women' might lead one to surmise that it is about US gender politics, is in fact an article about the impact on women around the world of the Bush administration's policies, such as its refusal to fund the United Nations Population Fund and his reinstatement of the 'global gag rule,' which prohibited US funds from going toward any foreign organization that supports (even if it does not perform) abortions. Returning to his familiar theme of using shock to highlight the plight of women 'over there,' Kristof writes: 'If I'm angry, it's because those figures conjure real faces of people I've met: Aisha Idis, a Sudanese peasant left incontinent after giving birth at fourteen, with no midwife or prenatal care, to a stillborn child; Mariam Karega, a young woman nursing her dying baby in a Tanzanian village far from any doctor; Sriy, a smart and vibrant thirteen-year-old Cambodian girl who was sold into prostitution by her stepfather and by now is probably dead of AIDS' (Kristof 2002).

13 Examples of collections of refugee images, which she likens to coffee-table books, include *Images of Exile* (UNHCR 1991) and *Migrations* (Salgado 2000).

14 Those who argued that the cover photograph and lead article were propaganda asserted that the true intention of *TIME Magazine* was to bolster US occupation, especially at a time when public support appeared to be waning. The timing of the issue's release also struck many as slightly too coincidental – coming out just days after WikiLeaks released 91,000 documents, many of them containing damaging information about failures in the Afghan campaign, putting the US government on the defensive. (The *New York Times* reported that 'administration officials acknowledged that the documents, released on the Internet by an organization called WikiLeaks, will make it harder for Mr. Obama as he tries to hang on to public and congressional support until the end of the year, when he has scheduled a review of the war effort' [Schmitt and Cooper 2010].) Some critics found the timing of the article and photograph suspicious for other reasons, coming as it did a week before congressional house leaders were set to hold a vote on a critical war-financing bill and two weeks after Richard Holbrooke, the then US Special Representative to Afghanistan and Pakistan, began making an argument that the Afghan war effort required a significant troop build-up. Taken together, these timing issues led critics to view the *TIME Magazine* cover as a deliberate media strategy to justify continued, and even increased, US military involvement in Afghanistan.

Most of the propaganda charges zeroed in specifically on the title that accompanied the photograph, 'What happens if we leave,' making the statement one of fact rather than a question. The title is also problematic, some argued, because the type of violence depicted on the cover wasn't poised to occur 'if' the United States left; it happened while the United States was there. 'What happens if we leave??? Didn't this girl meet this fate after we'd been there nine years?' asked Shaw (Shaw 2010). The false dichotomy suggested by the title – either we stay and women's rights are ensured, or we leave and abandon them to a terrible fate – also struck some as propagandistic. Irin Carmon, writing for the feminist online news site *Jezebel*, for example, writes 'there is an elision here between these women's oppression and what the US military presence can and should do about it, which in turn simplifies the complexities of the debate and turns it into, "Well, do you want to help Aisha or not?"' (Carmon 2010). Finally, the title is based on an empirically false premise, some argued – that is, that staying was actually having the effect of weakening an insurgency hostile to women's rights (Crowe 2010).

In terms of the content of Aryn Baker's accompanying article, Derrick Crowe offered an analysis that mirrors Alison Jagger's critique of gender-based HR PSAs: the magazine's framing of the issue obscures our own complicity in violence against women in Afghanistan; it implies that only we (i.e. the West) can save them; it argues that it is their culture/tradition that is killing Afghan women, and it is the task of US media to 'expose' their cultures (i.e. through HR PSAs such as the *TIME Magazine* Aisha issue) (ibid.).

15 Kristof cites an experiment by Slovic in which people were asked to donate to help hungry children in West Africa. One group was asked to help a seven-year-old girl named Rokia. A second was asked to donate to help millions of hungry children, while a third group was asked to help Rokia but was provided with statistical information that contextualized the problem of child hunger. People donated more than twice as much to help Rokia alone than a group of children. Surprisingly, he notes, providing the context

for the request actually decreased empathy: 'people were less willing to help Rokia when she represented a broader problem' (Kristof 2009b).

16 The ethics of profiting from PSAs is one that affects public-health PSAs as well. On the very lucrative cause branding associated with breast cancer awareness, see Fempeace 2011. Obviously, the commercial use of images of suffering are nowhere more apparent than in the Benetton ads described in note 1 above, in which pictures of atrocities were used to sell clothing.

17 Deemed one of the most iconic photos of suffering of all time, the image can be viewed at http://iconicphotos.wordpress. com/2009/08/12/vulture-stalking-a-child/.

References

Addario, Lynsey. 2010. 'Maternal mortality in Sierra Leone: The story of Mamma.' *TIME Magazine*, 4 June. www.time.com/time/ photogallery/0,29307,1993805,00. html.

Baker, Aryn. 2010. 'Afghan women and the return of the Taliban.' *TIME Magazine*, 29 July. www. time.com/time/magazine/ article/0,9171,2007407,00.html.

Boyle, Elizabeth Heger, and Andrea Hoeschen. 2001. 'Theorizing the form of media coverage over time.' *The Sociological Quarterly* 42(4): 511–27.

Carmon, Irin. 2010. 'A visual introduction to an Afghan woman's mutilation.' *Jezebel*, 29 July. http://jezebel.com/5599482/a-visual-introduction-to-an-afghan-womans-mutilation.

Change.org. 2011. 'About us.' www. change.org/about.

Chouliaraki, Lilie. 2006. *The Specta-*

torship of Suffering. London: Sage
Publications.

Cortright, David. 2010. 'War: What
Afghan women "want?"' *24
Peace Scholars* (blog), 3 August.
www.24peacescholars.net/?p=68.

Crowe, Derrick. 2010. '*TIME*'s epic
distortion of the plight of women
in Afghanistan.' *SpeakEasy* (blog),
31 July.

Daily Mail Reporter. 2011. 'From
drugs to mugs: Shocking before
and after photos show how drug
addiction takes devastating toll
on faces of users.' *MailOnline*,
25 February. www.dailymail.co.uk/
news/article-1360586/From-drugs-
mugs-shocking-photos-drug-
addiction-takes-toll.html.

Emery, David. 1999. 'Petition for
Afghan women's rights.' *About.
com*. http://urbanlegends.about.
com/library/blafghan.htm?p=1.

Fempeace. 2011. 'Pink-washed
profits.' *Feminist Peace Network*,
2 October. www.feministpeace
network.org/2011/10/02/pink-
washed-profits/.

Gulliver. 2010. 'What's hard to look
at.' *Ink Spots* (blog), 29 July.
http://tachesdhuile.blogspot.
com/2010/07/whats-hard-to-look-
at.html.

Human Rights Watch. 2010. *The 'Ten-
Dollar Talib' and Women's Rights:
Afghan Women and the Risks of
Reintegration and Reconciliation*.
New York: Human Rights Watch.

Imaginis. 2000. 'Breast cancer
ad campaign features models
with mastectomy scars.'
Imaginis.com, 31 January. www.
imaginis.com/breast-health-news/
breast-cancer-ad-campaign-fea-
tures-models-with-mastectomy-
scars-dateline-january-31-2000.

Jagger, Alison M. 2005. '"Saving
Amina": Global justice for women

and intercultural dialogue.' *Ethics
and International Affairs* 19(5):
55-75.

Kilkenny, Allison. 2010. '*TIME
Magazine* uses exploitive
photo to pimp nation-building.'
Unreported (blog), 29 July. http://
allisonkilkenny.com/2010/07/
time-magazine-uses-exploitive-
photo-to-pimp-nation-building/.

Kleinman, Arthur, and Joan
Kleinman. 1996. 'The appeal of
experience; the dismay of images:
Cultural appropriations of suffering in our times.' *Daedalus* 125(1):
1-23.

Kristof, Nicholas. 2002. 'Bush
vs. women.' *New York Times*,
16 August.

Kristof, Nicholas. 2005. 'The secret
genocide archive.' *New York
Times*, 23 February.

Kristof, Nicholas. 2008. 'Terrorism
that's personal.' *New York Times*,
30 November.

Kristof, Nicholas. 2009a. 'New life
for pariahs.' *New York Times*,
31 October.

Kristof, Nicholas. 2009b. 'Nicholas
Kristof's advice for saving the
world.' *OutsideOnline*, 30 November. www.outsideonline.com/
outdoor-adventure/Nicholas-
Kristof-s-Advice-for-Saving-the-
World.html?page=all.

Kristof, Nicholas. 2010. 'Westerners
on white horses ...' *New York
Times*, 14 July.

Kristof, Nicholas. 2011a. 'When a girl
is executed ... for being raped.'
New York Times, 30 March.

Kristof, Nicholas. 2011b. 'What
about American girls sold on the
streets?' *New York Times*, 23 April.

Kristof, Nicholas. 2011c. 'A rite of
torture for girls.' *New York Times*,
11 May.

Kristof, Nicholas, and Sheryl

WuDunn. 2009. *Half the Sky: Turning Oppression into Opportunity for Women Worldwide*. New York: Knopf.

Lorch, Donatella. 1993. 'Sudan is described as trying to placate the West.' *New York Times*, 26 March.

Los Angeles Times. 2011. 'FDA's new warning labels for cigarettes.' *Los Angeles Times*, 21 June. www.latimes.com/health/boostershots/la-he-smoking-cigarette-warning-labels-pictures,0,6757388. photogallery.

Manchandra, Rajesh V., Kristina D. Frankenberger, and Darren W. Dahl. 2003. 'Does it pay to shock? Reactions to shocking and nonshocking advertising content among university students.' *Journal of Advertising Research* 43(3): 268–80.

Marketplace. 2009. 'Do ads with high shock value work?' American Public Media. Original air date 14 October.

Mayer, Ann Elizabeth. 1995. 'Cultural particularism as a bar to women's rights: Reflections on the Middle Eastern experience.' In *Women's Rights, Human Rights: International Feminist Perspectives*, edited by Julie Peters and Andrea Wolper, 176–88. New York: Routledge.

McNicholl, Duncan. 2010. 'Perspectives on poverty.' *Water Wellness*, 28 April.

Merry, Sally Engle. 2009. *Gender Violence: A Cultural Perspective*. Malden, MA: Wiley-Blackwell.

Moeller, Susan D. 1999. *Compassion Fatigue: How the Media Sell Disease, Famine, War and Death*. New York: Routledge.

Narayan, Uma. 1997. *Dislocating Cultures: Identities, Traditions, and Third World Feminisms*. New York: Routledge.

Owens, Maggie. 2001. 'FCUK: Four letters too far.' *ABCNews.com*, 25 April. http://abcnews.go.com/Business/story?id=88278&page=1.

PetitionOnline.com. n.d. 'Save the life of Amina Lawal Kurami petition.' *PetitionOnline.com*. www.petitiononline.com/amina1/.

Priests for Life. n.d. 'The use of graphic images: Re-thinking the pro-life strategy.' *PriestsforLife.org*. www.priestsforlife.org/ resources/abortionimages/abortion graphics.htm.

Pulitzer Prizes. 2006. 'The 2006 Pulitzer Prize winners: Commentary.' *Pulitzer.org*. www.pulitzer.org/citation/2006-Commentary.

Salgado, Sebastiao. 2000. *Migrations: Humanity in Transition*. New York: Aperture.

Schmitt, Eric, and Helene Cooper. 2010. 'Leads add to pressure on White House over strategy.' *New York Times*, 26 July.

Sengupta, Somini. 2003. 'When do-gooders don't know what they're doing.' *New York Times*, 11 May. www.nytimes.com/2003/05/11/weekinreview/the-world-when-do-gooders-don-t-know-what-they-re-doing.html.

Shaw, Michael. 2010. 'What happens if we leave Afghanistan? ... Try, what's happening on this cover?' *Bag News Notes*, 29 July. www.bagnewsnotes.com/2010/07/your-turn-what-happens-if-we-leave-afghanistan/.

Slack, Allison T. 1988. 'Female circumcision: A critical appraisal.' *Human Rights Quarterly* 10(4): 437–86.

Slovic, Paul. 2007. '"If I look at the mass I will never act": Psychic numbing and genocide.' *Judgment and Decision Making* 2(2): 79–95.

Stevenson, Seth. 2006. 'Wham! Bam! Buy a VW, Ma'am!: The violent new Jetta ads.' *Slate*, 8 May. www.slate.com/id/2141286/.

Szörényi, Anna. 2006. 'The images speak for themselves? Reading refugee coffee-table books.' *Visual Studies* 21(1): 24–41.

TIME Magazine. 2010. Front cover. 9 August. www.time.com/time/covers/0,16641,20100809,00.html.

UNHCR (United Nations High Commissioner for Refugees). 1991. *Images of Exile: 1951–1991*. Geneva: UNHCR.

Volpp, Leti. 2001. 'Feminism versus multiculturalism.' *Columbia Law Review* 101(5): 1181–218.

Warah, Rasna. 2010. 'Images of the "Dying African" border on pornography.' *The Citizen*, 8 July. www.thecitizen.co.tz/editorial-analysis/19-editorial-comments/2856-images-of-the-dying-african-border-on-pornography.html.

White House. 2001. 'Radio address by Mrs. Bush,' 17 November. http://georgewbush-whitehouse.archives.gov/news/releases/2001/11/20011117.html.

Wilson, Duff. 2011. 'US releases graphic images to deter smokers.' *New York Times*, 21 June. www.nytimes.com/2011/06/22/health/policy/22smoke.html.

6 | Celebrity diplomats as mobilizers? Celebrities and activism in a hypermediated time

ANDREW F. COOPER AND JOSEPH F. TURCOTTE

Celebrities in the 'network society'

The early twenty-first century has been a time of unprecedented growth for communications and media industries. The established 'broadcast' forms of media – including the radio, television, and even the newspaper – that disseminate media content in a hierarchical and one-to-many way have been joined by a whole host of digital and networked communications media and content distribution platforms. Facilitated by the rise of the Internet, these technologies are based largely on platforms of the World Wide Web, which allows for greater interactivity among users and producers of information. These technologies have afforded activist movements new forms of outreach and coordination: 'The global Internet, then, is creating the base and the basis for an unparalleled worldwide anti-war/pro-peace and social justice movement during a time of terrorism, war, and intense political struggle' (Kahn and Kellner 2004, 88). The globally networked nature of the Internet allows content to be transmitted transnationally at unprecedented rates. It is safe to say, then, that the 'global village' that Marshall McLuhan (1962 and 1964) famously envisioned fifty years ago has come to pass.

This 'global village' in all its complex manifestations is being built upon the infrastructure of what Manuel Castells (2009a, 2009b and 2009c) describes as 'the network society,' a place where individuals as well as economic, cultural, and social flows and forces are associated with one another in different ways than in earlier generations. In particular, networks are the new orienting factor for how individuals interact with one another and organize the various aspects of their lives. This networked situation has resulted in new forms of citizen engagement and activism, facilitating the questioning of the legitimacy of various forms of government across the world. It is no surprise that recent uprisings in the Middle East and North Africa have been facilitated by networked communication technologies that disrupt the rigid hierarchies of established broadcast media models. As Riyaad Minty (quoted in Williams 2011), the head of social media at Al Jazeera, has described the process, use was made of traditional 'boots-on-the-ground' reporting from its correspondents that was also amplified through media sourced from Facebook, Twitter, and Flickr. By creating hashtags such as #sidibouzid (the Tunisian city where a street vendor set himself on fire and ushered in the events of the Arab Spring), a means was created to sidestep either restrictions on reporting or government tampering with the Internet, which, of course, remain serious concerns and possibilities.

While it is tempting to see these events as technologically driven uprisings, McLuhan reminded us long ago that the global village can be 'a place of very arduous interfaces and very abrasive situations' (McLuhan 1977, xx). Technological achievements alone are not enough to cause social change and the betterment of living conditions across the globe. Technologies can be implemented to restrict access just as easily as to enable it. A global village will be just as contested, dangerous, or disinterested a place as the citizens who occupy it. However, as Robert David Sack (1997, 257) points out, our current era of globalization with the accompanying technological advancements and increased interdependence among nations has brought new attention to the concerns of people in distant countries. Understanding media and activism in the early twenty-first century, then, requires a broad acknowledgment of the various ways in which social, economic, and productive flows and forces operate in the media realm of the day.

In this sea of widely dispersed and abundant media forms are new 'gatekeepers' that have the ability to disseminate and direct the narrative of the day. Whereas in previous generations these gatekeepers consisted of political, economic, and media elites, in the networked era a new form of gatekeeper is emerging. A diverse group of civil society actors, digital entrepreneurs, and activists now have the technological tools necessary to spread information to large groups of society with the click of a button. Remaining near the top of these forms of digital outreach are familiar faces: those of cultural celebrities. As a recent *Newsweek* article put it: 'In the age of Twitter-shortened attention spans, fame is an increasingly powerful weapon of diplomacy' (Avlon 2011) and for motivating change. Since the early days of Hollywood, celebrities have held a special place in the public imagination and 'In this new environment – fueled by social networking – fame is a potent commodity that can have more influence on public debate than many elected officials and even some nation-states' (ibid.). It is not too surprising then that in a hypermediated time such as the early twenty-first century – or what Jean Baudrillard (1994) would describe as 'hyperreality,' a time of a greatly expanded use of images and simulations in culture and society – celebrities remain prominent forces for capturing attention and initiating action.

However, as intimated above, spurred by networked and digital technological innovations, the twenty-four-hour news cycle, the ascendancy of soft media (in terms of the style and content of programming, especially in the mainstream news sector where focus has shifted from in-depth reports to gaining viewers), and the celebrity-dominated nature of consumer culture have undergone a radical shift. In place of the message-dissemination model of communication that predominated in the broadcast era, the emerging social and networked media society is developing into a more collaborative space where individuals interact with one another directly on an unmediated basis. In recent years, these converging circumstances have coalesced around a number of high-profile and tragic circumstances. From the tsunami that swept through Southeast Asia in 2004, to the ongoing humanitarian crisis in Sudan/Darfur, to the earthquake that decimated Haiti in January 2010, the responses to these crises-turned-media-events have highlighted the intersecting nature of media, culture, and celebrity. At play in such situations is the social and networked nature of contemporary culture, which allows individuals to become mobilized in a variety of ways. Facilitated by technologies such as Twitter, Facebook, and other online social networks, individuals have assembled and directed their efforts and resources toward responding to these crises.

Contained within this emerging collaborative space is the influence of celebrities and celebrity-driven culture. Situated at a privileged point within this networked world, celebrities are often arbiters and drivers of the topics of conversation. In response to humanitarian crises, celebrities have become active participants in the dialogues surrounding these events as well as in efforts to engage and respond in the front lines. From Sean Penn in Haiti to Angelina Jolie's 'Ripples of Genocide: Journey through Eastern Congo' (and activism in other places including Iraq and Chechnya), the efforts of George Clooney in Sudan/Darfur, and the U2 frontman, Bono, in a number of well-publicized efforts across the African continent, these celebrity diplomats are able to mobilize a great deal of attention to and engagement with human rights causes.

Building on the topics explored by one of the authors of this chapter (Cooper 2008a), this chapter explores the ways in which celebrities mobilize and/or demobilize activism and engagement. This chapter begins by highlighting the ways in which the structure of the media and star systems of the early twenty-first century provide celebrities with a privileged position from which to attract attention and generate responses. We then explore how these celebrity diplomats are implicated within international affairs generally and particular episodic situations more specifically. While celebrity involvement can generate increased attention and activism, the star system that develops these celebrities also entails a number of problematic elements. The chapter will then focus on the ways in which celebrities can serve to mobilize activism in its various forms. Ultimately, this chapter will contend that celebrities play an important role in helping to mobilize responses to human tragedy as well as for coalescing public attention around various global causes and initiatives.

Media and society: the role of the celebrity

In the media-driven society that is now dominant in most parts of the Western or industrialized (developed) world,[1] news and information are largely circulated within networks of the media or cultural industries. As Douglas Kellner (2010, 121) points out, under this framework news and information are often relayed in the form of a 'media spectacle,' that allows celebrities to act as influencers of what stories are and are not covered. For Kellner (ibid.), 'when daily cable news, presidential campaigns, and major media events are presented in the form of media spectacle it is likely that the media attention and often spectacle produced by celebrity activism will publicize their issues, and make such celebrity diplomats more public and perhaps effective advocates for their causes than normal diplomats.' Because of their privileged position(s) in this media ecosystem, celebrities are able to garner attention, and potentially support, for the causes they decide to promote. Celebrities 'can reach into people's lives and speak to them in ways that Oxfam [and other] spokesmen cannot,' says Phil Bloomer (quoted in Ford and Goodale, 2005), head of advocacy for Oxfam UK: 'they can reach out to people who might not normally listen to what Oxfam [or another advocacy group] has to say.' It is this intertwining of celebrities with the cultural imaginary, and their ability to address members of the public, that provides celebrities with such a prominent pulpit from which to address the world. The phenomenon of celebrity mobilization in domestic and international arenas, then, can be attributed to broad causes that include 'a psychological/emotional development linked to celebrity culture in more generalized terms' and the 'structure or environment in which celebrities operate' (Cooper 2008a, 10).

The relationship that celebrities have with the public at large can be attributed to the ways in which the media landscape uses these personalities to generate attention and desire. Public interest in celebrities – or celebrity personas – is not new (Lowenthal 1961). Prior to the advent of mass electronic media systems, the written word – largely in the form of newspapers and magazines – helped to sensationalize the news by framing stories and individuals in ways to elicit interest among the public, ultimately to generate sales and profits (see Cohen 2000). However, with the birth of electronic media, celebrity stars truly began to shine. The photographic image, which was deployed in print media previously, gained new import with the birth of the moving picture. Directors, producers, and filmmakers exploited this technology and developed the now ubiquitous close-up, helping to draw heightened levels of association between the viewer and on-screen personalities (Powdermaker 1947, 85). The Hollywood star system capitalized on this and developed what we would now call marketing and branding strategies to leverage the popularity of movie stars (see Dyer 1979). No longer were these celebrities removed from the public. Instead, the availability of film screenings along with magazine and press clippings generated increasing desire and affection from fans. In a harbinger of today's media-saturated, celebrity-obsessed situation, at the time 'the fans, usually a relatively young group, [were] obsessively and possessively interested in their particular stars' (Powdermaker 1947, 85). Soon other entertainment industries would follow suit as athletes and musicians, among others, had their images widely circulated (see Jermyn 2006). With the power of the image, these personas were manufactured and disseminated widely, thus instigating and building on their desire.

In this way, a new form of media-driven celebrity culture was added to the general cultural milieu. In the past, culture writ large included many manifestations of cultural life – art, handicrafts, language, tradition, community, story-telling, etc. Celebrity culture, however, focused on the relationship that individuals had with celebrities whom they would rarely (if ever) meet and with whom they shared little to no direct interaction or relationships. Instead, this culture was based upon voyeuristic desires to see others. These 'others' were then valorized, or disparaged, according to changing times and preferences. As Daniel Bronstein (1962, 63) rightly points out, under this scenario 'the celebrity is a person well-known for his [or her] well-knownness.' Joseph Epstein (2005, 9) reminds us, though, that celebrity in the sense described by Bronstein must be distinguished from fame: 'Fame, then, as I prefer to think of it, is based on true achievement; celebrity on broadcasting that achievement, or inventing something that, if not scrutinized too closely, might pass for achievement. Celebrity suggests ephemerality, while fame has a shot at reaching the happy shores of posterity.' This distinction is important to recall when describing 'celebrity culture.' A celebrity can be famous for being famous or for also having some discernible talent, while fame can be achieved without an accompanying level of celebrity. In a media entertainment-driven society, celebrity is highly ascribed as opposed to achievement-oriented (Rojek 2001), dependent on the ability to circulate messages and images of the star to others and to have recognition from the public.

Public interest in celebrities can be attributed to how they are represented and reproduced in cultural situations. In the contemporary situation, 'the cult of the individual – in which relatively few celebrities have a huge name and activity recognition – is supreme' (Cooper 2008a, 15). Following the lives of idolized individuals allows for a form of escape: 'Celebrity in America has always given us an outlet for our imagination, just as the gods and demigods of ancient Greece and Rome once did' (Neimark 1995). However, escapism is not the sole factor that contributes to the privileged position that celebrities hold in the cultural imaginary. The media involved in the dissemination of stories and images of celebrities contribute to a sentiment of attachment between the watcher and those being watched. Paul McDonald (1998, 176) summarizes this by arguing that 'cinema circulates the images of individual film performers and how those images may influence the ways in which we think of the identity of ourselves and others.' Celebrity images and narratives attract the attention of members of the public and also reorient the attitudes and ideas of those members of the public: 'it [is] *because* of the apparatus of manipulation and hype that stars could operate as a site for the working through of discourses on the construction of identity' (Holmes 2005, 14). This relationship between identity, ideas, and their celebrity offers celebrity activists an opportunity to influence public opinion and to effect change.

The hypermediated reality of the contemporary situation lends itself and contributes to this ability. Traditional media forms of broadcast distribution and advertising frame their content to attract the audience and invite them into the meaning-making processes. Intertextual references across various media and cultural situations encourage the audience to become more actively engaged in the creation and determination of meaning (Morris 2005, 698). In the network society this interpretation is furthered by the existence of social media and networked communication forms. Twitter, for example, provides a channel where the distributor of content and information has a personalized link or attachment to the receiver. The format of Twitter – where individuals or outlets follow one another – creates a form of intimate bond between the two parties, where an increased attachment, when compared with previous broadcast media that relied upon imagined forms of attachment (Anderson 1991), can be represented in a seemingly tangible way. At the same time, 'digital distributed networks like the web and Twitter do not exist as the only medium in any society, but work alongside older mass media that take the form of centralized broadcast systems' (Hands 2011, 119). Due to this interconnected relationship between emerging and established media forms, attention and attachments can be magnified through intertextual references. The bonds developed through media and communication technologies can be used to foster communities of members that can organize around a specific cause or purpose.

In the political realm, the mixing of celebrity persona into the campaign equation is not new (see Kamons 2007), but what *is* new are the technologies and strategies that can be employed. This was evident during the Democratic primary and US general election campaigns of Barack Obama. Capitalizing on the nature of media industries and the media spectacle, the Obama campaign was able to develop an unprecedented level of celebrity for its candidate – who had previously been a relatively unknown US senator – and help propel him to the office of the US presidency (Kellner 2010). In doing so, the campaign effectively used the rationale behind contemporary advertising by creating an association and relationship between Obama and the public so that the campaign could continue to attract attention and support (for more on this advertising technique, see Morris 2005, 705). The Obama campaign demonstrates how media, culture, and political savvy can be combined to promote a specific cause – in this case, the election of Barack Obama. For celebrity mobilizers who already have a developed following and position in the cultural sphere, similar techniques can be deployed to shape public opinion toward their causes.

The celebrity, citizens, and activism in a star-obsessed culture

Whereas Barack Obama began his journey to the US presidency as a relative unknown, celebrities in the realm of popular culture are able to exploit their privileged positions to achieve their desired goals. The aim is to address their audience and increase awareness of specific causes while also encouraging participation and action toward initiating change. In many cases, this participation or action comes in the form of creating shifts in public opinion that they hope will then be reflected in governmental decisions. The impetus, then, is to maximize awareness and acceptance of the need for action and to have this reflected in public opinion and ultimately public and state policy.

Celebrities are able to leverage the preferential attachments that they have with members of the public and have their messages easily received. In this sense, 'preferential attachment is the process wherein links are made not because of random factors, but for specific, determinate reasons' (Hands 2011, 112). The preferential attachments that celebrities enjoy are based upon the privileged position they hold in a culture obsessed with their lives and actions. Celebrity endorsements have long been used as a means of selling products through advertising, and the role of celebrities in political and social activism can be viewed in this light. At the same time, with more personal power and awareness, celebrities have begun to understand the reciprocal value that their involvement in policy and activist discussions can have: 'one reason for the newfound global agendas of celebrities is simply that today's stars have more autonomy than previous generations and many of them recognize the benefits of being a popular saint' (Drezner 2007, 23). The cadre of celebrities who endorsed Obama throughout his campaign may not have had an easily quantifiable effect on the outcome of the election but their involvement can certainly be viewed as helping to shape the narrative and attention given to the candidate (Hands 2011, 116). This celebrity boost was especially visible in the impact provided by the gradual ramping up of the support Obama received from Oprah Winfrey, through her signal on CNN's *Larry King Live* in May 2007 that she was endorsing Obama, to her hosting a successful fundraiser in September 2007 at her Santa Barbara home, and eventually her announcement in November 2007 that she would campaign for him in Iowa, New Hampshire, and South Carolina. Message control can be mixed with sentiments of attachment and admiration to enhance the relationship between the celebrity, their cause, and the members of the public with whom they communicate.

Through their mix of star power, attraction, and attachment, celebrities are able to generate public attention in ways that traditional actors in activist and international circles cannot. As Cooper (2008a, 7) has argued elsewhere, 'the advantages of linking individual star power to a collective project are clear. Celebrities have the power to frame issues in a manner that attracts visibility and new channels of communication at the mass as well as the elite levels.'

In a culture dominated by mass as well as emerging media forms, the ability of the celebrity to frame discussions is profound. As such, 'celebrities would appear to have a huge head start. They not only have the advantage of name recognition, but they can channel media focus onto their activities in a way that few NGOs [non-governmental organizations] and firms can' (ibid., 11). Celebrity culture and the structures of globalization and the media industry offer avenues for connecting with the public that cannot be matched by very many others in different positions. However, credibility remains a prime concern.

Celebrity activists who are seeking only publicity – or perhaps more importantly, those *perceived* in this way – can become a source of embarrassment for international organizations and global causes. Such celebrities can detract from the overall goals of the cause, attract attention only to themselves, misallocate scarce resources, and complicate on-the-ground efforts by their very presence. The United Nations has experienced instances of this with its selection of stars such as Geri 'Ginger Spice' Halliwell, who seemed ill suited for the complex role (see Cooper 2008a, 29–30) and did not seem credible in the eyes of the public. In the same sense, shortly after her release from prison in 2007, celebrity socialite Paris Hilton made an attempt at promoting the cause of animal rights and also planned a trip to Rwanda to draw attention to the plight of Africa's poor (see Hammel 2007). However, the public's apparent cynicism and dismissal of Hilton's activities ultimately caused the trip to be postponed (Reuters 2007). Other celebrities, including pop superstar Michael Jackson, have had mixed results trying to balance their public and private personas alongside social causes (see Van den Bulck and Panis 2010). Even an experienced celebrity activist such as Richard Gere has committed cultural gaffes, notably when he kissed an Indian Bollywood star on stage during a 2008 anti-AIDS event in New Delhi. Celebrity alone is thus not enough to make a personality a credible activist or mobilizer, yet it is dangerous to dismiss outright the intentions and actions of *all* celebrities based upon the poor results of a few.

Despite the failings of some ill-advised and misguided attempts by celebrities to capitalize on humanitarian efforts to extend their personal brands, there are significant instances where celebrities have positively impacted policy changes. As seen with George Clooney's efforts in Darfur and the establishment of South Sudan (Avlon 2011), the efforts of the late Princess Diana in the anti-landmine campaign (Cooper 2008a, 26–8), and the activist efforts of Bono as well as Angelina Jolie's efforts in Africa (ibid.), adept celebrity diplomats have demonstrated their ability to draw attention to serious issues in the public consciousness as well as in policy circles. Jolie's ability to use her celebrity status to draw attention to critical issues and also to frame her experiences in a way that the public can relate to (Barron 2009) demonstrates this. Angelina Jolie has upgraded the traditional format of celebrity activism through her involvement with the Council on Foreign Relations and the Clinton Global Initiative. On a fundamental level, nonetheless, Jolie's style remains grounded in the style developed by Audrey Hepburn in the late 1980s and built on in the 1990s by Princess Diana in the landmine campaign. Empathy for those on the front lines of disaster or conflict areas is pronounced. A huge amount of personal time and money is allocated to try to alleviate suffering. While the actions of celebrities cannot easily be correlated to public policy developments, their efforts can have a positive impact in having these issues added to the agendas of domestic and international discussions. There is also empirical survey evidence that indicates that the efforts of celebrities can influence public as well as political opinion.[2] For example, in Canada, which has relatively fewer instances of celebrity involvement in politics than in the United States, 'a survey of 456 young Anglophone Canadians indicated that Bono's beliefs influence the political beliefs of young Canadians, and he has helped to set the agenda for politicians' (Jackson 2007, 75). Efforts from celebrities to mobilize public and political action, then, can influence policy debates when performed in an effective way.

Celebrity diplomats and the international arena

Just as the media and communication industries are changing in the face of dramatic technological advances and the increased spread of globalization in the network society, the international relations arena is undergoing similar shifts. The global financial crisis of the late 2000s has underscored that rising states and emerging economies, whether termed BRICs (Brazil, Russia, India, and China) or BRICSAM (the BRICs plus South Africa, the ASEAN [Association of Southeast Asian Nations] states, and Mexico), are increasingly important actors at the global level. At the same time, traditionally state-centric modes of operation are being challenged by a host of civil society and NGOs that are negotiating for increased attention and involvement in decision-making processes. The international arena is no longer confined to the traditional clubs of Western, developed states and their governments. International affairs are increasingly open to a network of divergent and diverse interest groups. Jorge Heine (2008) describes this emerging tendency in international diplomacy as a shift toward 'network diplomacy' where a multi-stakeholder approach to decision-making and problem-solving is necessary. In this networked scenario there is room for new forms of actors in the international arena. As described above, due to their position in the contemporary hypermediated environment and their ability to attract and focus the attention of the public, celebrities – in the form of celebrity diplomats – have become actively involved in crafting narratives and pushing for policy changes.

When speaking about celebrity diplomats it is important to underscore the distinctions that separate them from traditional diplomats. We are not contending that celebrities are or should be the new and sole diplomats in international affairs. Neither are we suggesting that celebrity diplomats hold a dominant position in the sphere of agenda-setting and debate-framing. Instead, we contend that celebrity diplomats maintain a unique position in the public and international setting that can help bring public attention to important issues. One of the most obvious differences between celebrity diplomats and their traditional counterparts is that celebrity diplomats have the luxury of not having to represent a nation-state or intergovernmental institution. This means that celebrity diplomats can focus on causes as they see fit without having to clear their positions with their host governments. However, this independence does create drawbacks in terms of the representation that celebrity diplomats can provide. Whereas state-based and institutional diplomats can approach situations claiming to represent the interests of their countries and public at home, celebrity diplomats must cultivate their followers, and any associations or representations that they claim may be subject to challenge from national governments: 'The biggest gap has to do with the criterion of representation, where there is no basis for seeing any of the celebrity diplomats as members of a formalized guild of diplomats. Celebrities, unlike official diplomats, cannot easily claim that they speak for a constituency, whether defined as a cause or a people' (Cooper 2008a, 2). This drawback can be countered through effective engagement with communities of members and by assembling groups of people and interest groups behind a certain cause. To claim that a celebrity diplomat is ineffective because he or she does not formally represent a certain group fails to take into account the ways in which these celebrities help frame and focus debates and narratives toward causes and situations that can then be leveraged through formal groups and NGOs.

There are, of course, celebrity diplomats who have moved into more formalized roles – specifically in the case of the United Nations' Goodwill Ambassador program and the 'Celebrity Advocacy for the New

Millennium' (CANM) program (see ibid., 28–31). During his tenure, former UN Secretary-General Kofi Annan embraced the role that celebrities could play in helping to gain attention and promote progress. When speaking of celebrity involvement at a meeting of the CANM, Annan (quoted in Agence France-Presse 2000) spurred celebrities into action by telling them, 'you have the personality to capture the imagination of people and policymakers alike.' It is this mixture of celebrity gravitas and informed discussion that enables celebrity diplomats to pierce the clutter of our hypermediated society and focus public attention. As Ronald Mendoza (2006), formerly of the United Nations Development Programme (UNDP) Development Studies division, has put it, 'to their credit, Bono and Angelina Jolie have probably done more to make the world aware of the Millennium Development Goals than most development experts.'

Celebrity involvement in the international arena is not without its detractors, and views of it are mixed:

> For sympathizers, this form of public engagement by celebrities represents an inexorable force tied in with the onward rush of globalization with all its attendant elements of mass technology in global communications. It also reflects the wider crisis of credibility and efficiency that currently affects international organizations, whether international financial institutions (IFIs), the World Trade Organization (WTO), or the G8. For the resisters, the challenge is cast as part of a spillover from the wider gauge of celebrity culture, with the global sphere providing an inviting stage for opportunistic self-indulgence (Cooper 2008b, 265).

Detractors of celebrity diplomacy highlight how the actions of some celebrities are merely attempts to promote their individual importance and remain in the public eye. Others contend that celebrities are not the proper vehicles for conveying and addressing complex issues, arguing that 'there is a case to question the legitimacy of celebrities to speak with authority on development and other international issues' (Dieter and Kumar 2008, 262). At the same time, the effectiveness of celebrity efforts is called into question by focusing on whether they directly influence policy and cause change. However, as Louise Fréchette (2008, vii), former Deputy Secretary-General of the United Nations, nicely puts it:

> neither the demands nor the actions of celebrities are going to save the world, but their engagement (and often their generosity) can help convince many in the younger generations that solutions to problems

come in unpredictable but robust guises. Their activities also serve as a valuable signaling device that the status quo in terms of the global health/poverty/debt agenda remains contested by some who could easily enjoy rich, private, and even frivolous lives.

That the rich and famous would devote time and effort to various causes that do not appear to be their concern can help galvanize public opinion and support. For this reason, politicians as well as international organizations, institutions, and NGOs are turning to celebrities as a way of promoting their respective causes and interests. This interaction between celebrities and traditional international actors is a two-way street: 'As celebrities push for recognition and support by becoming plugged into transnational policymaking, the political elite use celebrities to boost their own credibility. This interplay is consolidated by the combination of publicity and symbolic and material resources that celebrities can generate' (Cooper 2008a, 3). To dismiss celebrity activists and mobilizers as mere extensions of a celebrity-obsessed culture who serve to dilute domestic and international policymaking by their presence as media and entertainment stars is to miss the point. These celebrities use the structures and institutions of the hypermediated contemporary situation to expand the debates and narratives of celebrity culture to include pressing issues at home and abroad.

The successful celebrity diplomat: NGOs, civil society, and the public at large

As described above, there is no one-image-fits-all recipe for a successful celebrity diplomat just as there is no guarantee that the efforts of a celebrity will be perceived as anything other than a scheme to garner personal attention. One consistent way of recognizing and predicting successful celebrity diplomacy is the level of engagement and interaction the celebrity has with state officials on the one hand and experts and policy advocates from NGOs and civil society on the other. Successful celebrity diplomacy must not detract from the cause at hand or monopolize the scarce resources of NGOs and international task forces and missions. Celebrities such as Bono, Jolie, and Clooney use their celebrity to focus debate and attention on the issues at hand. Rather than becoming the story themselves, these successful celebrity diplomats use the spotlight of media and public attention to highlight causes and advocate for change.

Linking process to substantive policymaking clarifies the line separating the few celebrities who can be termed celebrity diplomats from activists. The top-tier celebrity diplomats do not concentrate on only one geographically focused issue. Rather, they engage in mainstream diplomatic activities – communications and negotiations – with some degree of global reach. Bono has attended a number of G8 meetings. Jolie has gone inside the Green Zone of Baghdad as well as Washington DC. Clooney has focused on Sudan/Darfur but has also gained access to policymakers in a range of other countries extending from the US to India.

The links between top-tier celebrities and policy advisors from the NGO world have also been magnified in recent years. The relationship of Bono and Jamie Drummond, the executive director of ONE, is at the forefront of this trend because of their prior involvement with the Jubilee 2000 'Drop the Debt' campaign. A more apparent trend is the shift toward what can be termed freelance advisors. Some of these are extremely well-connected Hollywood insiders, such as Donna Bojarsky, a political consultant close to the Obama administration who runs an influential Foreign Policy Roundtable, which encourages the entertainment industry's leaders to engage with international affairs and the US's role in the world (see Horowitz 2009). Another example is experienced foreign policy experts who straddle a number of advisory roles. A good illustration of this type of person is Morton H. Halperin. Long associated with a set of leading Washington DC-based think tanks, such as the Carnegie Endowment for International Peace and the Brookings Institution, Halperin also acts as a consultant to George Soros' Open Society Foundations and is a board member of ONE (see Open Society Foundations 2011).

Other consultants focus on specific issues. John Prendergast is arguably the best known of this type of advisor, coaching and navigating a number of celebrities (including Don Cheadle, George Clooney, Javier Bardem, and Ryan Gosling) through the complexities of dealing with African issues such as Darfur. More generic is the work of Trevor Neilson, who set up the Global Philanthropy Group, a firm that connects celebrities and causes. Although Neilson has a wealth of experience in advocacy as executive director of the Global Business Coalition on HIV/AIDS, and as the director of public affairs and director of special projects for the Bill & Melinda Gates Foundation, Global Philanthropy Group is explicitly commercially oriented, operating on a fee-for-service basis.

Especially significant in the context of this chapter is how some of Neilson's key initiatives have incorporated new media. A case in point is the campaign Ashton Kutcher and Demi Moore have launched against child sex-trade trafficking, which combines Kutcher's massive Twitter profile (he was the first user of Twitter to have more than 1,000,000 followers) with Neilson's overall strategizing (Gray 2010).

Rocking the boat from within: sites of tension for celebrity mobilizers

In many respects the global economy is structured to promote and perpetuate the status quo. Dissent and activism are discouraged in explicit and implicit ways, making the task of mobilizing activism at times daunting. Economic, social, and surveillance mechanisms are employed to entrench values that support the democratic and business ideals of society (for more on these structural manifestations, see Elmer and Opel 2008). Operating from a position that is firmly connected to the media and communication industries, celebrities must navigate the complexities of this political-economic system. Celebrity mobilizers still operate 'within a framework in which [their work] is oriented towards a market, and [they] must reproduce expectations [of] popular formats and themes to attract a sufficient audience in order to satisfy this market' (Hands 2011, 63).

Two critiques of this contestation must be taken into account. The first expresses frustration concerning the very attractiveness of celebrity diplomacy. In providing a new vehicle for mobilization, it defuses, drains, or even suffocates more radical forms of protest. Because of its ability to act as a magnet for attention, any success of this form of celebrity activity comes at the expense of alternative voices not only from the North (the anti-globalization or social justice movement) but also the diverse elements of civil society from the South. As one critic puts it:

celebrities exert immense influence in the public sphere. They attract attention not only from television news, but from every popular medium ... They can and do set agendas that empower some actors and disempower others. They offer solutions and celebrate heroes. Because celebrities are regarded as trendsetters, they create, reinforce, and promulgate our popular 'truth' about Africans: who they are, what their problems are, how those problems can be solved, and who can and should come to their aid (Elliott 2010, 147).

To reach and maintain a level of celebrity that affords the freedom and audience for social action, these personalities must work within the systems of the media and communication industries. Celebrity mobilizers, then, must work from within the boat while trying to 'rock' it in various directions. Tensions thus emerge when celebrities look to capitalize on their popular status to mobilize change.

The increased reach of the media and entertainment industries has fundamentally changed the ways in which celebrities operate in activist fields. Stars of the 1960s, including musicians John Lennon and Bob Dylan, 'understood themselves to be engaged in a rather subversive, radical, anti-establishment kind of politics' (Panton 2007, 5). However, 'since the 1990s celebrity activism has become less radical' (Huliaras and Tzifakis 2010, 262). In some cases, celebrity activism can be seen as an attempt to ensure that the celebrity remains relevant and in the public consciousness. As Huliaras and Tzifakis (ibid., 261) note, some 'celebrities embrace global causes or take political initiatives in order to remain celebrities. We live in a world where fame cannot be retained without continuous publicity. And the image of a star in a war-torn African country, surrounded by undernourished black children and thus making a nice contrast for photographers, attracts immediate attention.' Cynicism about the motivations behind celebrity activism and diplomacy are not unwarranted (see Littler 2008). After all, as has been argued above, celebrities operate in a hypermediated environment that valorizes and thrives on public attention and the ability to turn that attention into a commodity. Celebrity involvement in efforts to promote change are therefore limited in terms of scope and subject matter.

Dependent upon the established media and communication industries for their livelihoods and fame, celebrities are unlikely to advocate changes that call into question the legitimacy of corporate and neoliberal economic structures. As Ilan Kapoor (2010, quoted in Faculty of Environmental Studies) argues, 'celebrity humanitarian work legitimizes capitalist democracies, which often cause the very violence and inequalities that celebrities purport to be addressing.' From this perspective, celebrity advocacy for change in domestic and international circumstances does not address structural inequalities in the international economy but seeks to address issues that are easily describable and apparent to the public and do not threaten the status quo at large. Perhaps this is why, then, that we have seen the nature and tactics of celebrity activists change since the early 1960s, when artists advocated for radical changes in public policy, especially in relation to the Vietnam War.

Again, though, it is important to note how the actions of celebrity activists reflect the general sentiment of society at large. Counter-cultural heroes in the 1960s and 1970s were the faces of a generational shift in terms of looking at the world and public policy, which eventually became *de rigueur* and mainstream – at least in the United States. Today, the efforts of celebrity diplomats reflect the structures and institutions of the time (see Marsh, Hart, and Tindall 2010). The mainstream consensus today has shifted away from these sorts of activities and toward ways of improving existing institutions and structures without challenging the overarching dimensions that support them. To challenge the activities that celebrity activists and diplomats undertake, then, is to highlight how commercial culture in the early twenty-first century is structured and how the public at large is implicated within these systems. From their privileged position within these networked structures, celebrity diplomats work to expose problems across the world and advocate for action to address them. Under these circumstances, it may be too much for celebrities to take the lead in advocating more radical types of change, especially when significant portions of the public are not doing so themselves. Celebrity diplomats may be the faces and voices of social causes, but they too are implicated within larger social, cultural, economic, and political networks that serve to shape the types of causes that can be advocated for. Returning to Louise Fréchette's sentiment from above, celebrities alone are not going to save or change the world, but their actions and efforts can help to remind the public that a better world is possible.

The second critique of celebrity diplomats concerns their autonomy. Instead of viewing celebrities as networked actors in their own right, some critics view them as co-opted by either NGOs or state authorities. The former takes its point of reference from the position that some big global NGOs benefit from the endorsement they get from celebrities who mobilize on their behalf – in the form of a tacit endorsement – as much as they do from the results of the mobilization itself. Such activities show the extent to which celebrities have advantages over NGOs. Adding celebrities to the mix allows them to win renewed momentum for their campaigns. One pay-off comes in the form of heightened leverage with state officials, who want to identify with celebrities. Attention also allows for an acceleration of fundraising activities.

Another side of this point of contestation is whether celebrity diplomats have been co-opted by state authorities – what Bianca Jagger (2005) in an article for the UK's *New Statesman* termed 'sleeping with the enemy.' Through this alternative perspective, the dots are connected in a very different fashion from the image of networked 'boundary spanners' serving as a bridge and sharing information between various organizations. Instead of privileging the dynamics of Bono's own hub via ONE and other activities, the exclusive focus is on what is taken to be the 'cozying up' behavior toward major Western leaders at G8 summits.

Such a view, nonetheless, plays down the subtle nature of Bono's approach. His approach is to continually play key political leaders off one another, balancing intense involvement with an eye to keeping the boundaries of access open to as many decision-makers as possible. Nudging and cajoling go hand in hand with maintaining a presence in core policy circles and mimic many similar efforts at the traditional diplomatic level. Public rebukes are reserved for the smaller players or those who are on their way out of power. The G8 summit provides a state-centric target. Davos provides the core site for deepening the logic of the network society.

The potential problem with the Bono network is not the intrusion into public space. The bilateral relationship Bono forged with leaders such as George W. Bush and Tony Blair – and his privileged access to Bob Geldof at the 2005 Gleneagles summit both physically (via helicopter) and symbolically (in their presence at the communiqué signing) – may indicate an appreciation of the mobilization, channeling, and mediation role highlighted by the sociological theory. But it did not create a crisis in governance, in that Bono's meetings were media-driven and hoisted on the back of the unique Live 8 'mandate' that a message on debt and development assistance be delivered to the G8 leaders.

The greater potential difficulty with the network encompassing not only Bono but the Gates Foundation (infused with the astronomical gift of over $31 billion from Warren Buffett) and the Open Society Foundations is not the dynamics of its relationship with state officials at the apex of power but the nature of its own inner workings as an expression of the ascendancy of private authority on global public policy. The unbundling of the state and the filling of the role of filter or conduit between citizens and sites of authority by celebrities is one thing. Questions about accountability and the representative form of this network with its privileged access not just to policymakers but also to the mass media, with its combination of popular legitimacy and massive material resources, is another thing entirely.

Moreover, there are indeed other celebrities in the anti-diplomatic category who stretch the limits to a far greater extent than Bono – Angelina Jolie and George Clooney come to mind; Jane Fonda has continued to be vilified as 'Hanoi Jane,' and Sean Penn was widely viewed through a similar frame as an apologist for Saddam Hussein by the vehemence of his anti-war activities (complete with an attention-grabbing trip to Baghdad in December 2002). The critical reactions to these types of effort have seemed to limit the number of celebrities willing to get involved in activism. Significantly, a number of prominent African-Americans have as much potential to be celebrity diplomats as the cohort depicted in this chapter. Some stars from this background, however, avoid such activities, mindful that such associations could put restrictions on their autonomous activities or generate unwarranted criticism. Danny Glover, the well-known Hollywood star, is perhaps the best exemplar of this type of thinking. Asked by a South African journalist whether he was 'the new Bono,' the star of *Lethal Weapon* and other box office hits demurred, saying that his preferred role was to act as 'an obnoxious radical' and spokesperson for the dispossessed. In tune with this alternative role, Glover traveled with Harry Belafonte to the World Social Forum where they met Hugo Chávez (quoted in Madondo 2004).

Belafonte epitomizes the more radical stream among celebrities. Appearing with President Hugo Chávez in the 2006 meeting noted above, Belafonte condemned President George W. Bush while praising Chávez's Bolivarian revolution. He added that 'not hundreds, not thousands, but millions of the American people ... support your revolution' (quoted in Associated Press 2006).

Conclusion: celebrity mobilizers as a generative force

The ability of celebrities to mobilize activism in a hypermediated time is not clear or straightforward. As described above, celebrities' relationships with the public at large are based upon an intricate and complex milieu of social, cultural, economic, and media flows and forces. The privileged position that (many) celebrities maintain in the cultural imaginary provides them with impressive access and the ability to influence public opinion. Routinely seen on television, the web, or other media platforms, celebrities have a stage from which they can articulate their opinions and/or advance their positions or interests with little competition. For instance, in a 2007 report, media watchdog group Fairness and Accuracy In Reporting (FAIR) examined the current state of Africa-related television network news coverage and concluded that African issues were increasingly viewed 'through the prism of celebrity' (Elliott 2010). This ability is based upon the way in which celebrity culture is used as a vehicle for attracting attention. In the developing network society, this attention can be derived through an array of media sources and sites that do not necessarily rely upon the broadcast formula of the past. Social networking and web-based platforms enhance the opportunities for disseminating messages (see Mangold and Faulds 2009) and further the connections between celebrities and members of the public by presenting the feeling of increased intimacy and interaction. The ephemeral nature of these connections and messages is well suited to the ways in which celebrities are implicated within the cultural milieu.

At the same time, the ability of celebrities to mobilize various forms of activism is restrained by their various positions in this context. From an economic perspective, media industries use these images and expressions to construct a narrative that can be employed to attract greater attention and further promote efforts of various projects. Due to this, activist mobilization that is dependent upon the status and role of celebrities is likely to remain associated with issues that are deemed popular or that can generate popularity among the public as well as agreement and endorsement from associated interests within the media industry. As we have seen, celebrity diplomats as mobilizers for causes, therefore, are involved in projects and efforts to improve the living conditions of others while working within the structures and institutions of mainstream society. As witnessed by George Clooney's efforts on the Sudan referendum and Angelina Jolie's push on the Iraqi refugee issue, celebrities have ramped up the scope of their activities in terms of tough cases. Yet, it would be an exaggeration to suggest that celebrities have moved to a position where they are doing everything and everywhere: their niches are in particular areas, but above all in areas of public good.

This restricted scope is a marked departure from the 1960s and 1970s, when celebrity 'activists' such as John Lennon challenged power and political regimes. Instead, today's celebrity activists tend to work for change from within the system (see Easterly 2010). However, today's celebrity mobilizers, epitomized by Bono, are more adept at massaging the levers of government and public opinion to bring about the changes that they and their cadre of policy experts advocate.[3]

The sometimes-fleeting nature of celebrity further complicates the ways in which these personas can work to affect improved outcomes and situations. Based on the image (either static or moving), celebrity culture is best suited for encouraging and generating action for relatively brief periods of time. Public responses to humanitarian crises that call for donations and few other forms of involvement are the prime example. For celebrities to transcend their positions as short-term mobilizers, greater effort and commitment is necessary. This is what we find in the case of celebrity diplomats such as George Clooney, Bono, Angelina Jolie, and the late Princess Diana. These celebrity diplomats, and others like them, commit substantial amounts of time and effort to the projects that they endorse. Working with a network of NGO and civil society organizations, celebrity diplomats transcend the fleeting nature of celebrity culture to establish and promote sustained effort, involvement, and institutions encouraging change. Leveraging the commitment and resources of these NGO and civil society actors and adding their own celebrity status to these initiatives allows for greater promotion and awareness of these various causes among the general public. Also, 'in addition to drawing media attention, celebrity participation may draw in other participants and potential supporters' (Meyer 1995, 185). The work of celebrities in activist situations helps garner support from the public, from politicians, and from other celebrities, thus helping to generate further attention and awareness.

As *Newsweek*'s '21st Century Statesman,' George Clooney, describes it, 'celebrity can help focus news media where they have abdicated their responsibility. We can't make policy, but we can "encourage" politicians more than ever before' (quoted in Avlon 2011). At the same time, these successful celebrity diplomats are often able to directly interact with world leaders to promote the alleviation of the suffering of others. Ultimately, though, any state-based initiatives will be directed and followed up by national governments and/or international institutions. Celebrity diplomats can help to set and frame an agenda in the public consciousness and then promote that agenda to global leaders in the hope that the issue will be addressed. These personalities will not be able to change the world themselves, but by working within networks of individuals, institutions, state officials, NGOs, and advisors, celebrity diplomats can help to frame important discussions about policy changes that can help better the lives and conditions of people across the globe.

Notes

1 This is not to say that celebrity mobilization is a purely Western phenomenon. For an account of the emergence of celebrity diplomats in the developing, or non-Anglo-Saxon, world, see Cooper 2008a, 91–112.

2 Scholarly attempts to find analytical evidence of celebrity influence remain fairly rare but are a useful area of inquiry.

3 Furthermore, it is far too simplistic and problematic to compare activist movements/movers from different eras as they are rooted in different times and social situations. It is important to

recognize that celebrity mobilizers of the early twenty-first century have adapted their techniques to current circumstances in an effort to generate change.

References

Agence France-Presse. 2000. 'UN-celebrities: Annan says UN goodwill ambassadors counteract cynicism.' *Agence France-Presse*, 23 October.

Anderson, Benedict. 1991. *Imagined Communities: Reflections on the Origins and Spread of Nationalism*, revised edition. New York: Verso.

Associated Press. 2006. 'Belafonte says Bush is "greatest terrorist in the world," praises Venezuelan dictator.' *Associated Press*, 8 January. www.foxnews.com/story/0,2933,181030,00.html.

Avlon, John. 2011. 'A 21st century statesman.' *Newsweek*, 21 February. www.thedailybeast.com/newsweek/2011/02/20/a-21st-century-statesman.html.

Barron, Lee. 2009. 'An actress compelled to act: Angelina Jolie's *Notes from My Travels* as celebrity activist/travel narrative.' *Postcolonial Studies* 12(2): 211–28.

Baudrillard, Jean. 1994. *Simulacra and Simulation*. Translated by S. F. Glaser. Ann Arbor: University of Michigan Press.

Bronstein, Daniel. 1962. *The Image: Or, What Happened to the American Dream*. New York: Atheneum.

Castells, Manuel. 2009a. *The Rise of the Network Society (The Information Age: Economy, Society and Culture, Volume I)*, 2nd edition. Hoboken, NJ: Wiley-Blackwell.

Castells, Manuel. 2009b. *The Power of Identity (The Information Age: Economy, Society and Culture,*

Volume II), 2nd edition. Hoboken, NJ: Wiley-Blackwell.

Castells, Manuel. 2009c. *End of Millennium (The Information Age: Economy, Society and Culture, Volume III)*, 2nd edition. Hoboken, NJ: Wiley-Blackwell.

Cohen, Daniel. 2000. *Yellow Journalism: Scandal, Sensationalism and Gossip in the Media*. Breckenridge, CO: Twenty First Century Books.

Cooper, Andrew F. 2008a. *Celebrity Diplomacy*. Boulder, CO: Paradigm Publishers.

Cooper, Andrew F. 2008b. 'Beyond one image fits all: Bono and the complexity of celebrity diplomacy.' *Global Governance* 14: 265–72.

Dieter, Heribert, and Rajiv Kumar. 2008. 'The downside of celebrity diplomacy: The neglected complexity of development.' *Global Governance* 14: 259–64.

Drezner, Daniel W. 2007. 'Foreign policy goes glam.' *The National Interest*, November–December: 22–8.

Dyer, Richard. 1979. *Stars*. London: British Film Institute.

Easterly, William. 2010. 'John Lennon vs. Bono: The death of the celebrity activist.' *Washington Post*, 10 December. www.washingtonpost.com/wp-dyn/content/article/2010/12/09/AR2010120904262.html.

Elliott, Rebecca. 2010. 'Contesting the spectacle: Global lives as counterpublic in the context of celebrity activism.' *Cultural Analysis* 9: 146–50.

Elmer, Greg, and Andy Opel. 2008. *Preempting Dissent: The Politics of an Inevitable Future*. Winnipeg: Arbeiter Ring Publishing.

Epstein, Joseph. 2005. 'Celebrity culture.' *The Hedgehog Review* 7(1): 7–20.

Ford, Peter, and Gloria Goodale. 2005. 'Why stars and charities need each other.' *Christian Science Monitor*, 13 January. www.csmonitor.com/2005/0113/p01s04-wosc.html.

Fréchette, Louise. 2008. 'Foreword.' In *Celebrity Diplomacy*, by Andrew F. Cooper. Boulder, CO: Paradigm Press, vi–vii.

Gray, Kevin. 2010. 'The king of Hollywood philanthropy.' *Details*, 30 November. www.details.com/culture-trends/critical-eye/201012/humanitarian-power-broker-trevor-neilson-global-philanthropy-group?currentPage=1.

Hammel, Sara. 2007. 'Paris Hilton plans a trip to Rwanda.' *People*, 26 September. www.people.com/people/article/0,,20058640,00.html.

Hands, Joss. 2011. *@ is for Activism: Dissent, Resistance and Rebellion in a Digital Culture*. London: Pluto Press.

Heine, Jorge. 2008. 'On the manner of practising the new diplomacy.' In *Global Governance and Diplomacy: Worlds Apart?*, edited by Andrew Cooper, Brian Hocking, and William Maley, 271–87. Basingstoke, UK: Palgrave Macmillan.

Holmes, Su. 2005. '"Starring ... Dyer?": Re-visiting star studies and contemporary celebrity culture.' *Westminster Papers in Communication and Culture* 2(2): 6–21.

Horowitz, Lisa. 2009. 'Engaging Hollywood with world policy.' *The Wrap*, 4 November. www.thewrap.com/movies/article/engaging-hollywood-world-policy-9662.

Huliaras, Asteris, and Nikolaos Tzifakis. 2010. 'Celebrity activism in international relations: In search of a framework for analysis.' *Global Society* 24(2): 255–74.

Jackson, David J. 2007. 'Star power? Celebrity and politics among Anglophone Canadian youth.' *British Journal of Canadian Studies* 20(1): 75–100.

Jagger, Bianca. 2005. 'Real people power, or pernicious platitudes?' *New Statesman*, 11 July.

Jermyn, Deborah. 2006. 'Bringing out the * in you: SJP, Carrie Bradshaw and the evolution of television stardom.' In *Framing Celebrity: New Directions in Celebrity Culture*, edited by Su Holmes and Sean Redmond, 67–86. London: Routledge.

Kahn, Richard, and Douglas Kellner. 2004. 'New media and Internet activism: From the "Battle of Seattle" to blogging.' *New Media & Society* 6(1): 87–95.

Kamons, Andrew. 2007. 'Of note: Celebrity and politics.' *SAIS Review* 27(1): 145–6.

Kapoor, Ilan. 2010. 'Celebrities: Humanitarians or ideologues?' Faculty of Environmental Studies, York University. www.yorku.ca/fes/community/news/archive/666.htm.

Kellner, Douglas. 2010. 'Celebrity diplomacy, spectacle and Barack Obama.' *Celebrity Studies* 1(1): 121–3.

Littler, Jo. 2008. '"I feel your pain": Cosmopolitan charity and the public fashioning of the celebrity soul.' *Social Semiotics* 18(2): 237–51.

Lowenthal, Leo. 1961. 'The triumph of mass idols.' In *Literature, Popular Culture, and Society*, edited by Leo Lowenthal, 109–40. Palo Alto, CA: Pacific Books.

Madondo, Bongani. 2004. 'Lethal

weapon.' *Sunday Times* (South Africa), 7 November.

Mangold, W. Glynn, and David J. Faulds. 2009. 'The new hybrid element of the promotion mix.' *Business Horizons* 52: 257–65.

Marsh, David, Paul 't Hart, and Karen Tindall. 2010. 'Celebrity politics: The politics of late modernity?' *Political Studies Review* 8: 322–40.

McDonald, P. 1998. 'Reconceptualising stardom.' In *Stars*, 2nd edition, edited by Richard Dyer, 175–200. London: British Film Institute.

McLuhan, Marshall. 1962. *The Guttenberg Galaxy: The Making of Typographic Man*. Toronto: University of Toronto Press.

McLuhan, Marshall. 1964. *Understanding Media: The Extensions of Man*. New York: McGraw Hill.

McLuhan, Marshall. 1977. 'Global village.' Interview excerpt from *McLuhan Speaks*. www.marshallmcluhanspeaks.com/sayings/1977-global-village.php.

Mendoza, Ronald. 2006. 'You don't have to be an aid expert to make a difference.' *Financial Times*, 3 February. www.ft.com/cms/s/0/00331f82-945b-11da-82ea-0000779e2340.html#axzz1SmQ6n5gf.

Meyer, David S. 1995. 'The challenge of cultural elites: Celebrities and social movements.' *Sociological Inquiry* 65(2): 181–206.

Morris, Martin. 2005. 'Interpretability and social power, or, why postmodern advertising works.'

Media, Culture & Society 27(5): 697–718.

Neimark, Jill. 1995. 'The culture of celebrity.' *Psychology Today*, 1 May. www.psychologytoday.com/articles/199505/the-culture-celebrity.

Open Society Foundations. 2011. 'Morton H. Halperin.' *OSI-Washington*, staff listing. www.soros.org/initiatives/washington/about/bios/halperin.

Panton, James. 2007. 'Pop goes politics.' *The World Today* 63(6): 4–6.

Powdermaker, Hortense. 1947. 'An anthropologist looks at the movies.' *Annals of the American Academy of Political Science* 254: 80–7.

Reuters. 2007. 'Paris Hilton's Rwanda trip postponed.' *Reuters*, 26 October. http://uk.reuters.com/article/2007/10/26/uk-hilton-idUKN2532366720071026.

Rojek, Chris. 2001. *Celebrity*. London: Reaktion.

Sack, Robert David. 1997. *Homo Geographicus: A Framework for Action, Awareness and Moral Concern*. Baltimore, MD: Johns Hopkins University Press.

Van den Bulck, Hilde, and Koen Panis. 2010. 'Michael as he is not remembered: Jackson's "forgotten" celebrity activism.' *Celebrity Studies* 1(2): 242–4.

Williams, Greg. 2011. 'Wired's five highlights from the 2011 Red Innova tech conference.' *Wired*, 4 July. www.wired.co.uk/news/archive/2011-07/04/red-innova-conference?page=2%20.

7 | Amplifying individual impact: social media's emerging role in activism

SARAH KESSLER

Social media are not, as they are sometimes portrayed, magic pixie dust that can be sprinkled on complex problems to make them better, but they are beginning to impact activism in ways beyond 'likes' and Tweets.[1] Social media make available to all individuals certain aspects of activism that were once most accessible to members of centralized organizations. They do not cause revolutions, but they are beginning to revolutionize the way that activists approach them.

The argument that social media foster feel-good clicking rather than actual change has been around long enough to generate its own derogatory term. 'Slacktivism,' as defined by contributor '1Spectre4U' in the *Urban Dictionary* (2003), is 'the act of participating in obviously pointless activities as an expedient alternative to actually expending effort to fix a problem.'

Many skeptics of social media's impact on activism focus narrowly on the clichés of slacktivism. Malcolm Gladwell (2010, n.p.), for instance, writes that 'boycotts and sit-ins and non-violent confrontations – which were the weapons of choice for the civil-rights movement – are high-risk strategies. They leave little room for conflict and error … Enthusiasts for social media would no doubt have us believe that [Dr Martin Luther King, Jr.'s] task in Birmingham would have been made infinitely easier had he been able to communicate with his followers through Facebook, and contented himself with tweets from a Birmingham jail.'

What is somewhat unfair about this viewpoint is that social media are a relatively new tool in the activist arsenal. SixDegrees.com, considered by many the first social network, was launched in 1997 (Boyd and Ellison 2007). Facebook was launched in 2004, YouTube in 2005, and Twitter in 2006. Today's primary social tools have been around for only a little more than five years. As with any new technology, the full potential of social media has not been immediately realized and their use is still evolving.

Many activists I have interviewed, however, provide examples of how social media are beginning to shift the world of activism from one in which organizations and centralized movements are the most effective change agents to one in which individuals and decentralized collections of individuals are equally effective or more effective at completing activist tasks.

Spreading the word: how boundary crossing and 'strong weak' ties make social media powerful cause-communication mechanisms

One in seven girls is married before she turns 15. If you know this statistic, it is probably due to the efforts of the United Nations Foundation's 'Girl Up' campaign. The campaign is designed to empower girls in the United States to raise money and awareness for the education, health, and safety of girls at risk of being forced to marry as children. While its website (www.girlup.org) encourages girls to host events offline and donate their own money, its guidelines for spreading awareness of the issue are largely focused on sharing through social media.

'[Social media] is a cross-demographic and cross-generational way for me to publicly align myself with a cause,' says Aaron Sherinian, the executive director of communication at the United Nations Foundation (personal interview with the author, 9 June 2011). 'In the past, I would need to bumper sticker myself to say to random individuals on the highway that I cared about the environment, children, or health.'

Bimber, Flanagin, and Stohl (2005, 377) apply the term 'boundary crossing' to the digital bumper-stickering Sherinian describes:

> Individuals maintain a realm of private interests and actions. When they make these interests or actions known to others in some way, they cross a boundary between private and public realms ... When it is costly, boundary crossing typically takes on the characteristics of a discrete decision: Should I bear the costs of expressing myself or acting in order to enter the public domain in pursuit of a particular public good? ... When boundaries between private and public domains are porous and easily crossed, however, people's negotiation of the boundary typically involves less intentionality and calculation. Moreover, formal structures designed to broker the private to public transition become less crucial.

In other words, the easier it is to publicly align with an issue, the easier it is for that issue to transfer from private to public discourse without actions that are coordinated by a central organizer. The expansion of social media has helped make boundaries significantly more 'porous.' Before their development, an individual may have publicly expressed an alliance with a cause by handing out fliers, writing letters or, yes, bumper-stickering her car. Social media make it easier for individuals to publicly state that they align with a cause: no printing fliers, no addressing letters, no ruining a car's paint job. That is one reason why they are an excellent tool for elevating the visibility of an issue.

The other reason is that a public statement can be easily shared with acquaintances or 'weak ties.' Friends from high school who haven't spoken in years are more likely to be exposed to each other's public alliance with a cause through social networks than they would be otherwise. This is particularly important because acquaintances are more likely to create bridges to new ideas than are close friends, who tend to be exposed to similar ideas.

Mark Granovetter (1983, 202) has gone so far as to say that it would be impossible to organize a movement without weak ties. 'While members of one or two cliques may be efficiently recruited, the problem is that, without weak ties, any momentum generated in this way does not spread *beyond* the clique,' he writes. 'As a result, most of the population will be untouched.' Developing collective identities and helping to identify common concerns are, Granovetter argues, two necessary components of a movement. Social media allow a collection of individuals to meet these requirements rather than structuring a campaign around traditional media outlets.

Instead of coordinating a media strategy, many activists are handing the burden of spreading the word to a decentralized collection of individuals. The United Nations Foundation did not control how its 'Girl Up' campaign spread to include more than 16,000 participants. It simply created a message for individuals to spread.

Online petitions, boycotts, and letter-writing campaigns: how social media organize collective action and recruit participants in a cause

Social media's advantages as a communication mechanism – minimal barriers to public alignment with a cause and easy access to weak ties – can also help coordinate collective actions. 'If the Internet didn't exist, Barack Obama would not be president of the United States,' says Ben Rattray, the founder and CEO of the online petition and information platform Change.org (personal interview with the author,

5 October 2010). 'The fact that the most powerful person in the world wouldn't be in that position without the Internet and online organizing says something.'

The power of the Internet in President Obama's case, Rattray says, was its unique ability to organize thousands of people to work together. While 100,000 people ranting on Twitter might not be worth anything, organizing those 100,000 people in a simultaneous action can have significant impact. Before social media, getting them all on the same page would have required a massive effort and the resources of a top-down, hierarchical organization. If an organization utilizes social tools, however, it doesn't need to send representatives from local bureaus door to door to collect signatures. It doesn't even need to create an email list. Instead, an organization – or a single person – can use social sharing tools to put the burden of distributing a petition, letter, or boycott onto a decentralized collection of individuals.

'The goal here is social change, it's not to make things difficult,' Rattray says. 'It may be really difficult to go protest in person, but it might be more effective to mobilize a hundred other people using the web to simultaneously send letters to a single target.'

Calls for digital collective actions such as petitions and letter-sending are not just easier to distribute through social media, they are also easier to complete. Because of the relatively high cost of time, money, or personal safety involved in organizing or participating in many traditional tools of activism, individuals who can receive the benefits of a movement without actually participating themselves are likely to accept a 'free ride' by remaining inactive (Olson 1965). Bimber, Flanagin, and Stohl (2005) have argued that the low cost of online participation mitigates this effect, and that people who sympathize with a cause but would usually 'free ride' will participate in collective action if doing so is inexpensive.

An analysis of online protest sites by Jennifer Earl and Katrina Kimport (2011) supports this theory. They found that those sites with higher levels of automation and tasks that could be completed completely online had more participants than those on which participation was not fully online or that were less automated. Putting the burden of distributing a call for collective action on a social network not only makes top-down organization of the task less important, but it also successfully brings more participants to the task.

While using social media to spread a call for digital collective action may lower the cost of participation enough to increase the number of people who become involved, instinct suggests that the resulting action must be less effective. Thousands of people consenting to a statement with a click does not seem as though it could possibly be as effective as twenty people attending a protest outside or collecting signatures door to door. But evidence that offline protest is an effective change agent is, as with its online counterpart, largely anecdotal. 'Empirically documenting the causal influence of protest on policy or culture is notoriously hard,' write Earl and Kimport (ibid.). 'While some have demonstrated that various combinations of factors matter, empirically evidencing the effects of major movements or specific protests is a tricky business ... It might be fairer to say that the consequences of both conventional street protest and e-tactics are relatively unknown at this point.'

Change.org and organizations like it, however, use anecdotal evidence to argue that online organizing is both efficient and effective. Rattray says that Change.org wins a campaign – changes an unjust law, policy, or practice – at least once a week. Similar organizations, such as MoveOn.org and PetitionOnline.com, which encourage the sharing of boycott instructions or online petitions to government officials, offer similar success stories. Avaaz.org, for instance, coordinated a petition that convinced Hilton to train 180,000 of its hotel employees to spot and prevent sex slavery (see www.avaaz.org/en/hilton_sign_now/).

'[Non-profit organizations] have traditionally treated people not as those who might organize, but as those who might by proxy express their support through donations,' Rattray argues. 'The web's ability to network those people, to connect them and to channel them to specific action together, is absolutely powerful.'

Even if so-called 'five-minute activism,' in which large numbers of people are mobilized within a short period of time at minimal cost (Bennett and Fielding 1999, 27), were effectively useless, there is another reason why giving individuals an easy way to express their alliance with a cause could be valuable: small actions might eventually lead to bigger ones.

Before Claire Diaz Ortiz became the head of corporate social innovation and philanthropy at Twitter, she founded a non-profit organization that uses running to empower AIDS orphans in Kenya. *Runner's World* wrote an article about it, which piqued widespread interest in her cause. 'We did get some donations from it, but basically thousands and thousands of runners just wanted to send us their dirty running shoes,' she says (personal interview with the author, 12 July 2011).

Signing an online petition might be much like adding to Diaz Ortiz's pile of running shoes. Although the action stems from good intentions, more people taking it does not necessarily make it more impactful. Yet, Diaz Ortiz does not consider her pile of shoes a waste. 'The ROI [return on investment] on awareness exists,' she says. 'Of a hundred people that sent me used running shoes, which I wouldn't even want to drag to an orphanage in Africa, maybe one of those people did somehow become, in turn, more involved in AIDS awareness work.'

The argument that mailing a pair of old running shoes can lead to deeper engagement in an AIDS awareness organization is often referred to as 'the ladder of engagement.' Social media's prominence did not create a need for such a term – the ladder is a metaphor that can be applied to all activism throughout history.

When Craig Kielburger was twelve years old, for instance, he saw a newspaper article about a child slave who was about his age. The article eventually inspired him to found Free The Children, an organization that fifteen years later has student groups in 3,500 Canadian schools that have helped build 650 schools around the globe. Kielburger didn't wake up one day and discover he was an activist. His deep engagement with the cause of children's rights began with a rather low-commitment action of reading a newspaper article.

Many argue that something like signing an online petition, clicking a 'like' button or retweeting a message about malaria can function, like the article did for twelve-year-old Kielburger, as the first step in a relationship with a cause. 'You're not going to get everyone who liked your Facebook page to volunteer their summer building schools and helping out, but it's still part of that journey,' Kielburger says (personal interview with the author, 6 October 2010).

The more commitment Free The Children asks for, the fewer people they get to participate. Some 174,000 people 'liked' the Free The Children Facebook page in the first month after it was posted. About 20,000 people showed up to Free The Children's 2010 'We Day' event in Toronto. And 2,000 people actually committed to a trip overseas to help the cause. Even so, Kielburger says, social media 'opens the megaphone so much wider ... when you finally look at that spectrum, we've got more people who are finally making that journey.'

The more people who casually engage with a cause, the more opportunities there are to engage individuals past that first step. Accumulating piles of so-called 'slacktivists' isn't necessarily a wasted effort if there are steps they can take to deepen their minimal commitment. Unremarkable actions such as signing an online petition can, in theory, be a 'gateway drug' for deeper engagement. In this way, individuals who spread messages and easy online activities through their networks are in some ways taking on a recruitment role for the movement.

Everybody can broadcast: how bypassing traditional media can facilitate change

Every new medium has played some role in major movements that were taking place at the time. The rise of the printing press in the fifteenth century accelerated the Protestant Reformation by allowing for the dissemination of bibles in local languages and making it possible for Martin Luther to distribute his list of complaints about the Catholic Church to a wide audience. Clay Shirky describes the printing press's role in the Protestant Reformation in *Here Comes Everybody* (2008, 67) as follows: 'Two things are true about the remaking of the European intellectual landscape during the Protestant Reformation: first, it was not caused by the invention of movable type, and second, it was possible only after the invention of movable type.'

A similar statement could be made about television and the civil rights movement of the 1950s and 1960s. While nobody would call it a 'television' movement, it is hard to argue that television didn't play a role. Images of non-violent protestors – and the violence being committed against them – reached audiences in places far away from the South and helped elevate what was previously an isolated concern into a mainstream issue.

'There's a reason why so many of the actions taken by Congress and by the federal government took place in the 1950s and 1960s as opposed to the 1920s and 1930s,' says Alec Ross, Senior Advisor for Innovation to Secretary of State Hillary Clinton (personal interview with the author, 9 August 2011). 'The treatment of African-Americans was not necessarily worse in the 1950s and 1960s than it was in the 1920s or 1930s but more Americans knew about it because of the images that were shared.'

Similarly, Shirky (2008, 143–60) argues that the rise of email and digital media was an essential aspect of the mainstream revolt against abusive priests in the early 2000s. While most reports of abuse were filed in the 1950s and 1960s, he points out, a mainstream revolt didn't occur until 2002 after the *Boston Globe* published a story about a local Catholic priest who had abused more than 100 boys during a thirty-five-year period in which the Catholic Church, despite reports of abuse, kept moving him from parish to parish.

Sharing this story was a matter of clicking a 'forward' button. Fifty years ago scandals may have erupted in local communities when abuse was reported, but Catholics had no easy way to share the story with Catholics in other areas. When sharing a news story became a simple matter of forwarding, it was more difficult for the Catholic Church to isolate individual scandals. When any parishioner could use a search engine to dredge up dozens of these articles, it was much harder to deny the abuse and shelter abusers.

In the case of social media, what has changed about the way that news spreads is that a major news network does not need to be involved – just a collection of individuals with an accessible network of weak ties. Bypassing the news outlet makes it easier to broadcast what is happening in places where the government heavily censors traditional media.

Esra'a Al Shafei lives in Bahrain, where this is the case. She started a website called Crowdvoice.org in 2010 that crowdsources social media content surrounding controversial topics that are rarely covered in state-controlled media. Discussion on the website originally focused on the abuse of migrant workers in the Middle East, but when protests against then-President Hosni Mubarak erupted throughout Egypt in January 2011, traffic on Al Shafei's site exploded as people searched the public billboard for information about the revolution. When protests started in Yemen, it became a source for information there. And three days after protestors seized a Bahrain landmark known as Pearl Square, the government found Crowdvoice.org enough of a threat to shut it down.

'It makes it difficult for governments to deny it,' Al Shafei says (personal interview with the author, 28 June 2011). 'It's there. And people can find it. When this stuff was happening in Bahrain, people were going on TV and saying, guys, this is not happening, this is not real. This is all exaggerated propaganda. But then people would go to Crowdvoice and say, wait a minute, this is actually happening. I can see it on the site. People are disseminating this kind of information on here. And it's tons and tons of people doing it. It's not just one or two people.'

Dissent in places such as Tunisia, Egypt, Yemen, and Bahrain is not new. But social media have helped make it more visible by giving individuals the power to broadcast. People inside and outside these countries no longer rely solely on the information from government-controlled or highly censored news organizations.

How social media are decentralizing leadership

During a speech that Alec Ross gave to more than 180 of the United States' foreign ambassadors, he asked if any of them could name a revolutionary leader in Tunisia. Not one of them raised their hands.

Similarly, no iconic leader has emerged in Egypt, Libya, Bahrain, Syria, or Yemen. 'The Che Guevara of the twenty-first century is the "network,"' Ross says. 'There is not a single figure organizing the masses in a hierarchical fashion. Rather, there are nodes of influence' (personal interview with the author).

Just as communication and collaborative action have in some cases shifted from top-down control to networks of individuals, so too has leadership been decentralized in many movements. Not all of the factors that contribute to decentralized leadership are attributable to social media, but many are. Digital sharing makes it easier for leaders of small nodes to loosely coordinate actions rather than receiving orders from a single point person. Instead of investing control in one individual at the top of a hierarchy, leadership is distributed through decentralized networks, which are significantly more difficult to assassinate or shut down. Social media's impact on activism thus should not be viewed only through the lens of casually involved participants and low-cost actions. These media are also contributing to the way movements are organized.

Conclusion: everyone is a potential activist organization

Social media are not creating movements. They are, however, shaping how activists approach movements by empowering a collection of individuals to carry out activist tasks that have historically been accomplished through centralized organizations.

With social media, activist actions such as signing a petition or passing on a disturbing statistic can easily gain more participants even in the absence of deliberate organization. The low cost of publicly aligning with a cause and the ease of sharing across weak ties make social media as effective, or more effective, as an institutionally driven media campaign, and the ability of individuals to self-publish elevates to the world stage movements that may not have been as visible previously.

My argument is not that traditional activist organizations are about to disappear or have no role in how social media change activism. Many of the efforts I discuss in this chapter were initiated by organizations leveraging social networks to do work they may have once managed more closely. It is too early to know to what extent activist organizations will continue to leverage social media or how effective new media's tactics are in comparison with traditional tools. Rather, my argument is that an individual, holding his or her involvement level constant, can contribute more to activist goals with social media than he or she could without them. Many are succeeding as activists without an established organization to back them up.

Shawn Ahmed, for instance, is fond of reminding people that, 'I'm not a charity. I'm just a guy' (personal interview with the author, 9 September 2010). While plenty of 'just guys' in the last generation also traveled to less privileged countries for altruistic purposes, Ahmed has the leverage of YouTube.

When people view videos that are part of Ahmed's 'Uncultured Project' (http://uncultured.com/), they are often inspired to pitch in and help the people they see. After more than 140,000 YouTube viewers saw a Bangladeshi school that was destroyed in a cyclone, for example, many sent money to help rebuild it. Before the donations, the village had only enough money to replace the roof of the school. With the donations, Ahmed was able to help them rebuild the school, buy supplies for fishermen, provide assistance to single mothers, and build a well. Ahmed's work may be just a drop in the bucket, but it is arguably a much bigger drop than would have been possible without his ability to engage an audience in North America via tweets and YouTube videos from Bangladesh.

Beth Kanter and Allison Fine (2010, 4) called 'just guys' like Shawn 'free agents' in their book, *The Networked Nonprofit*. Social media have enabled many of them. Mark Horvath, for instance, has helped expose the complexity of homelessness by posting homeless people's stories on YouTube and teaching them how to use social tools to tell their own stories. Dan Savage's one story about growing up as a homosexual became a movement when he was inspired to post it on YouTube following the suicides of several young homosexual men. Eleven months later more than 25,000 people – including President Barack Obama – had created their own videos to tell homosexual teenagers that 'It Gets Better,' and the project outgrew YouTube and has been relocated to its own site (www.itgetsbetter.org/). At the time of writing, the videos have been viewed more than 40 million times.

Activists who are deeply engaged in a cause have always been able to make a difference, but in the past most of them have done so through traditional non-profit organizations or in relative isolation. Now they can amplify their individual actions through social media.

'Free agents' are, I would argue, becoming microscopic organizations that can broadcast their causes, solicit support, and invite others to contribute without the resources a large, hierarchical structure provides. At the same time, social media maximize the impact of 'casual activists' by allowing them to participate easily in activist tasks such as communication, collective action, and recruitment.

Notes

1 In this chapter, the term 'social media' broadly refers to tools that enable the average Internet user to create and distribute content to a network. These include blogs, social networks such as Facebook and Twitter, photo- and video-sharing sites, and social features of websites such as comments sections. In some cases, viral email can fit this definition.

References

1Spectre4U [pseudonym]. 2003. 'Slacktivism.' *Urban Dictionary*, October 21. www. urbandictionary.com/define. php?term=slacktivism.

Bennett, Daniel, and Pam Fielding. 1999. *The Net Effect: How Cyberadvocacy Is Changing the Political Landscape*. Washington, DC: Capitol Advantage.

Bimber, Bruce, Andrew J. Flanagin, and Cynthia Stohl. 2005. 'Reconceptualizing collective action in the contemporary media environment.' *Communication Theory* 15(4): 365–88.

Boyd, Danah M., and Nicole B. Ellison. 2007. 'Social network sites: Definition, history, and scholarship.' *Journal of Computer-Mediated Communication* 13(1): article 11.

Earl, Jennifer, and Katrina Kimport. 2011. *Digitally Enabled Social Change: Activism in the Internet Age*. Cambridge, MA: The MIT Press.

Gladwell, Malcolm. 2010. 'Small change: Why the revolution will not be tweeted.' *The New Yorker*, October 4. www.newyorker.com/ reporting/2010/10/04/101004fa_ fact_gladwell.

Granovetter, Mark. 1983. 'The strength of weak ties: A network theory revisited.' *Sociological Theory* 1: 201–33.

Kanter, Beth, and Allison Fine. 2010. *The Networked Nonprofit: Connecting with Social Media to Drive Change*. San Francisco, CA: Jossey-Bass.

Olson, Mancur. 1965. *The Logic of Collective Action: Public Goods and the Theory of Groups*. Cambridge, MA: Harvard University Press.

Shirky, Clay. 2008. *Here Comes Everybody*. New York: Penguin Books.

8 | The spectacle of suffering and humanitarian intervention in Somalia

JOEL R. PRUCE

Introduction

Since the liberation of Nazi concentration camps, a central organizing principle of human rights advocacy has been that information is the key to stopping atrocities in progress and preventing those that are imminent: if only the public knew what was going on behind those walls, something could have been done. The photographs that emerged from Bergen-Belsen and Buchenwald in 1945 were so startling they led observers to optimistically opine that, should future atrocities become known and visible to the public, the audience would be sufficiently motivated to speak out in defense of the vulnerable. By virtue of their visceral response to grotesque and brutal imagery, ordinary citizens would be stirred from complacency to become politically engaged. But is this actually what happens? Does our ability to see human rights abuse portrayed in visual media increase the likelihood that audiences become politically involved to alleviate suffering?

This dilemma plays itself out on two levels. Witnessing, in the sense that non-governmental organizations (NGOs) including the International Committee of the Red Cross and Médecins Sans Frontières (MSF, or Doctors Without Borders) employ it, is a critical act in and of itself because by being present, by bearing witness to crimes, violators are denied impunity. Geopolitically, being labeled as an abusive regime has negative effects on legitimacy and reputation and, therefore, witnessing may discourage abuse. Witnesses thus raise the cost of human rights abuse and expose tyrants to the world. With the initiation of digital technology and satellite communication in the 1990s, the human rights community gained a new arsenal of tools with the potential to transform an entire general audience into an active crowd of witnesses. With the bright lights of globalized media shining into the darkest corners, actors can be held up to international human rights standards, the global public bearing witness to their crimes.

Additionally, seeing human rights abuses on television and online may also motivate a response that goes beyond that act of witnessing:

audience members could decide to become active in campaigns to remedy the situation portrayed before them in the imagery. Human rights and humanitarian engagement can take many forms, from texting a monetary donation to a foreign aid agency and contributing to a canned food drive, to calling elected officials, urging state action, and attending a protest event for the cause. These activities exist on a spectrum of political engagement with witnessing at one end of the spectrum and direct action tactics at the other, and they vary widely based on personal investment, exposure to risk, and effect.

This chapter examines the types and degree of engagement cultivated by the exposure to graphic imagery of suffering. Do audiences maintain their passivity and remain on the couch? Are they moved to give of themselves financially? Is footage of suffering sufficient to mobilize political activism? If so, for how long? The relationship between seeing and acting is neither natural nor linear, but is at times disjointed and operating at cross-purposes. The cautionary tale that follows indicates how the converse of the mantra may well be true: the claim that information deficit is at the root of inaction ignores the possibility that information overload may be equally detrimental.

With the onset of neoliberal globalization and specific advances in information and communications technology, the channels were in place for the transmission of ideas and images in an increasingly open and permissive environment. The medium that exemplifies this period is the television, because, while the Internet was still in the process of maturation in the 1990s, television had reached a critical mass of households and, with the expansion of global media conglomerates, content on television was expanding as well. Yet this rapid shift toward visual media resulted in an excessiveness that eventually gave way to an age of hypersaturation aptly described as an age of spectacle (Debord 1983; Kellner 2003).

Through new media, images stream at the audience with omnipresent and overwhelmingly spectacular displays designed to entice, intrigue, and attract, pummeling our eyes and our minds with information and entertainment. At once, visual media generate amusement and distraction from daily life and provide a necessary, if temporary, escape into the realm of fantasy. At the same time, television serves the public with invaluable access to far-off places that details stories of human struggle and sheds light on matters of great international importance. However, if 'the medium is the message' (McLuhan 2003), or even if 'the medium is the metaphor' (Postman 1985), what is the effect on the audience when serious content is communicated through a platform such as television that is so thoroughly fraught with levity and commercialism? Perhaps the profit motive compels media companies to provide emotive stories for the audience that speak to the common denominator in all of us, human frailty. This may set into motion a process whereby our moral communities – those we consider ourselves close to and close enough to act on behalf of – are expanded to include suffering strangers. Or, perhaps the medium itself consolidates distance and alienates us from the suffering 'other' because of the nature of television and our associations with it as a realm of diversion and fiction.

Crises and conflicts of the past provide an insight into the possible effects that the imagery of a war zone has on its audience: the experience of observing the pain of others, even at a distance, has the ability to touch the audience in a deeply personal way. Audience members as a group are not affected evenly, but a connection can be forged through witnessing the suffering of other humans – a psychological bond that hinges on a sensibility of human sameness. Even if a television viewer has never been the parent of a starving child or has never been tortured, he or she can empathize with the suffering other because of his or her familiarity with less severe hunger and pain. An emotional response is evoked with a myriad of subsequent effects that are reflected back on the viewer and range from dismissal and disgust to outrage and protest. From a human rights perspective, a question to be explored in this chapter is whether the audience's experience of images of suffering on television translates into political action for intervention on behalf of the sufferer, or whether the emotional reaction is merely a fleeting feeling that evaporates quickly.

This chapter details the impact of graphic imagery of suffering on the ability of the human rights movement to mobilize behind humanitarian intervention, specifically in the case of Somalia. Following the expansion of the movement during the 1970s and 1980s, the 1990s presented new opportunities for growth, specifically due to developments in visual mass media. However, these new platforms for activism also produced stumbling blocks. While atrocity coverage can engage the audience and motivate a civil society response, audiences may also tune out imagery of distant suffering, literally and figuratively. The interplay between the media and the audience with respect to human rights encapsulates a dialectic of the global information age: on the one hand, it is clear that this period presents an amazing opportunity for social solidarity, democratization of foreign policy, and cosmopolitanism. However, these same forces can be turned against themselves as firms shape new networks as avenues for advertising, consumerism, and distraction from politics. A critical look at the effect of technology and media on human rights activism evidences the potential for progress even in the face of deep structural obstacles. What becomes clear is that the sensational coverage can be used to serve the interests of the powerful as well as those of the victimized. The battle over spectacle is waged by geopolitical players, commercial media outlets, and human rights advocates, with the former two often demonstrating greater mastery for spinning and manipulating the substance of suffering on television.

This calls into question the classic human rights concept that raising awareness is a precursor of political action. If bearing witness is no longer a powerful human rights tool, exactly *what kind* of engagement is provoked by graphic imagery of suffering? Are audiences entertained? Are audiences outraged? Are audiences ambivalent? Are audiences numb? And what types of action are taken in response to these emotional states? The case of Somalia evidences a range of vacillating audience reactions to the media representation of suffering. Overall, the story that unfolds is one of emotional outpouring of sentimentality for the plight of innocents on television in the context of ascending norms surrounding the use of force for humanitarian goals. What results is a splintered human rights community held hostage by mediated spectacles. The spectacle of suffering is sufficient to provoke an emotional response from the audience but fails to serve as the foundation for a sustained effort for human rights protection. Instead, the spectacle provides only a snapshot and glimpse into a crisis, focusing on the human catastrophe but obscuring the political dynamics behind the catastrophe. Television, by its nature, objectifies its content, fictionalizes reality, and alienates the audience from the real world. Graphic imagery of suffering makes the audience aware of famine and war but does not transcend mere superficial awareness in favor of political commitments able to withstand the news cycle and geopolitical manipulation. Thus, viewers are moved but not motivated to commit themselves or their governments to the kind of interventions required to remedy dire suffering. To dissect and justify this reasoning, this chapter explains the use of the term 'spectacle'; provides context in social, economic, and technological terms; and proceeds with the case study of the Somali intervention set against the backdrop of antecedent events in Biafra and Ethiopia transmitted to the world through images.

What is the 'spectacle of suffering'?

The era of spectacle emerges as a product of globalization, primarily associated with technological developments in the field of information communications. Facilitating this shift was an infrastructure of fiber-optic cables, satellite link-ups, and corporate media outlets that formed an enmeshed global network. Through these channels, content traveled instantaneously across great distances, at low costs. Twenty-four-hour cable news with live video feeds fueled a demand for content and provided the wherewithal to transmit it. However, the spectacle is not only a matter of speed and access; the nature of visual information also marks a transformation in the media landscape. Due to technological capacity and the drive for market share and viewership inherent in corporate-owned media, the spectacle is born of developments in global capitalism, which has social effects on the audience. That global audiences can see imagery of others' suffering is not new; newspapers and magazines have been the preferred platforms in previous eras. What is new is the intensity of moving images compared with still photography, and the coming ubiquity of the imagery itself: the culmination of a historical trajectory that captures circumstances of vulnerability and indignity on film. The spectacle is a thoroughly mediated environment that expresses a promise of globalization: the ability for audiences across large distances to experience each other's lives and be part of a single, transnational moral community that shares care and concern for fellow members.

Yet, this promise went unfulfilled. The 1990s actually saw a relative decline in the coverage of foreign affairs on television newscasts and an inverse rise in stories about scandal, entertainment, and lifestyle, suggesting not only the replacement of the latter for the former but broader qualities of the evolving milieu in which foreign news must compete (Doyle 2007, 190–1). This relationship indicates a trend in television and cable news in favor of content of a light nature, instead of the pressing crises that would unfold throughout the decade. Furthermore, due to its commercial demands, this medium was never intended to cultivate cosmopolitan human rights defenders, but instead consumers and spectators. Information takes the form of breaking news headlines, but it also takes the form of advertising. Television is a vehicle for creating and targeting the demographics of consumers and provides access for corporations to these consumers in their homes. Global capitalism at the beginning of the twenty-first century is increasingly personalized and prepackaged, and the individual is ever more accustomed to constant confrontation with advertising and commercialism. It has become part of daily life and slips easily into the backdrop of all environments; while not necessarily overt, information as advertising takes on an inconspicuous presence, constantly operating but rarely noticed. Whether these channels can be shaped to serve the interests of the downtrodden is one question that motivates the argument in this chapter and the conceptualization of the spectacle of suffering.

The 'spectacle of suffering' presents a new lens through which to view a familiar, modern phenomenon, namely a tendency in mass media to traffic heavily in images of suffering to the point of becoming rote, repetitive, and predictable. This terminology illustrates a qualitative aspect of the media environment of the post-Cold War era and describes the subject matter of discrete media events, often described as 'pornography of war,' 'pornography of violence,' or 'disaster pornography' (Baudrillard 2008; Mamdani 2007; Omaar and de Waal 1993). The allusion to pornography in this context relates to at least two characteristics: the way imagery of brutality and violence appeals to our prurient interests and the exploitative nature of graphic imagery of suffering victims. Drawing comparisons between atrocity photography and pornography suggests a certain self-indulgence in observing others in vulnerable, intimate, and sensitive positions, while also injecting a power dynamic that connects the subject and object. The current analysis focuses on less conspicuous effects of the visual image on the audience, however, in a distinct way compared with other deployments of the term 'spectacle.' In cases where scholars use the language of spectacle, it is often to signify something spectacular and visually stunning, without necessarily addressing political consequences (Boltanski 1999; Chouliaraki 2006). While my use of 'spectacle' will obviously apply to its visuality, I deploy this term in a specific manner associated with Guy Debord and the Situationist International.

For Debord, 'the society of the spectacle' was a particular description of modern times as obsessed and mystified by appearance.

> The first stage of the economy's domination of social life brought about an evident degradation of being into *having* – human fulfillment was no longer equated with what one was, but with what one possessed. The present stage, in which social life has become completely dominated by the accumulated productions of the economy, is bringing about a general shift from *having* to *appearing* ... (Debord 1983, para. 17).

Herbert Marcuse, Theodor Adorno, and other Frankfurt School scholars originated the critique of the society of mass consumption and Debord continues in this tradition, identifying the spectacle as an extension of capitalism and 'the image' as a new plane of commodification for the exercise of social control. For Debord, 'the spectacle is a permanent opium war designed to force people to equate goods with commodities and to equate satisfaction with a survival that expands according to its own laws' (Debord 1983, para. 44). Debord sees late industrial capitalism as a system that suffocates radical politics and preserves the status quo at all costs. Therefore, by applying the spectacle of suffering to a human rights context, there is an attempt to coherently discuss the impact of the spectacle on the audience's capacity to engage in a political movement and upend traditional power relations, as human rights advocacy does.

The fact that nightly news coverage features human rights issues is not inherently a bad thing; on the contrary, cable television is an essential medium through which the public stays connected to world events. However, a concern arises when nightly coverage of human rights abuse is transformed by the medium and the saturation of the medium with spectacular imagery. In the post-Cold War era, there has been no shortage of spectacular suffering beamed into the living rooms of Western viewers: refugees in flight, starving African children, burnt American Ranger corpses, mortal machete wounds, mass graves, concentration camps, planes flying into skyscrapers, and degrading detainee torture, to name several. The impact of spectacle on the recipient is complex – provocative, yet paralyzing; fascinating, yet redundant. The spectacle of suffering is responsible for the ubiquity of graphic coverage of brutality and humiliation in ordinary settings. Viewing suffering on television during the prime-time dinner hour provides a complicated context in which to digest material of such a severe nature. Night after night, and story after story, the repetition of imagery of suffering makes it so familiar to the audience as to affect how this news and information are absorbed and processed, and how the reaction is induced. Western audiences become attuned to coverage of children, women, and the elderly fleeing war zones and natural disasters. At what point does the endlessness of ghastly, brutal imagery transform both the subject and object, and how? Is the audience able to separate the difficult reality of events from the otherwise light content on television? Is there a point at which human rights becomes mere human interest? Can the audience distinguish between coverage of a humanitarian intervention and that of the rescue of a cat stuck in a tree? The spectacle transforms the nature of the content on television and informs the viewer's relationship to it.

In the age of global media spectacle, there is a tangible shift in the way audience members relate to the world. Viewing graphic imagery creates the opportunity for proximity and participation. To reiterate, while television is not new, the immediacy with which its broadcasts are transmitted and the depth and breadth of its reach were unique to the early 1990s. Whether it was the invasion of allied forces in Somalia or another mediated crisis, television coverage of human rights events provided the wherewithal for civil society to monitor action in progress. The narrative below details how this tension played out during the period, whose interests were served, and how the human rights community was affected. Departing from Debord's rigid proposal, the thesis advanced in this chapter is that spectacle opens space for empathic engagement and the expansion of the moral community but ultimately seals off terrain for committed political activism. This chapter pivots on the proposition that a connection is forged between the individual audience member and the individual suffering on television through spectacle – but this connection does not transform the audience member into a witness in the traditional sense, nor does more active engagement flow from this experience. Audience members may be better informed and even more interested but remain unwilling to bear the weight of personal or national investment in human rights interventions. Despite the potential inherent in global media for the founding of a moral community willing to sustain the costs of human rights protection, the spectacle proves ineffective in achieving this end.

Despite the way in which this phenomenon bloomed in the 1990s, even through pre-spectacle media audiences have demonstrated a curiosity about and attraction to atrocity photographs that provide historical precursors for what will follow. A longer historical look at this phenomenon would probably begin with Congo in 1960 through Biafra in 1968, continue in Ethiopia in 1984 and then into Somalia in 1991. The role of imagery in each of these cases was absolutely critical. This chapter will emphasize the famine in Biafra and the intervention in Somalia as events that suggest the prominence of the spectacle of suffering in the mediation of atrocity. The case of Biafra demonstrates most clearly how the image constitutes a fluid arena in which interested parties contend for the upper hand in the struggle for media supremacy.

The iconography of famine: Biafra 1968

The emergence of the spectacle of suffering in the 1990s, as I trace it, is the product of an aggregate of factors: developments in information and communications technology, corporate media consolidation, geopolitical space created by the end of the Cold War, and competition among NGOs for air time and donor attention. However, it is also the consequence of a historical trend that manifested itself again during this decade. Public response to media coverage of previous humanitarian crises set the tone for future incidents. Specifically, events in Nigeria in 1968 provide an early case of the effect of visual imagery of suffering on the audience's mobilization in support of human rights by demonstrating the crucial role photography can play in elevating a crisis to the status of *cause célèbre*. Furthermore, this case suggests how 'the image' can become an alternate plane for contestation in which two parties to a conflict, great powers, and civil society can all be drawn in. There is a great deal at stake even in a conflict waged in the realm of the visual.

The civil war in Nigeria, also known as the Biafran War, was introduced into Western homes in the form of photographic evidence of the starvation of civilians among the secessionist Igbo people. War photography by Gilles Caron of France and Don McCullin of the United Kingdom has come to epitomize the ability of an image to frame a conflict and communicate the desperate predicaments of the subjects of the photograph for an unsuspecting audience. Beginning in the spring of 1968, news of the conflict began to flow to Western news outlets through Caron's and McCullin's journalism. On 4 May 1968, Caron's photographs were published in *Paris Match*, and were thereafter syndicated in *The New York Times Sunday Magazine*, *Manchete* (Brazil), and *Kwick* (Germany) (Cookman 2008, 227 and 238). On 12 June, similar photographs were plastered on the cover of *Life* magazine and in *The Sun* (Heerten 2009, 5–6). These photographs have been, over time, elevated to iconic status because of their impact on the public and the way in which they have laid the foundation for atrocity coverage to follow.

The images from the region of Biafra portray the debilitating effects of chronic malnutrition on women and children. In a raw fashion they capture the physicality of suffering by focusing the viewer's attention on the extreme toll taken on the body:

> In one, a child attempted in vain to suckle his mother's withered breast. In another, a group of naked boys stood intently watching some action ... Caron focused on a boy in the front rank, gently grasping a slender stick; its thinness emphasizes the boy's wasted limbs ... The other photograph shows a girl of indeterminate age, who seems little more than a tissue of skin stretched tautly across ribs and shoulders (Cookman 2008, 238).

Effectively, the photographs break down the experience of suffering into its most visceral and base form in a way that translates well to an audience. Through the process of mediation, the coverage strikes at the sentimental core of the audience: 'Caron humanized his subjects ... gave his subjects dignity despite their suffering ...' (ibid., 239). The relationship that photojournalists hope to establish with viewers is primarily on the level of emotions – a response to the way the images make them feel. Because of the nature of the still photograph, there are many contextual assumptions required of the viewer that cannot be made explicit through the medium. For instance, there is a presumption of victim innocence in the Biafra coverage that has continued across other cases. The use of women and children as subjects communicates the notion that there are powerful, external forces acting upon them, due to traditional narratives of female and child passivity. Starvation itself is illustrated in simple terms, as a natural disaster, more akin to an earthquake than a calculated political strategy. In the case of Biafra, as well as the famed/infamous 1984 Ethiopian famine, this simplicity is in fact a distortion because of the use of food as a weapon of war to punish civilian populations. The combination of childlike victim innocence and denial of subsistence rights, beginning in 1968, cast a shadow on future incidents of visual media representation of suffering.

However, these 'innocent victims' were not merely passive subjects in the frame of the photographs – they were in fact active participants in the global trafficking of their own atrocity images. Under the leadership of Colonel Odumegwu Ojukwu, the secessionist Biafrans employed the services of MarkPress, a Geneva-based public relations firm, to assist in their marketing and publicity. In addition to 700 press releases sent to 'British MPs, newspaper editors, radio and television correspondents, businessmen and academics,' MarkPress was more generally tasked with casting 'the Biafran case in the most heartrending light' (Harrison and Palmer 1986, 22; Black 1992, 121). In the television coverage of 12 June on British outlet Independent Television News (ITN), the figure of 3,000 deaths per day was quoted, despite having been drawn from 'partisan' sources (Black 1992, 120–1). Ojukwu, aware of the power of the image and of the press, leveraged the 'starvation card' to sway British public opinion and hopefully encourage a cessation of support for the federal government with which the Biafrans were at war (ibid., 121).

This proved to be an overwhelmingly successful strategy as the images of starving Biafrans galvanized British civil society and awoke a remarkable, if short-lived, movement. 'The eventual breaking of the famine story provoked a massive popular campaign which began in Britain and spread quickly throughout the west ... The pictures of Biafran children clearly touched a sensitive spot ... Thousands of people in the west marched, protested and demonstrated, went on hunger strikes, collected money, took out whole-page advertisements in newspapers and other opinion-formers' (Harrison and Palmer 1986, 34). Local 'Support Biafra' groups surfaced in the United Kingdom, Belgium, France, Holland, Ireland, and the US, and advocacy editorials appeared in major publications (ibid., 34–5). Tanzanian President Julius Nyerere quipped: 'If I'd been a Jew in Nazi Germany, I'd feel the same as an Ibo in Nigeria' (quoted in ibid., 34). The British *Daily Sketch* called Biafra 'today's Belsen,' an unsubtle reminder of the famed photographs of liberated Nazi camps (ibid., 31). It is central to the Nigerian case that the images of famine, as influential as they were, cannot be seen as neutrally filtered throughout the global mass media of the late 1960s. One party to the conflict was able to manipulate the substance to serve its own interests – as well as the interests of humanitarian agencies.

Worldwide publication of Caron's and McCullin's photographs stirred the conscience of the global public and had a range of cascading effects on the NGO community. Aid agencies, such as Caritas Internationalis and Oxfam, used these images in their print advertising, attempting to play off empathetic sentiments in their solicitation for donations. Caritas literally reprinted Caron's photograph of a starving baby on its posters (Cookman 2008, 240); Oxfam cleverly took out ads in newspapers such as the *Guardian* that were reluctant to print the brutal photographs in their coverage of the crisis (Heerten 2009, 7). Famously, Biafra was the point of origin of Médecins Sans Frontières when Bernard Kouchner, then a doctor on location with the International Committee of the Red Cross (ICRC), refused to maintain his silence in line with the ICRC dictum of neutrality in conflict zones. Kouchner declared the starvation an act of 'genocide,' imploring the world to act and reprimanding all actors for failing to take a stance against the guilty parties in this conflict (de Montclos 2009, 71–2). The photographic evidence of the humanitarian emergency in Biafra had the effect of spurring public outcry and generating financial contributions to agencies but also retaining simplistic storylines about the crisis instead of delving into the political mire.

Visual mediation of the conflict brought tales of suffering to new sectors of Western societies and, therefore, 'from a media point of view, Biafra was a success story, the first major famine to be addressed through media images of starving Africans, before Ethiopia in 1984 or Somalia in 1992' (ibid., 72). Photography brought an element of reality to viewers far removed from the crisis. Similar to coverage of the liberation of the Nazi concentration camps, Biafra jostled a generation from its complacency. The combination of photographs in daily papers and weekly news magazines with the use of stills in the nightly broadcast news illustrated for Western affluent classes the depths of the ongoing peril in Biafra. Biafra is important in cultural media history because of the way in which African children specifically were featured as subjects of war photography. While many photographs had famously captured historical cases of suffering – from Hiroshima to My Lai – Biafra introduced the world to African famine using a frame that would be replicated into ubiquity.

Viewers were becoming prepared to absorb imagery of starving Africans and to accept certain claims about the issue (presumed innocence, appropriate remedies, etc.). However, the repetitious nature of starving African children on television created a context in which, while an audience could be temporarily shocked, especially due to the timeliness of the coverage, it could not be surprised. As these images became routinized in print advertisements and television commercials for causes and organizations, their effect on the audience was transformative. For the audience member, just a flash of an image of an African child on television conjures memories of Biafra, Ethiopia, famine, and charity. Observers remark on the ascent of this image in the public psyche with overlapping language: 'By the mid-nineteen-sixties ... the powerful image of the starving African child with haunting eyes and skeletal limbs had become a universal icon of human suffering' (Cohen 2001, 178); 'Starving children are the famine icon' (Moeller 1999, 98). But what does it mean for an image of suffering to become 'iconic'? Does it mean that starving children symbolize all suffering and give suffering children voice and visibility? Does it evoke the same meaning for all viewers? Ultimately, from a human rights perspective, the question is what is the effect of icon status on the dignity of the subject? Is the starving child merely a *symbol* of something to someone or a real human being who deserves our care and concern? Has the child been reduced to a symbol, whose worth is limited to his or her ability to generate public attention and donations? The answers to these questions are wrapped up in the contradictions inherent in the spectacle of suffering.

From Biafra to Somalia, we witness an expanding role of the image in prompting a civil society response and a growing intensity in the response. It is my contention that this trajectory is attributed to changes in the technological capacity for communication, as well as in the cultural associations that are nurtured over time through the repetition of crisis. However, until the end of the Cold War, starvation was treated as remediable through donation and provision of aid. As we will see in the case of Somalia, coverage of child malnourishment on the Horn of Africa did not produce a telethon or pledge drive; instead, military intervention was initiated that expanded into a nation-building exercise. Distinguishing this episode from those that preceded it are the heightened media context and the means used to alleviate suffering of others. If Biafra was mediated through black-and-white photographs, Somalia is the African famine that occurred live and in full color before the public for all to experience simultaneously. The frenzied and frenetic pace at which events occurred in this case is a metaphor for the rapidly shifting public opinion that shaped and was shaped by the media coverage.

Emergence of the spectacle: Somalia 1991

Much has been written about the humanitarian intervention in Somalia in the twenty years since it took place. The state remains essentially failed and plagued by violent turf wars. Two decades of incapable governance have provided a safe haven for terrorists affiliated with al Qaeda, as well as the home-grown organization, al Shabab. Piracy, the scourge of centuries past, has returned in the Gulf of Aden as local opportunists attempt to make a life for themselves in the midst of an otherwise stagnant economy. All the while, Somali civilians remain squeezed between hardcore Islamist ideologies and geopolitical battles waged intermittently on its shores. The country remains an incredibly dangerous place, a policymaker's worst nightmare, and the situation is as ripe today for chronic famine as it was before the fall of the country's last government in 1991.

'Operation Restore Hope,' as the US intervention was termed, is a crucial landmark in the checkered history of humanitarian inter-vention in the post-Cold War era. The debate surrounding Somalia generally consists of two central questions: what was the media's role in motivating the intervention, and what was the subsequent effect on the West's response to mass atrocity? With advancements in information and communications technology and the innovation of the twenty-four-hour cable news network, viewers witnessed these events in real time, and foreign policy appeared to shift in lockstep with media coverage and public opinion. As images of famine-stricken children appeared, the public called for intervention; as these images were replaced by those of dead American soldiers the following year, the public swung to favor withdrawal. The blowback from Somalia negatively affected the ability of human rights advocates to lobby governments for humanitarian intervention for fear of making a repeated spectacle out of the deaths of their own soldiers. The CNN Effect, as it was termed, was an attempt by commentators to describe the role played by media coverage of the event in driving foreign policy. However, when social science caught up with the commentators, the CNN Effect was largely debunked (Robinson 2002; Western 2005).

The most convincing evidence of its inaccuracy is the simple sequencing of events. As this narrative describes, the mobilization for intervention in Somalia had more to do with controlling the spin of the spectacle than it did with national interest or humanitarian relief. In late 1991, news of the famine in Somalia came into view on Western television screens, mostly as part of a larger story about famine on the Horn of Africa. *Africa Watch* reported 'wanton and indiscriminate' violence in the fallout from the government collapse (quoted in Western 2005, 139). Major news coverage would not return until late summer 1992, even though international organizations (IOs) and human rights groups would continue their alarm-sounding advocacy. In July 1992, ICRC cited the figures of 300,000 casualties from famine since 1989, and 'reiterated its six-month-old estimates that 95 per cent of the population of Somalia was malnourished' (ibid., 135). The Office of the United Nations High Commissioner for Refugees (UNHCR) 'estimated that as many as 4.5 million of the country's 6 million civilians would be subject to death by starvation without some form of immediate assistance' (ibid., 139). While reporting from IOs does not often reach the average news consumer, inside the US administration there were officials such as Andrew Natsios who were also advocating forcefully for intervention. Natsios, then assistant administrator of the US Agency for International Development (USAID), sought to make the crisis more public with a series of press conferences on the topic of the 'humanitarian catastrophe' (ibid., 135). Yet, with all this discussion, there was very little graphic coverage of the famine in Somalia. Most news outlets had pulled out due to insecurity and it was not until the Bush administration chose to make the famine an issue that media sources began covering it.

Still, the fact that there was an ongoing debate between IOs, State Department officials, the Pentagon, and the executive branch is not a mass-media matter. However, nearly simultaneously, news emerged from the Balkans and reports of concentration camps in Europe stole the headlines temporarily. For the duration of the summer of 1992, the Bush administration was under pressure from all sides to intervene somewhere: either in Somalia or in Bosnia. Photographs of concentration camps in Bosnia had surfaced and the human rights community demanded action. Yet, the Bush administration ultimately executed the proverbial bait-and-switch. On 14 August, President George H. W. Bush authorized a military airlift of food aid and of the Pakistani guards representing the UN security force (Moeller 1999, 135). 'The decision to launch the airlift to Somalia did divert media and liberal attention away from critical coverage and commentary on Bosnia and to sympathetic stories on Somalia ... The airlift had given the administration a slight reprieve from the pressure on Bosnia' (Western 2005, 163). This calculated move helped 'deflect attention away from ... inaction over Bosnia' (Wheeler 2000, 181), which was seen as a much more difficult conflict and a less favorable context for intervention, and mobilized the press corps to cover Somalia in full stride. By initiating the airlift, 'the White House saw an opportunity to demonstrate it had a heart ... and do it relatively cheaply' (Power 2007, 286).

From late summer 1992 through the fall, Somalia was the humanitarian story covered by all outlets. 'Stories on and photographs of the famine's victims, heroes and villains became ubiquitous. The tales of woe – especially of child victims – led the coverage on air and in print' (Moeller 1999, 137). Pleas for further and more sustained action occupied the editorial pages, as calls escalated from aid delivery to a more extended presence and a revised set of rules of engagement. Philip Johnston, president of CARE-US, as well as other officers from that organization, continued vocal calls until the 'drumbeat for intervention reached its crescendo' (de Waal 1997, 185). In September, US Marines were deployed to support the airlift mission, while concurrently news magazines carried stories with graphic imagery of starving children. Somali supermodel Iman and UNICEF Goodwill Ambassador Audrey Hepburn made trips to the country (Moeller 1999, 140). Of all the grief and suffering on the Horn of Africa (or elsewhere, for that matter), Somalia had clearly arrived.

Yet, contrary to popular opinion, upon close inspection public attention and media coverage *followed* official policy decision-making, *not vice versa*. The calculations of the Bush administration, especially following his electoral defeat at the hands of Bill Clinton, consisted of the expectation that the public supported and would continue to support military activity in Somalia on behalf of humanitarianism. By effectively mobilizing the media to cover stories of the famine, the administration could maintain the storyline: 'media coverage enabled humanitarian intervention by ensuring domestic legitimacy ...' (Wheeler 2000, 180). With US interests being affected by the introduction of troops, and the emotional narrative of starving children, public support would help President Bush set himself up for a memorable legacy. Slowly, over the course of the fall, the storyline shifted from the starving children and aid delivery to the more heroic, patriotic vision of the role of US troops and the thuggish locals (Moeller 1999, 138). However, despite the rousing support for the troops among the American public, 'it was not easy for the administration to control the subsequent coverage, which focused on the fact that over 1,000 Somalis were dying daily' (Wheeler 2000, 179). The spectacle enabled by the administration's decision to intervene – and on which it depended – would become the bane of the mission.

The night before Thanksgiving 1992, the shape of the mission changed when outgoing President Bush, with President-elect Clinton's approval, declared he would send 15,000 to 30,000 troops to bolster the UN mission. At that announcement, civil society awoke to the cause. Relief organizations saw a remarkable response in donations, and media outlets began to position teams on the scene to cover the next stage of the intervention. However, unlike in late summer, the facts on the ground would not be allowed to drive the story; there would be more coordination from the center. On 8 December, Marines landed on the shores of Mogadishu to be greeted by journalists and cameras (estimates of news personnel on the scene range from 75 to 300). The Pentagon had arranged for these media representatives to be on site by issuing invitations, even positioning them appropriately (Moeller 1999, 143; Keenan 2004, 440). Reminiscent within Western cultural memory of the landing on Normandy Beach in World War II, the Somali expedition was designed to be a display of American power and intentionality in the post-Cold War period, a controlled environment in which to make such a pronouncement, and medi-ated to an extreme so as to message the event clearly to enemies and allies alike. As dazed as the Marines were to be welcomed with conspicuous television studio lighting, US forces would be faced with an equally jolting reality when the same cameras would capture their exit months later.

Coverage of the landing boosted television news ratings to their highest levels since the 1991 Gulf War (Moeller 1999, 143). Public opinion of the intervention was extremely favorable, with 81 per cent supporting the mission from a moral position and 70 per cent willing to sacrifice American blood and treasure for the cause (ibid., 145). The spectacle of Somalia had been transformed from that of suffering to that of militaristic heroism in a way that resonated with the audience and generated support for the administration's humanitarian, political, and geopolitical goals. Messaging through visualization was being controlled in a masterful way. Media outlets were reaping profits through an increase in television viewership and in print sales. All parties were content to continue behind the mission in Somalia because all of their interests were being well served. However, the unfolding events tested the limits of spin and demonstrated the difficulty of managing image in an age of spectacle. As public opinion turned against the mission, the US government learned the lesson of the fickle nature of the audience for humanitarian expeditions.

By early 1993, with the end of drought and resumption of the rainy season, the famine was effectively over, making it a 'straightforward task to declare victory over starvation' (ibid., 145; de Waal 1997, 185). While the original impetus for intervention had been removed, the mission evolved rapidly to respond to facts on the ground. In the summer of 1993, aid delivery was no longer the force's *raison d'être*. Due to an escalation in violence, prompted by attacks against the Pakistani peacekeepers, the militarized humanitarian expedition took on a singularly military function. Infamously, in the fall of that year, American forces faced significant opposition from troops under the command of General Mohamed Farrah Aidid, the president of Somalia. On 25 September, a US helicopter was downed in Mogadishu and on 3 October two more helicopters were shot down over the capital. The second attack resulted in eighteen US Army Rangers killed, one taken captive, and one of the bodies of the deceased dragged through the streets by children (Moeller 1999, 146). Fallout from the transmission of photographs of the fierce battle and brutal treatment of American casualties was immediate and dramatic. President Clinton pledged a withdrawal of American troops from the UN mission in direct response. Graphic imagery of suffering had provoked a change in foreign policy, but the suffering subjects in this case were not African children – they were American servicemen acting on humanitarian grounds. While thousands of Somalis were dead or wounded when the dust settled in Mogadishu, their suffering had been cast aside in favor of the American narrative. This narrative was driven by lingering symptoms of the Vietnam syndrome, in which the nation's military gets bogged down in a quagmire. Of course, the Vietnam syndrome would give way to a 'Somalia syndrome' that framed the West's approach to Rwanda, Bosnia, and Kosovo (Brooks 2006).

Conclusion: bearing witness to distant suffering in an age of spectacle

The spectacle of suffering that emerged in the 1990s continued trends in visual media receptivity, but in a heightened state. Technology made it possible for distant suffering to be a regular feature of nightly news broadcasts and introduced average viewers to extraordinary situations. Images of suffering civilians influenced debate and framed the crisis in a certain way. For Western audiences, to witness suffering at a distance is to be involved in a central human rights process traditionally reserved for relief workers, medical personnel, and staff on the ground in conflict zones. From a human rights perspective, witnessing is a political act because it disables the abuser from operating in secrecy; accountability for gross violations can occur only when the veil of obscurity has been lifted. This is 'a fundamental axiom of the human rights movement in an age of publicity: that the exposure of violence is feared by its perpetrators, and hence that the act of witness is not simply an ethical gesture but an active intervention' (Keenan 2004, 446). To reiterate Amnesty International's founding motto: 'Better to light a candle than curse the darkness.' It is no coincidence that in 1992 the Lawyer's Committee for Human Rights began its Witness program, which distributes video cameras throughout the world to capture human rights abuse for documentary purposes (Cohen 2001, 186).

The spectacle is equivalent to the lighting of a million candles, but transforming ordinary people into witnesses through television does not have the effect ICRC and MSF intend in their conceptions of witnessing, nor does it simply transform viewers into human rights activists. The episodes detailed above evidence the potential for the spectacle to be a force for the expansion of moral community, but only on the basis of emotional appeal.

This is the power [of television] to make spectators witnesses of human pain by bringing home disturbing images and experiences from far-away places ... The tension between a knowing yet incapable witness at a distance is the most profound moral demand that television makes on Western spectators today (Chouliaraki 2006, 18).

Visually, television has a unique impact on its audience that radio and print never could have. In terms of transmitting content, the ability to see the faces of the affected cuts deeper than just reading or hearing about their plight, and this experience brings the viewer closer to the person on television in a morally relevant way. Witnessing distant suffering is a symptom of globalization in the sense that ordinary audience members can participate in global happenings through the process of watching. Television provides a bridge across which irrelevant differences seemingly evaporate. Because one party is sitting comfortably at home and one party is struggling to stay alive does not make either party any less a part of the same moral category – and visual media allow one to make this argument to a broader community. Communities of care and concern can be expanded through products of globalization, such as global media, which impact the demands that citizens make on their governments for human rights policy. It is possible for Western audiences to have solidarity with suffering people in another part of the world and feel a moral compulsion to restore and uphold human dignity.

However, this moral claim – that a Somali, for instance, deserves assistance because he or she is part of the same human community as I am – originates as an emotional plea. Empathy motivates a series of cascading emotions that may range from sadness and grief to anger, but generally all contribute to a comprehension of what it would be like to be the victim of severe suffering. An understanding of sameness drives the desire to act on behalf of others, and this sameness is communicated forcefully through visual media. However, the emotional response expressed by audiences to distant suffering is a distinct form of witnessing. Journalists, aid workers, and other conventional human rights witnesses remark on the role of feelings in their work, but also are consciously hopeful of the political effect of witnessing. Even those reporters covering conflict zones, who are supposed to remain impartial in their coverage, acknowledge daily the intervention they are making when reporting a story of suffering. Adapting this into a mass perspective is rare in history, but the 1990s demonstrate the potential for this sensibility to be mainstream, widespread, and normalized. As such, there is reason for hope that the power of the image can at times serve as a source of support for international action for human rights ends. This leads some to be optimistic about the possibility for cultivating a mass human rights movement that stands up against abuse and brutality, in defense of the oppressed and vulnerable. Many advocates of the hopeful view point to the role of emotion in compelling average people to become involved in activism and claim that the 'human capacity for compassion is the key to global solidarity' (Linklater 2007, 24).

Yet, the spectacle of suffering serves neither the interests of bearing witness, nor of more participatory forms of human rights engagement, as laid out in the introduction. There is a qualitative difference between the new form of witnessing underwritten by the spectacle of suffering and those forms customary in the field of human rights. Witnessing from the vantage of one's living room and witnessing from within a refugee camp are not equivalent, and they have widely varying consequences. While they may each evoke similar emotions, absent from the former is a concrete comprehension of the reality of suffering. Mediation can transmit images and information, but only a replication of reality. As Stanley Cohen (2001, 187) remarks:

> The increased international awareness of atrocities and suffering, the spread of new information technologies, and the globalization of the mass media indeed mean that sovereign states (some of them) are being 'watched' as never before. But representing this information is more difficult than ever. There is a profusion of similar images; lines are blurred between fiction and fact ... 'reality' is always in inverted commas ...

If this is the case and the audience confronts *imagery* of human suffering at an alienating distance from the *reality* of human suffering, then it becomes clear how the emergence of the spectacle affects the audience from the outset. By presenting a mediated version of reality, 'it makes us voyeurs of the suffering of others, tourists amidst their landscapes of anguish' (Ignatieff 1985, 59). It is the illusion of unity that the spectacle creates, and when this euphoric feeling of solidarity through television attempts to be translated into political action, it generates a fickle, shallow constellation of actors.

An audience cannot be transformed into a social movement through emotions alone. Emotions do not account for politics, and human rights abuse is inherently political. 'What determines the possibility of being affected morally by photographs is the existence of a relevant political consciousness. Without a politics, photographs of the slaughter-bench of history will likely be experienced as, simply, unreal ...' (Sontag 1977, 19). Graphic news coverage of atrocity may be a necessary condition for awareness, but awareness is not a sufficient condition for action. If witnessing in this form does not compel abusive regimes to check their behavior, then effective human rights advocacy depends upon a subsequent step that translates awareness into action – a step that the spectacle of suffering does not sustain. The emotional reaction experienced by the audience does not translate into the commitment and investment necessary for a persistent effort with a long-term positive effect on the conflict.

This effort may have taken many forms in the case of Somalia. Had the audience been committed to the alleviation of the suffering of Somalis, we might have seen continued support for the intervention force until a proper government had been re-established that was better suited to serve the needs of civilians. We may have seen popular forms of protest emerge, urging President Clinton to keep US troops in Somalia until the causes of the famine were corrected and prevented from reappearing. Instead, the audience turned away from its previous posturing in support of intervention as soon as the Black Hawk Down incident was broadcast. This indicates that the spectacle of suffering Somalis had very concrete limits and that suffering Americans trump suffering Somalis. Therefore, this example refutes the suggestion that global media can help individuals overcome national bias and be a platform for the broadening of moral communities, fulfilling a promise of globalization.

Instead of witnesses, in the traditional sense, the spectacle of suffering produces spectators: those audiences who watch without engaging, willfully detached from reality. Television proves it is no panacea. Human rights and humanitarian crises are treated as newsworthy, and even given serious coverage over an extended period of time, but the mediated version beamed into the homes of the viewers maintains moral and geographical distance. There is an acknowledgment of the suffering of others and an emotional response is provoked, but the emotional experience does not translate into sustained political participation. While forces of globalization demonstrate an ability to expand moral capacity across boundaries, facilitating for new communities the recognition of others, that feeling tends to be limited to empathy, devoid of full consciousness.

Without political consciousness, an emotional mass outpouring is vulnerable to manipulation, evidenced notably in Somalia. While human rights organizations seek to capitalize on sensational reporting of human rights abuse, power elites and media outlets also wrestle for control of the message:

> The stakes of this mediatic scenario are high; we cannot understand, nor have a properly political relation to, invasions and war crimes, military operation and paramilitary atrocities – both of maximal

importance for human rights campaigners – in the present and future if we do not attend to the centrality of image production and management in them. We will be at an even greater loss if we do not admit that the high-speed electronic news media have created news opportunities not just for activism and awareness, but also for performance, presentation, advertising, propaganda, and for political work of all kinds (Keenan 2004, 442–4).

Foreign policymakers attempt to secure domestic legitimacy for international operations through the deployment of the spectacle. Corporate media conglomerates seek to bolster ratings and advertising revenue with the use of imagery of suffering. The emotional appeal of a humanitarian narrative serves both sets of interests. And, while it could also serve human rights interests, the spectacle consolidates the gaps between the moral, the emotional, and the political, complicating the prospects for a sustained response. Since witnessing and other forms of human rights interventions are necessarily political acts, the spectacle of suffering does not provide an obvious venue for efforts of this kind. Instead, the spectacle spews content over which no actor has ownership: neither the human rights movement, nor the government.

From the perspective of the human rights community, in its perpetual quest to bolster its base, the risk inherent in the use of graphic imagery to attract audience members is providing an unintended substitute for activism: *the spectacle effectively replaces political action with the act of looking*. Viewers feel empathy and compassion for those suffering on television and participate through their voyeurism. However, driven by the imperative that knowledge of atrocity fosters cessation of atrocity, the steps in between are taken for granted. The experience of the audience is limited to an emotional response to imagery that curtails further commitment, either personal or political. Television circumscribes the extent of political engagement by the very virtue of its nature, and human rights organizations do not demonstrate the aptitude to supplement the coverage with actionable operations. The age of spectacle proves to be a challenging media environment to navigate, providing the tools for compassionate cosmopolitan engagement in human rights crises, yet built on foundations fraught with obstacles to overcome and contradictions to transcend.

References

Baudrillard, Jean. 2008. 'Pornography of war.' In *The Jean Baudrillard Reader*, edited by Steve Redhead, 199–202. New York: Columbia University Press.

Black, Maggie. 1992. *A Cause for Our Times: Oxfam: The First 50 Years*. Oxford: Oxford University Press.

Boltanski, Luc. 1999. *Distant Suffering: Morality, Media and Politics*. New York: Cambridge University Press.

Brooks, Rosa. 2006. 'Somalia's deadly lessons.' *Los Angeles Times*, 23 June. http://articles.latimes.com/2006/jun/23/opinion/oe-brooks23.

Chouliaraki, Lilie. 2006. *The Spectatorship of Suffering*. London: Sage Publications.

Cohen, Stanley. 2001. *States of Denial: Knowing About Atrocities and Suffering*. Cambridge: Polity Press.

Cookman, Claude. 2008. 'Gilles Caron's coverage of the crisis in Biafra.' *Visual Communication Quarterly* 15(4): 226–42.

de Montclos, Marc-Antoine Pérouse. 2009. 'Humanitarian aid and the Biafra War: Lessons not learned.' *Africa Development* 34(1): 69–82.

de Waal, Alex. 1997. *Famine Crimes: Politics & the Disaster Relief Industry in Africa*. London: African Rights and the International African Institute.

Debord, Guy. 1983. *Society of the Spectacle*. London: Rebel Press.

Doyle, Mark. 2007. 'Reporting the genocide.' In *The Media and the Rwanda Genocide*, edited by Allan Thompson, 145–59. London: Pluto Press.

Harrison, Paul, and Robin Palmer. 1986. *News Out of Africa: Biafra to Band Aid*. London: Hilary Shipman.

Heerten, Lasse. 2009. 'The Biafran War in Britain: An odd alliance of late 1960s humanitarian activists.' *Journal of the Oxford University History Society* 7 (Special Issue: Colloquium 2009). http://sites.google.com/site/jouhsinfo/issue-7specialissueforinternetexplorer.

Ignatieff, Michael. 1985. 'Is nothing sacred? The ethics of television.' *Daedalus* 114(4): 57–78.

Keenan, Thomas. 2002. 'Publicity and indifference: Media, surveillance, "humanitarian intervention."' In *CTRL [SPACE]: Rhetorics of Surveillance from Bentham to Big Brother*, edited by Thomas Y. Levin, Ursula Frohne, and Peter Weibel, 544–61. Cambridge, MA: MIT Press.

Keenan, Thomas. 2004. 'Mobilizing shame.' *South Atlantic Quarterly* 103(2/3): 435–49.

Kellner, Douglas. 2003. *Media Spectacle*. London: Routledge.

Linklater, Andrew. 2007. 'Distant suffering and cosmopolitan obligations.' *International Politics* 44(1): 19–36.

Mamdani, Mahmood. 2007. 'The politics of naming: Genocide, civil war, insurgency.' *London Review of Books* 29(5): 8.

McLuhan, Marshall. 2003. *Understanding Media: The Extensions of Man*. Berkeley, CA: Gingko Press.

Moeller, Susan D. 1999. *Compassion Fatigue: How the Media Sell Disease, Famine, War and Death*. New York: Routledge.

Omaar, Rakiya, and Alex de Waal. 1993. 'Disaster pornography from Somalia.' *Media and Values* 61: 13–14.

Postman, Neil. 1985. *Amusing Ourselves to Death: Public Discourse in the Age of Show Business*. New York: Viking.

Power, Samantha. 2007. *'A Problem from Hell': America and the Age of Genocide*. New York: Harper Perennial.

Robinson, Piers. 2002. *The CNN Effect: The Myth of News, Foreign Policy, and Intervention*. London & New York: Routledge.

Sontag, Susan. 1977. *On Photography*. New York: Farrar, Straus and Giroux.

Western, Jon. 2005. *Selling Intervention and War: The Presidency, the Media, and the American Public*. Baltimore, MD: Johns Hopkins University Press.

Wheeler, Nicholas J. 2000. *Saving Strangers: Humanitarian Intervention in International Society*. Oxford: Oxford University Press.

About the contributors

Dan Chong (MA, University of Notre Dame; PhD, American University) is assistant professor of political science at Rollins College in Winter Park, FL. His recent book is titled *Freedom from Poverty: NGOs and Human Rights Praxis* (2010). He has published in journals such as *Human Rights Review*, *Development and Change*, and *Global Environmental Politics* (forthcoming), and wrote a chapter for a book called *The International Struggle for New Human Rights* (2008). Outside academia, Dan has worked for several organizations involved in human rights, peace, and social justice work. His work for Save the Children brought him to a refugee camp in Thailand, and his work for Catholic Relief Services brought him to field offices in Burkina Faso, Eritrea, and Ecuador. He has also served with policy advocacy organizations in Washington DC, such as the Burma Fund, the Peace Tax Fund, and the United States Institute of Peace.

Andrew F. Cooper (DPhil, University of Oxford) is a distinguished fellow at the Centre for International Governance Innovation, and professor in the Department of Political Science, University of Waterloo in Canada. In 2009 he was the Canada-US Fulbright Research Chair, Center on Public Diplomacy, University of Southern California. Recent books include: as author, *Internet Gambling Offshore: Caribbean Struggles over Casino Capitalism* (2011) and *Celebrity Diplomacy* (2007); and, as co-editor, *Rising States, Rising Institutions: Challenges for Global Governance* (2010), *Which Way Latin America: Hemispheric Politics Meets Globalization* (2009), and *The Diplomacies of Small States: Between Vulnerability and Resilience* (2009). His scholarly publications have appeared in *International Organization*, *World Development*, *International Studies Review*, *International Affairs*, *Washington Quarterly*, *Journal of Democracy*, *Global Governance*, and *New Political Economy*.

Michael Galchinsky (BA, Northwestern University; PhD, University of California at Berkeley) is professor of English at Georgia State University in Atlanta, GA. He is the author and editor of books on Jewish culture and sociology, including *The Origin of the Modern Jewish Woman Writer* (1996) and *Insider/Outsider: American Jews and*

Multiculturalism, co-edited with David Biale and Susannah Heschel (1998). In 2007 he published a legal and political history of Jewish human rights activism, *Jews and Human Rights: Dancing at Three Weddings*. His current research focuses, on the one hand, on human rights literature and, on the other hand, on a range of human rights issues in the post-9/11 international law relating to counter-terrorism. He is a faculty fellow at the Yale Center for Cultural Sociology and is currently at work on a book called *The Problem with Human Rights Culture*.

Sarah Kessler (BS, Northwestern University) is an associate editor at *Fast Company*, where she covers social media, technology, and web culture. Before joining *Fast Company*, she covered digital innovation for *Mashable*. Her articles have also appeared in *Sierra Magazine* and *Inc. Magazine*, and on ABCnews.com and CNN.com.

David Kieran (BA, Connecticut College; PhD, The George Washington University) is visiting assistant professor of American studies at Franklin and Marshall College and co-founder of the War and Peace Studies Caucus of the American Studies Association. His book project, *'Sundered by a Memory': Foreign Policy, Militarism, and the Vietnamization of American Memory, 1970–Present*, which is under advance contract with the University of Massachusetts Press ('Culture, Politics, and the Cold War' series) examines how the recent cultural memory of significant events in US culture have, during moments of significant debate over US foreign and military policy, drawn upon the discourses, representational strategies, and memorial practices that simultaneously dominated the construction of the Vietnam War's contested legacy. His publications include articles in *War and Society*, *Children's Literature Association Quarterly*, and *M/MLA: The Journal of the Midwestern Modern Language Association* and chapters in edited collections.

Ella McPherson (BA, Princeton University; MPhil and PhD, University of Cambridge) is a research fellow in sociology at the University of Cambridge's Wolfson College and an affiliated researcher of its Department of Sociology, where she lectures on media and politics. While completing her PhD, she was a resident research fellow at the Center of Inter-American Studies and Programs at the Instituto Tecnológico Autónomo de México as well as a Gates Cambridge Trust Scholar. Her dissertation, 'Human rights reporting in Mexico,' argues that human rights reporting is influenced by a struggle for credibility between the state, the media, and civil society in a democratizing context. Her current research is on NGO journalism, focusing particularly on how human rights NGOs engage with social media.

Joel R. Pruce is a post-doctoral fellow with the human rights studies program at the University of Dayton. He earned his PhD at University of Denver's Josef Korbel School of International Studies, where he subsequently served as lecturer in international human rights. Joel's research critiques the strategies and assumptions of advocacy organizations and their deployment of consumerism, popular culture, and mass media in campaigns.

Joseph F. Turcotte is a PhD candidate in the communication and culture program at York University (Toronto, Canada) and a researcher with the Centre for International Governance Innovation (CIGI). His research focuses on technological, social, political, and economic changes in the early twenty-first century with a particular emphasis on Internet governance and intellectual property rights in the digital and globalized era.

Index